2

The Scientific Practitioner, 1870–1918

Rosemary Stevens has asserted that "[i]n most, if not all countries, whether they have national health insurance or not, the organization of the health system lies as a direct outgrowth of the history and culture of the medical profession."[1] America was "no exception," she added. "Basic patterns of medical organization, including the relationships between physicians and hospitals and between generalists and specialists long antedate the growth of what we like to call modern medicine."[2] Stevens's insight provides a starting point for examining the central theme of this book, which is that the composition and configuration of America's doctors and hospitals significantly have hampered efforts by reformers to synchronize finance and delivery.

This chapter covers the period from about 1870 to 1918, from the onset of scientific medicine in the United States until the end of World War I. During this period, doctors began their successful quest for political, social, and economic hegemony. Under the leadership of the American Medical Association, they created a power structure – a professional arena. This chapter shows how they did it.

THE ACQUISITION OF LICENSING AUTHORITY

Scholars who have written about professional power and control have maintained that a professional group's success largely depends upon the "exclusivity" of its claim to a particular area of knowledge.[3] In seeking exclusivity, professions seek help from the "state," a word that scholars often use when emphasizing the coercive powers of government.[4] Professions need the state in order to establish their claim and to protect it.

US Health Policy and Health Care Delivery

The unique composition and configuration of doctors and hospitals in the United States is leading to a crisis in primary care provision. There are significantly more specialists than generalists, and many community hospitals and outpatient facilities are concentrated in affluent areas with high rates of comprehensive insurance coverage. These particular features present difficult challenges to policymakers seeking to increase access to care. Carl F. Ameringer shows why the road to universal health care is not built on universal finance alone. Policymakers in other countries successfully align finance with delivery to achieve better access, lower costs, and improved population health. This book explains how the US health care system developed, and why efforts to expand insurance coverage in the absence of significant changes to health care delivery will fuel higher costs without achieving the desired results.

CARL F. AMERINGER is retired Professor of Health Policy and Politics at Virginia Commonwealth University.

US Health Policy and Health Care Delivery

Doctors, Reformers, and Entrepreneurs

CARL F. AMERINGER

CAMBRIDGE
UNIVERSITY PRESS

University Printing House, Cambridge CB2 8BS, United Kingdom

One Liberty Plaza, 20th Floor, New York, NY 10006, USA

477 Williamstown Road, Port Melbourne, VIC 3207, Australia

314–321, 3rd Floor, Plot 3, Splendor Forum, Jasola District Centre, New Delhi – 110025, India

79 Anson Road, #06–04/06, Singapore 079906

Cambridge University Press is part of the University of Cambridge.

It furthers the University's mission by disseminating knowledge in the pursuit of education, learning, and research at the highest international levels of excellence.

www.cambridge.org
Information on this title: www.cambridge.org/9781107117204
DOI: 10.1017/9781316338117

First published 2018

Printed in the United States of America by Sheridan Books, Inc

A catalogue record for this publication is available from the British Library.

Library of Congress Cataloging-in-Publication Data
NAMES: Ameringer, Carl F., author.
TITLE: US health policy and health care delivery : doctors, reformers, and entrepreneurs / Carl F. Ameringer.
DESCRIPTION: Cambridge, United Kingdom ; New York, NY : Cambridge University Press, 2018. | Includes bibliographical references and index.
IDENTIFIERS: LCCN 2017059463 | ISBN 9781107117204 (hardback) | ISBN 9781107539846 (paperback)
SUBJECTS: | MESH: Health Policy–history | Delivery of Health Care–history | Universal Coverage–history | History, 19th Century | History, 20th Century | History, 21st Century | United States
CLASSIFICATION: LCC RA418.3.U6 | NLM WA 11 AA1 | DDC 362.10973–dc23
LC record available at https://lccn.loc.gov/2017059463

ISBN 978-1-107-11720-4 Hardback
ISBN 978-1-107-53984-6 Paperback

For Suzanne, Caroline, and Katie

Contents

Figure

Tables

Acknowledgments

This book reflects my thinking over the past several years concerning the problem of universal access to basic health care services in the United States. I am greatly indebted to the previous labors of others on this subject, many of whom are mentioned by name in this book. My perspective stems in part from their work, from my own experiences in the field, from frequent exchanges I have had with colleagues and students over the years, and from numerous interviews and conversations with patients, providers, and administrators in low-income rural and urban areas of central Wisconsin, central Virginia, and Omaha, Nebraska. I would like to thank Christine Reed, David Johnson, and William Osheroff for their thoughtful comments on early drafts of Chapters 1, 2, and 6, respectively. I also would like to thank my wife, Suzanne; my daughters, Caroline and Katie; and my parents, Charles and Jean, for their abiding love and support. Finally, I would like to express my deep appreciation to J. Woodford ("Woody") Howard, Jr. Woody was the quintessential Johns Hopkins professor, a brilliant scholar and gifted teacher who mentored numerous graduate students throughout his remarkable career. I was fortunate to be one of them. I still feel his presence every time I sit down to write.

Abbreviations

AAGP	American Academy of General Practice
AALL	American Association for Labor Legislation
ACO	Accountable Care Organization
ACP	American College of Physicians
ACS	American College of Surgeons
AHA	American Hospital Association
AMA	American Medical Association
ASC	Ambulatory Surgery Center
BME	Bureau of Medical Economics (American Medical Association)
CAH	Critical Access Hospital
CCMC	Committee on the Costs of Medical Care
CME	Council on Medical Education (American Medical Association)
CMS	Centers for Medicare and Medicaid Services
COGME	Council on Graduate Medical Education
CON	Certificate of Need
CPT	Current Procedural Terminology (Codes)
DOJ	Department of Justice
DRG	Diagnosis-Related Group
FMC	Foundation for Medical Care
FTC	Federal Trade Commission
GP	General Practitioner
HMO	Health Maintenance Organization
IDS	Integrated Delivery System
IOM	Institute of Medicine

IPA	Independent Practice Association
MCO	Managed Care Organization
MSO	Medical Staff Organization
NHS	(British) National Health Service
NP	Nurse Practitioner
OECD	Organisation for Economic Co-operation and Development
OPS	Oregon Physicians Service
PCP	Primary Care Physician
PPO	Preferred Provider Organization
PPS	Prospective Payment System
PSRO	Professional Standards Review Organization

Health Policy and Health Care Delivery

Health care delivery and finance are closely linked. Changes to one often call for changes to the other. Just as budget cuts for instance may require adjustments to the nature and amount of health care services provided, so new scientific discoveries, new technologies, and new diseases or the proliferation of old ones may lead to changes in finance or insurance coverage.

US politicians have focused most of their attention on health care finance; they have given lesser consideration to its delivery. Yet the second is just as important as the first when it comes to increasing access to care, controlling costs, and improving quality. Access to health care services does not depend solely on insurance coverage; individuals with insurance must be able to use it, and use it effectively. Similarly, controlling costs and improving the health of populations are not simply or even principally about finance. The composition and configuration of a country's health care industry largely determine what is possible – the type and range of services that can be provided and the amount of money needed to achieve certain results.

All countries with government-run or government-financed health care (collectively referred to as "universal health care countries") oversee, monitor, and regulate both its finance and its delivery to varying degrees. Universal health care countries, for instance, often monitor and control the size of medical school classes and the proportion of doctors who provide primary and specialty care. Universal health care countries, moreover, frequently monitor and control the purchase of medical equipment, the building of new hospitals or additions to them, and the type of doctors who work in them. Universal health care countries also typically monitor and control the geographic configuration of doctors and hospitals, and the conditions for gaining access to them.[1]

The exception to the general rule is the United States. Not only does the United States lack universal coverage, it also lacks a system designed to provide basic services to all its citizens. While delivery systems in other countries largely have developed in tandem with expanded insurance coverage, US health care delivery has not. Instead, government programs to increase insurance coverage since 1965 (Medicare, Medicaid, and expanded versions of them) all too often have encouraged, rather than discouraged, high-cost specialty care. The result is that America's health care industry is poorly equipped and designed to meet the challenges of universal access. Absent a significant course correction, universal health care will remain elusive, even if universal finance is achieved.

This chapter will examine the composition and configuration of America's health care system and compare and contrast it with those in certain countries (Australia, Canada, France, Germany, and Britain).[2] Next, it will assess the approaches these other countries use to align finance and delivery. Finally, this chapter will seek to explain why the composition and configuration of the US health care industry is so different from those in other countries, and why this composition and configuration has led to higher per capita costs and often poorer results in terms of population health.

THE CENTRAL COMPONENTS OF UNIVERSAL HEALTH CARE DELIVERY

There are two significant differences in health care delivery between the United States and universal health care countries: (1) the emphasis on primary care and (2) the coordination and distribution of doctors, hospitals, and related health care facilities such as clinics and community health centers.

Primary Care

Primary care, the foundation of health care delivery in universal health care countries, is weakly rooted in the United States.[3] Primary care has been defined as "the kind of care that is ambulatory and directly accessible to patients, with a generalist character, situated in the community that it serves and with a focus on the individual in his or her home situation and social context."[4] Countries with a strong foundation in primary care require or encourage patients to register with a primary care physician (PCP), typically a general practitioner (GP), who acts as the initial point of contact in the delivery system. Primary care physicians practice in office-based settings, clinics, or health centers located in communities in which their patients reside. Primary care physicians provide comprehensive, whole person care; they do not specialize in a single body part or disease. Finally, primary care physicians are coordinators as well as providers of care; they act as gatekeepers to hospitals and specialists.[5]

The importance of primary care has become more apparent in recent decades as chronic diseases have proliferated, straining all countries' financial resources. Often defined as lasting more than three months, chronic diseases typically limit individual performance and require ongoing medical treatment and care. Leading chronic diseases or conditions (most publications treat the terms as interchangeable) include cancers, diabetes, hypertension, stroke, heart diseases, asthma, and mental disorders. Almost 44 percent of US citizens, or 133 million people, have experienced at least one chronic disease.[6] That number is projected to increase to 171 million, or 48 percent of the population, by 2030.[7] Many persons, moreover, suffer from multiple chronic illnesses or comorbidities, the number increasing as they get older. About two-thirds of US citizens over age 64 currently suffer from two or more chronic diseases.[8]

Effective prevention and treatment of chronic diseases calls for regular and continuous monitoring, coordination, and concerted management on the part of primary care physicians, nurses, pharmacists, and other health care providers. Unfortunately, the US path of increasing specialization is at odds with the trajectory of chronic disease escalation. Stressing primary care and public health promotion, health systems in other countries have adapted more quickly and more seamlessly to the century-long shift from acute to chronic diseases. These countries achieve better results than the United States when it comes to controlling costs and obtaining good outcomes on measures of population health, such as life expectancy and infant mortality.[9]

Coordination and Distribution of Health Care Services

The second distinguishing feature of US health care delivery is the lack of a uniform strategy for rationalizing, coordinating, and distributing health care services throughout the entire nation. According to Daniel Fox, President Emeritus of the Milbank Memorial Fund, twentieth-century health planners held firm convictions about proper health system design.[10] Fox coined the term "hierarchical regionalism" to describe the pyramidal shape that many planners prescribed. By "hierarchical regionalism," Fox meant the geographic alignment of doctors and hospitals from small towns to big cities along a continuum of increasing task complexity – from primary to secondary to tertiary care.[11]

Lord Bertrand Dawson, England's first Minister of Health, was an early proponent of hierarchical regionalism. In a famous 1920 report (known as the "Dawson Report"), the Medical Consultative Council, which Dawson chaired, provided the blueprint for Britain's National Health Service (NHS).[12] Figure 1.1 reproduces the diagram contained in the Dawson Report showing the recommended locations and linkages among primary centres, secondary centres, and teaching hospital centres. Primary centres, the report stated, "would be staffed by general practitioners."[13] Secondary centres, on the other hand, would "be situated in towns where adequate equipment and an efficient staff of consultants and specialists exist ... [T]heir services would mainly be consultative; they would receive cases referred from the primary centres for diagnosis and special treatment."[14] Finally, teaching hospital centres, the report indicated, "would receive cases of unusual difficulty requiring specialised knowledge and equipment, and its laboratories and special departments would be a court of reference."[15]

All universal health care countries have implemented hierarchical regionalism to varying degrees. Physicians with salaried hospital positions are specialists in most countries, while those who provide ambulatory care in private offices or community clinics most often are generalists. In several countries, patients must register with a general practitioner who provides first-contact care. Unless the situation is emergent, patients often need a referral from their GP in order to see a specialist. Known as "gatekeeping," the requirement of a referral accomplishes several purposes. It promotes hierarchy by coordinating and managing access to services of increasing task complexity; it advances regionalism because generalists are responsible for the health of populations in local communities; and it bolsters primary care because it officially sanctions the role of generalists in health care delivery.[16]

The closest America has come to using gatekeeping on a wide scale was in the 1980s and 1990s. Private health insurers initiated gatekeeping and other cost-cutting measures (known as "managed care") in order to control expenditures. These efforts encountered heavy resistance from doctors and consumers. By the mid- to late 1990s, the political headwinds became too strong for most insurers, causing them to roll back or mitigate

DIAGRAM OF AN AREA
SHOWING ALL SERVICES

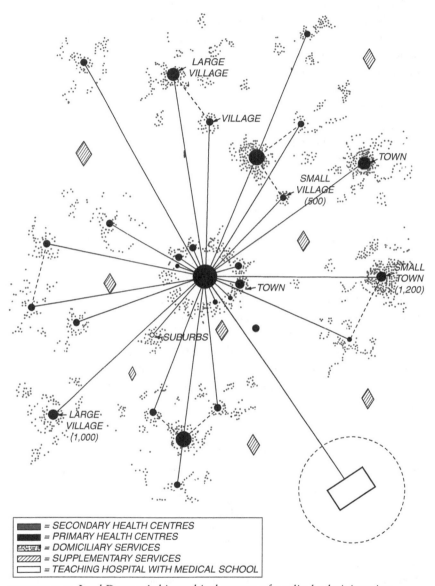

= SECONDARY HEALTH CENTRES
= PRIMARY HEALTH CENTRES
= DOMICILIARY SERVICES
= SUPPLEMENTARY SERVICES
= TEACHING HOSPITAL WITH MEDICAL SCHOOL

FIGURE 1.1 Lord Dawson's hierarchical system of medical administration.
Source: B. Dawson, *Interim Report on the Future Provision of Medical and Allied Services* (Ministry of Health, 1920).

their efforts.[17] Gatekeeping was drastically curtailed. As a result, most Americans today see a specialist with few restrictions.[18]

Neither "hierarchy" nor "regionalism" has been implemented systemically in the United States, though some have tried.[19] Some of the multihospital systems that have emerged in recent years contain features of hierarchy and regionalism, albeit to varying degrees.[20] While this may be promising, multihospital systems and their component facilities largely respond to economic, not social, cues. Whether for-profit or nonprofit, their main goals are to capture market share and increase revenues. Seeking to enhance income and market position, hospital systems generally organize and expand in regions of the country where large numbers of patients with comprehensive insurance coverage reside. Few hospital systems have established clinics or primary care practices in poor city neighborhoods or small rural towns.[21]

HOW OTHER COUNTRIES ADVANCE PRIMARY CARE AND COORDINATE HEALTH CARE DELIVERY

As indicated, countries that furnish health care to all persons not only provide a way to finance it, they also further the means to deliver it. Countries typically advance primary care and coordinate health care delivery in two ways. First, they seek to maintain an equivalent ratio of generalists and specialists, usually one-to-one. Second, they seek to uphold traditional boundaries between primary and specialty care, between care that generalists provide in the community and care that specialists provide in the hospital.

The Close-to-Even Split between Generalists and Specialists

As shown in Table 1.1, countries with a strong foundation in primary care have a close to even split of generalists and specialists. In the United States, on the other hand, specialists significantly outnumber generalists. Moreover, there are far fewer generalists in the United States based on population density than in the other countries listed in Table 1.1. While there are approximately 0.30 generalists per 1,000 persons in the United States, the range in other countries is 1.15 (Canada) to 1.61 (Germany), a difference of more than fivefold at the higher end.

Table 1.1 is based on data compiled by the Organisation for Economic Co-operation and Development (OECD).[22] The distinction between "generalist" in the OECD database and "primary care physician," the

TABLE 1.1 *Percentage of generalist and specialist physicians and their density for select countries, 2011*

Country	Total Physicians	% Generalists	% Specialists	Density per 1,000 Generalist/Specialist
Australia	73,980	47.31	49.47	1.57/1.64
Canada	74,526	46.98	53.02	1.15/1.30
France	199,920	47.28	52.72	1.56/1.74
Germany	312,695	41.86	58.14	1.61/2.23
United States	767,782	12.14	87.86	0.30/2.16

Sources: OECD Health Stats 2011; US Commonwealth Fund Survey 2009.
Note: "Generalist" is equivalent to family medicine practitioner in the United States.

preferred designation in the United States, calls for clarification. While the OECD's definition of "generalist medical practitioner" includes only general or family practitioners, the US definition of "primary care physician" typically includes general internists and general pediatricians as well as family practitioners.[23] If general internists and general pediatricians are counted as "generalist medical practitioners" in the OECD database, then the US share would increase to about one-third. A ratio of one-third PCPs to two-thirds specialists is consistent with most US compilations and estimates.[24] Unfortunately, OECD data do not provide information on each country's number of general internists, though the OECD does separate out pediatricians. Consequently, comparisons among countries using the US designation for PCP would be imprecise. Rough estimates based on existing data suggest that PCPs comprise close to one-half of the physician workforce in Australia, Canada, France, and Germany.[25] Despite these discrepancies, however, the point remains – the ratio of PCPs to specialists is much lower in the United States than in these other countries.

Because governments in universal health care countries pay all or a substantial portion of medical education, they can closely monitor and regulate student enrollments, residency placements, and practice locations.[26] In America, where many medical schools are private institutions and most students pay for all or a substantial portion of their medical school education, often accumulating large debts in the process, the federal government's influence over enrollments, residency placements, and practice locations is relatively weak.[27]

Britain uses quotas to fix medical school enrollments.[28] Following undergraduate medical study, students in Britain enter "vocational training," commencing with a two-year Foundation Programme or series of specialty rotations. After completing the two-year program, doctors pursue clinical training as generalists or specialists. Successful completion of generalist clinical training and examination leads to inclusion on the General Practice Registrar. GPs can practice independently at this point. Completion of training and examination in a particular specialty leads to inclusion on the Specialty Registrar. Only doctors on the Specialty Registrar can receive appointments as hospital consultants.[29]

France controls physician supply by restricting the number of students who can enter the second year of medical school (an approach known as *numerus clausus*).[30] In addition, French authorities allocate residency placements by area of specialization and training location.[31] Australian national, state, and territory governments also restrict medical school enrollments.[32] These governments further influence where students can practice after graduation.[33] Though Germany does not impose restrictions on medical school enrollments, "the number of practice permits for ambulatory care physicians in a specific region is limited, based on a national service delivery quota."[34] "Physicians need to obtain a permit to be reimbursed by the statutory health insurance," according to a 2014 OECD report on geographic imbalances in German doctor supply.[35]

Provincial governments in Canada oversee medical school enrollments and residency placements for the stated goal of maintaining an "equivalent proportion" of generalists and specialists.[36] To advance this goal, Canadian "[m]edical schools offer roughly half of all training opportunities in family medicine."[37] Canada also has policies in place that seek to address geographic shortages in rural and remote areas.[38]

The generalist/specialist mix in the United States has not always been different from those in other countries. In 1963, the proportion of PCPs to specialists in the United States was about 1:1. By 1988, the proportion of PCPs to specialists was about 1:2.[39] Almost coincident with this shift, health care costs began increasing in the United States well above those in other countries. Table 1.2 shows the growing divide in per capita spending between the United States and certain OECD countries.

Some analysts drew a connection between surging costs and disproportionate numbers of PCPs and specialists in the United States. They noted that as the spending gap between the United States and other OECD countries was expanding, so was the ratio of generalists to specialists.[40] In 1986, Congress tasked the US Council on Graduate Medical Education (COGME) with examining the situation and recommending any solutions. After about six years of study, COGME proposed that

TABLE 1.2 *Per capita health expenditures for select countries, 1970–2014*

Country	1970	1975	1980	1985	1990	1995	2000	2005	2010	2014
Australia	223*	401	615	880	1,153	1,555	2,157	2,842	3,607	4,289
Canada	289	476	769	1,236	1,694	2,002	2,422	3,282	4,228	4,502
France	193	365	655	1,012	1,412	2,053	2,505	3,124	3,872	4,464
Germany	263	567	960	1,400	1,757	2,251	2,709	3,331	4,413	5,200
United Kingdom	142	265	429	629	852	1,143	1,565	2,337	3,041	3,989
United States	355	605	1,108	–	2,843	–	4,559	6,445	7,932	9,036

* 1971 amount.

Sources: OECD Health Stats 2015; Centers for Medicare and Medicaid Services, *Trend Tables*, 2016.

Notes: All amounts are in US dollars/capita, 2015; US figures for 1970, 1975, 1980, and 1990 are from Centers for Medicare and Medicaid Services. All other figures are from OECD.

50 percent of all practicing physicians in the United States should be engaged in primary care and the other 50 percent in specialty and sub-specialty care. In support of its recommendation, COGME stated:

Increasing subspecialization in U.S. health care escalates health care costs, results in fragmentation of services, and increases the discrepancy between numbers of rural and urban physicians. A rational health system must be based upon an infrastructure consisting of a majority of generalist physicians trained to provide quality primary care and an appropriate mix of other specialists to meet health care needs. Today, other specialists and subspecialists provide a significant amount of primary care. However, physicians who are trained, practice, and receive continuing education in the generalist disciplines provide more comprehensive and cost-effective care than nonprimary care specialists and subspecialists.[41]

In another part of its report, COGME emphasized the link between overutilization of services and America's highly specialized physician workforce. "[P]atients undergo more intense medical services per visit because of the exceptionally high proportion of nonprimary care special-ists in this country," it stated.[42] Nor were higher spending and more specialty services producing better results, the Council observed. "Despite all the billions spent on health care and the remarkable increase in expenditures for biomedical research, new technology, and medical care, the United States has a rather dismal health status scorecard."[43] By "health status scorecard," COGME meant America's weaker results compared with OECD countries on certain key measures of population health – life expectancy and infant mortality.[44]

Over the course of the next several years, Congress sought to bolster funding for the education and training of primary care physicians, while decreasing it for specialists. Nothing really changed, however.[45] Market forces, not the federal government, dictated the course of events.[46] "[T]here seems to be little support in the marketplace for the goal of half of new graduates being in primary care specialties," analysts said.[47] "[E]ven in New York, where 68 percent of practicing physicians are non-primary care and, in California, with its high level of managed care penetration, the job market [in 2000] appears stronger for non-primary care physicians than for primary care physicians," researchers observed.[48]

Primary Care Gatekeeping and Practice Location

Just as governments in universal health care countries manage the pro-duction and placement of generalists and specialists, so they regulate access to specialists and the hospitals in which most specialists work. Government-imposed restrictions on patient access to specialists are crucial, many European experts maintain.[49] Without government restrictions, the boundaries between generalists and specialists will blur and the advantages of general practice will diminish. According to Wienke Boerma of the Netherlands and Ana Rico of Norway: "A strong position for general practice is not readily compatible with directly accessible medical specialists who compete with GPs to provide first contact care (this can be resolved by introducing a referral system). Similarly, continuity of care requires that patients have appropriate incentives to see the same GP for each new episode of care (this is usually realized with a patient list system; patients register with a GP of their choice)."[50]

The approaches that countries use to restrict access to specialists are linked to the financing scheme they employ.[51] Australia has a social insurance scheme known as Medicare, which, unlike most social insurance schemes, is administered by the central government. About two-thirds of hospital beds in Australia are public and the remaining one-third are private.[52] Medicare pays for primary care services in physicians' private offices. It also pays for inpatient specialty services in public hospitals and for outpatient specialty services if there is a referral from a general practitioner.[53]

Canada's social insurance scheme, also known as Medicare, consists of twelve separate provincial and territorial plans. Most Canadian hospitals are run by nonprofit entities. There are no truly private hospitals in Canada, however, because the national and provincial governments own the hospital beds.[54] While specialists can see patients in their private offices and are paid fee-for-service, strong financial incentives exist to encourage gatekeeping or primary care referrals.[55]

All French citizens receive comprehensive health insurance coverage under one of three different occupation-based funds. The Ministry of Social Affairs in France "closely supervises" all fund operations.[56] About 60 percent of hospitals and acute care beds are publicly owned.[57] In addition, France has regional hospital agencies that "coordinate public and private hospitals and allocate their budgets."[58] As of 2004, about 70 percent of GPs were self-employed and were paid fee-for-service.[59] By contrast, about 50 percent of specialists were salaried, many of them with hospital appointments.[60] France requires patients to register with a generalist and obtain a referral before seeing a specialist. Failure to obtain a referral reduces the amount of the reimbursement to the specialist under the public insurance scheme.[61]

Germany's national health insurance system is administered by 180 health insurance plans or "sickness funds." Though established and regulated by the German government, sickness funds are autonomous, not-for-profit, nongovernmental entities.[62] German hospitals obtain most of their funds for operations and capital expenditures from public sources.[63] Ambulatory care doctors in Germany cannot treat patients in hospitals, while hospital-based doctors, mostly specialists, cannot treat patients outside hospitals.[64] Though Germans do not need referrals to see office-based specialists, financial penalties exist.[65]

Established in 1948, Britain's National Health Service is a highly centralized health care system financed largely from general taxes. The British government owns the hospitals and employs or contracts with physicians. The pattern of delivery reflects the tiered structure outlined in Figure 1.1.[66] Community-based GPs, operating under government contracts, provide primary care services to persons residing in specific geographic areas. Most specialists ("consultants") are salaried employees of government-owned hospitals and do not have private offices. Local residents register with GPs (GP practices), who act as gatekeepers for hospital-based specialty or secondary (hospital) services. Patients typically need a referral from a community-based generalist in order to see a hospital-based specialist.[67]

Neither public ownership of hospitals nor the separation of doctors by practice location are common features of health care delivery in the United States. Instead, the lines between generalists and specialists, and between care that takes place in private offices and care that takes place in hospitals, are indistinct. This is not a recent phenomenon. It is a long-standing tradition, closely tied to the belief that all physicians of whatever background and training should be able to treat their patients in private offices and hospitals. While "closed staffing" is the norm in other countries, "open staffing" is the custom in the United States.[68]

THE THREE ARENAS AND THE CHALLENGE TO COMPREHENSIVE HEALTH POLICY IN THE UNITED STATES

Policymakers in all countries seek to improve access, control costs, and enhance quality. But the way they prioritize and balance these three goals, and the means they use to advance them, frequently differ. Tensions among the three goals often occur. Efforts to improve access may increase costs and lower quality, while efforts to control costs may reduce quality and hinder access. In universal health care countries, the balancing of these three goals takes place in the government or public arena, while in the United States balancing occurs in both the private and the public sectors. Because there are multiple sources of finance and multiple forms of delivery in the United States, reconciling tensions among the three goals is more challenging than it is in other countries.

The failure of the US government to construct a national health policy that reconciles diverse priorities means that there are no overriding principles to guide health care delivery. Neither the provision of care nor the financing of it targets the entire population. Rather, private entities and individuals – corporate boards and corporate managers, physicians, hospital administrators, accrediting bodies, and private insurers – establish the parameters and rules in local communities and regions. These stakeholders operate largely outside government control, exercising decision-making authority in certain key areas. Unchecked by government, private interests have taken the US health care industry in a very different direction from those in other countries. In a universal health care system, finance and delivery are interrelated and complementary. In the United States, on the other hand, finance and delivery are mostly separate and distinct.

Though physicians and hospitals have influenced the course of health policy in other countries, their impact has been significantly smaller than in the United States. This is because doctors and hospitals in other countries operate within, not outside, a government framework that establishes the parameters for their organization and operation. In the United States, on the other hand, myriad rules and regulations emanating from legislatures, courts, government agencies, professional associations, and private accrediting bodies, among others, have created and sustained the existence of three separate and autonomous policymaking arenas. The three arenas are the professional arena, the market arena, and the government or public arena.

The Professional Arena

The professional arena includes medical societies, licensing boards, specialty boards, accrediting bodies, teaching hospitals, medical staff organizations of hospitals, and advisory boards to government agencies, insurers, and other entities. Policymaking in the professional arena involves the education, training, licensing, and specialty certification of physicians; the rules and norms governing patient and professional relations; and to a great extent the amounts and methods of payment for professional services.[69] While doctors largely control the professional arena, other health professionals have made significant strides in recent years. As other health professionals have expanded their scope of practice (nurse practitioners (NPs) are a good example), so doctors' domination of the professional arena has diminished.[70]

The Market Arena

The market arena comprises corporate health systems, private insurers, laboratories, imaging centers, pharmaceutical companies, nursing homes, and various business enterprises. The market arena is where entrepreneurs reside. Despite numerous government regulations, entrepreneurs have more free reign than they do in other countries to devise innovative organizational forms. Policymaking in the market arena encompasses network formation by insurers, employers, and managed care organizations; strategic decisions concerning the configuration, distribution, and integration of physician groups and hospital systems; and the development of surgery centers, imaging centers, laboratories, and other outpatient facilities.[71]

The Government Arena

Prominent participants in the government arena include legislative bodies, government agencies, courts, and special interest groups. This is the arena where reformers and planners are located. Policymaking in the government arena involves lawmaking, rulemaking, enforcement actions, and court decisions. Government initiatives affecting health care delivery often are narrowly tailored and piecemeal.[72] Most are stop-gap measures enacted to plug holes in the delivery system.

Absent a single overarching framework for the generation and enforcement of a common set of rules for health care delivery, the US health care system has evolved in two ways: (1) through the interaction of groups and interests operating within each of the three arenas and (2) through confrontation, negotiation, and cooperation between dominant actors representing the different regimes. Those seeking to better understand the current delivery system and its effect on health policy should examine the pivotal events, developments, and conflicts occurring within and among the three arenas over time. This book is an attempt to do that.

OUTLINE OF THE BOOK

This book traces the development and evolution of the professional, market, and government arenas from about 1870 to 2015, from the emergence of the professional arena to the uneasy coexistence of all three today. Chapter 2 covers the medical profession's rise to hegemony and the foundations of US health care delivery in the years before World War I, from about 1870 to 1918. It examines the origins of the professional arena, its organizational underpinnings, its operating principles, and the incipient conflicts between generalists and specialists.

Chapter 3 examines the rules governing health care delivery and the internal and external challenges to them during the period 1919–1945. It explores the US government's attempts to establish universal health care; the hardening of positions concerning certain organizational forms; the challenge from reformers, many of them physicians who favored prepaid group practice; and the use of the federal antitrust laws to advance reformers' cause.

Chapter 4 traces the convergence of physicians around hospitals after World War II, from 1946–1964. It examines the decline of health centers for the delivery of primary and preventive care, the ascendance of voluntary hospitals and their links to medical specialization and medical technology, the development of private and public funding sources to support voluntary hospitals, the conflicts between generalists and specialists over hospital privileges, the formation of the Joint Commission, and the limitations of government planning.

Chapter 5 covers the decline of organized medicine and the creation of the market arena during the period 1965–1995. It explores health care delivery and practice patterns of hospitals and physicians following the enactment of Medicare and Medicaid, the use of government regulation to control rapidly escalating costs, the turn to market competition under the federal antitrust laws, the development of new rules for organizing health care delivery, and the accommodation of medical specialization and various corporate forms.

Finally, Chapter 6 examines the trajectory of the health care industry from 1996 to 2015. It covers the backlash against managed care, the rise of entrepreneurial specialism, the escalation of chronic diseases and the development of new delivery models to manage them, the emergence of multihospital systems, the struggle to provide care in rural and poor urban communities, the increasing use of hospitalists to coordinate inpatient care, and the creation of Accountable Care Organizations (ACOs) under the Patient Protection and Affordable Care Act (often called Oba-maCare) to address some of these problems.

In evaluating the course of health care delivery in the United States, this book views the policymaking process somewhat differently from most other historical and political accounts. While most scholarly works generally acknowledge the influence of doctors, hospitals, and their respective associations, they largely focus on political confrontations over the financing of health care.[73] By contrast, this book emphasizes, as some other books and writers do, that doctors, hospitals, and corporate health systems significantly influence US health policy through the principles, customs, and structural configurations they have imposed.[74]

Many scholarly works, moreover, largely fail to emphasize the role of US courts in fashioning health policy. Yet courts have been important forums for reconciling conflicts over rules and policies emanating from the three different arenas. By way of example, several confrontations occurred between state medical boards and managed care organizations in the 1990s over the accountability of medical directors for denials of insurance coverage. Medical boards argued that they could discipline company doctors who denied coverage for medical conditions. Managed care organizations, on the other hand, claimed that their medical directors were engaged in utilization review, a strictly "business function" that only state insurance commissioners should oversee. In a lawsuit filed in Arizona, Blue Cross/Blue Shield sued to stop the state medical board from disciplining its medical director for "unprofessional conduct" when the director refused to "precertify" a patient for gallbladder surgery. An Arizona appellate court ultimately decided that the state medical board had jurisdiction, that precertification involved a medical not an insurance decision.[75]

There are many other instances in which courts have reconciled conflicting views, rules, and norms that the three different arenas have advanced. While some of these conflicts have been over turf or jurisdiction as the above situation entailed, other disputes have involved the application of legal doctrines, such as the prohibition on the "corporate practice of medicine," a basic tenet of the professional arena that many states currently recognize and occasionally enforce.[76] In other instances, judicial rulings have resolved disputes over which set of rules or norms should prevail as happened when federal courts struck down professional constraints on advertising and contract practice in the 1970s, opening the health care industry to market competition.[77]

Finally, this book resists the notion that Americans can achieve universal health care through universal finance alone. Absent significant changes to its delivery system, the United States will continue to have difficulty providing basic medical services to much of its population even if universal insurance coverage is achieved. Costs will continue to escalate, and population health relative to most other OECD nations will continue to decline.

"The foundation of medicine's control over its work," sociologist Eliot Freidson has written, "is ... clearly political in character, involving the aid of the state in establishing and maintaining the profession's preeminence."[5]

The customary way that professions gain exclusivity is through professional licensing. Once a state-backed licensing scheme has been established, only those who have a license can do the types of things that the license allows. Professional licensing raises a number of important questions. What is the entity that issues the license? How closely does the state monitor, control, or oversee that entity? What are the criteria for licensure? How are the criteria implemented and administered? What is the scope of the license? What can the licensee do with the license? The answers to these questions involve the exercise of professional power.

Before the advent of science-based medicine, medical practice was often a primitive and haphazard affair. Several different schools of thought prevailed. These different schools produced a variety of healers, including allopathic physicians, known as Regulars, and eclectics and homeopaths, known as Irregulars. Allopaths attacked what they perceived to be the causes of disease, frequently using "heroic" measures such as purgatives and blood-letting. Eclectics used botanical or medicinal remedies to treat illness, while homeopaths employed diluted amounts of disease-causing agents to induce the body to treat itself.

Most Regular physicians stopped using heroic measures by the mid-nineteenth century and, with increasing success, applied the discoveries of modern science to detect and defeat the agents of disease.[6] Still, eclectics and homeopaths maintained a strong following until scientific medicine firmly took hold, which did not occur until the early twentieth century. Regulars founded the AMA in 1847 largely to combat their competitors. The quest for legal recognition through professional licensing was an important part of the AMA's strategy. In furtherance of this strategy, the AMA turned to the states. Professional licensing was a state, not a national, undertaking. West Virginia, the first state to license physicians, produced a test case that made it all the way to the US Supreme Court.[7]

In 1881, the West Virginia legislature created a state board of health, which had as its primary purpose the licensing of medical practitioners. Under West Virginia law, graduation from "a reputable medical college" was one of the ways that applicants could gain a medical license. The criteria that the state board used for determining whether a school was "reputable" came from the AMA. A challenger to the new board's authority soon emerged, Frank Dent, a graduate from an eclectic medical school in Cincinnati, Ohio. Dent continued to practice medicine in West Virginia even though the board refused to give him a license. The board's pursuit of an indictment against Dent for practicing without a license produced a misdemeanor conviction and a $50 fine.[8]

Resting his challenge on the equal protection and due process clauses of the Fourteenth Amendment to the US Constitution, Dent sought a reversal of his conviction in the US Supreme Court after West Virginia's highest court refused to overturn it. Dent claimed that the Fourteenth Amendment barred the state board from choosing one school of thought or approach to medical practice over another. The US Supreme Court took up Dent's case, but in an 1889 ruling affirmed the conviction.[9] "[T]here is nothing of an arbitrary character in the provisions of the statute in question," the Court held.[10] The board, the Court ruled, could deny medical licenses to eclectics, homeopaths, and other Irregular practitioners.[11]

Because the West Virginia law had been broadly crafted to favor Regular physicians, the Court's *Dent* decision was far-reaching. An important consequence of the Court's ruling was to make West Virginia's state medical society, founded in 1867 by Regular physicians, the state's de facto licensing authority. Under the West Virginia law, the state's governor appointed the members of the licensing board. James Reeves, a founding member of the state medical society and a chief proponent of the legislation that created the board, received a six-year appointment, as did several other medical society doctors.[12] West Virginia was far from unique in this respect. Indeed, many state laws called for governors to appoint board members from approved lists that state medical societies compiled. In a small number of states (Alabama, Maryland, and North Carolina), legislatures delegated the power of appointment directly to the state medical society, bypassing the governor entirely.[13]

Of further significance, the Supreme Court's *Dent* decision left standing the expansive definition of the "practice of medicine" contained in the West Virginia law. The practice of medicine, the law said, "include[d] anyone who treated or prescribed for the sick, including 'apothecaries and pharmacists.'"[14] Laws passed in other states were similarly expansive. Georgia defined medical practice to include "the diagnosis or treatment of disease, defects, or injuries of human beings";[15] Maryland's law encompassed anyone "who shall operate on, profess to heal, prescribe for, or otherwise treat any physical or mental ailment";[16] and Pennsylvania "cover[ed] and embrace[d] everything that by common understanding is included in the term healing art."[17] Definitions such as these arguably extended the profession's boundaries to the far reaches of medical science with few, if any, limits.

That the US medical profession, for all practical purposes, gained the legal recognition to issue licenses, to establish the criteria for their issuance, and to define the practice of medicine in very broad terms was of enormous consequence. No single group of physicians in other countries had achieved such extensive powers. The German and French governments, for instance, did not delegate licensing authority to physician associations. Beginning with Prussia in 1725, the German states removed licensing authority from the universities and medical schools and established "a system of state examinations." So too, the French government stripped away the "rank and privilege associated with the physicians and surgeons of the Old Regime." By the early 1800s, the new French republic had consolidated and centralized medical licensing.[18]

Though private entities exercised licensing authority in Britain, the power to issue medical licenses was divided among nineteen different entities, nine medical corporations (these included the Royal College of Physicians of London and the Royal College of Surgeons of London) and ten universities (these included Oxford and Cambridge).[19] While the nine corporations licensed individuals who received their training in hospitals, apprenticeships, or proprietary schools, the ten universities licensed those who received their education and training directly from them. This class-conscious approach accommodated "classical university study at Oxford and Cambridge" as well as "broom-and-apron apprenticeship in an apothecary's shop," historian Thomas Neville Bonner remarked.[20] Britain's Medical Registration Act of 1858, which mandated registration of all licensed physicians and established a General Medical Council for the issuance of minimum standards, did not change the issuing source. "A license to practice in midcentury Britain could still come only from one of the nineteen licensing bodies whose requirements remained as varied as ever," Bonner wrote.[21]

Unlike physicians in other countries, American doctors faced neither a central government as in Germany or France, nor diverse licensing bodies as in Britain. The state-based licensing scheme that the Supreme Court approved in the *Dent* case made it possible for a single well-organized group to seize control of much of what constituted the practice of medicine. After the Courts' ruling in *Dent*, Regulars had the legal authority to set the boundaries of medical practice and to enforce those boundaries.

THE STANDARDIZATION OF MEDICAL EDUCATION

While licensure was essential to the exercise of state authority, the medical profession still had to determine the standards for licensure and link those

to medical science. Only then could Regular physicians gain what sociologist Magali Sarfatti Larson has called "cognitive exclusiveness."[22]
"*[U]ntil the production of knowledge and the production of producers
are unified into the same structure,*" Larson contended, "[a] profession's
cognitive base can evolve in complete independence from the profession
itself and from its production of professional producers."[23] By "same
structure," Larson meant the modern university.[24] Universities linked the
production of knowledge and the production of producers.

The road to cognitive exclusiveness through university training was
slower to develop in America than elsewhere: first, because scientific
medicine was unproven and largely unaccepted in the United States until
the early 1900s;[25] and second, because the system of university education
itself had few precedents in America.[26] But when scientific medicine did
take hold, the US medical profession moved quickly to embrace it.
"Nowhere was the transfer of medical teaching to the university swifter
or more surprising than in the United States," Bonner noted.[27]

Before US medical schools embraced scientific medicine, prospective
physicians often traveled to Europe for their medical training, to Edin-
burgh in the late 1700s, to Paris in the early 1800s, and to Germany in the
mid-1800s.[28] The so-called Johns Hopkins Big Four, the founding professors of the Johns Hopkins School of Medicine depicted in John Singer
Sargent's 1905 portrait, all trained at various locations in England,
France, and Germany – William Stewart Halsted, the surgeon who pioneered antisepsis, scrub suits, sterile rubber gloves, blood transfusions, and
the "gentle handling" of human tissue; William Welch, the pathologist
and medical school dean who established the first surgical pathology lab
at Johns Hopkins; Sir William Osler, the internist and clinician, renowned
for his teaching skills and bedside manner whose 1892 book, *Principles
and Practice of Medicine*, became the landmark text of internal medicine;
and Howard Atwood Kelly, the father of surgical gynecology, inventor of
several medical devices, and among the first to use radiation therapy to
treat cancer.[29]

These and other physician-educators introduced laboratory techniques
and clinical instruction learned at European schools and hospitals, which
they then incorporated and refined upon their return to the United States.
A major refinement that these European-educated doctors introduced was
the merger of laboratory and clinical instruction. "The fusion of laboratory medicine with the clinic in a university setting proved to be the key
development on the shaping of twentieth century medical education,"
Bonner wrote.[30] The Johns Hopkins School of Medicine, founded in

1893, represented the new model. Welch viewed German universities as archetypes for scientific exploration, while Osler saw London's hospitals as crucibles of clinical instruction. Welch and Osler merged the two in establishing the medical school at Johns Hopkins.[31]

Another important feature that US medical schools pioneered was the use of full-time faculty to do much of the teaching rather than local practitioners. Though German universities employed full-time faculty for laboratory research and experimentation, students in Germany did not receive laboratory training until the last two years of their medical school education. American medical students, on the other hand, were taught by full-time faculty from the beginning. US schools "did not simply copy the German system but turned it upside down so that the beginning students got the kind of attention reserved for advanced students and graduates in Germany," Bonner stated.[32]

By the late 1800s, the AMA fully had embraced medical instruction in a university setting. In 1906, the AMA's Council on Medical Education (CME), formed in 1904 and comprising mostly academic physicians, conducted a nation-wide inspection of 160 medical schools, classifying them as acceptable, doubtful, or unsatisfactory.[33] The CME's inspection tour preceded the publication of Abraham Flexner's highly publicized 1910 report for the Carnegie Foundation on the inadequacies of medical school education.[34] Though not a physician, Flexner was a leading educator and Johns Hopkins graduate with deep roots in the medical community. His brother, Simon Flexner, was a medical school professor and the first director of the Rockefeller Institute for Medical Research. Accompanied by N. P. Colwell, CME's secretary, Flexner surveyed many of the same schools that the CME had examined, sometimes duplicating and frequently building on the CME's findings.[35]

Flexner took aim at schools run by private practitioners, proprietary schools, in small cities and rural areas.[36] He claimed that these schools "delegate[d] the teaching function to essentially unscientific practising physicians."[37] "The sciences were badly taught, not merely because they were ... prematurely and excessively conscious of application," Flexner wrote in his report, "but because the teachers lacked abundant scientific knowledge and spirit."[38] "In the effort to teach the modicum of chemistry or physiology or pathology that 'the family doctor needs to know,' [these schools] neglected to teach anything of permanent scientific value," Flexner asserted.[39] Flexner's report adopted the curriculum for medical school instruction that the CME earlier had formulated – a four-year course of study in which "the first two years are devoted mainly to laboratory sciences, – anatomy, physiology, pharmacology, pathology; [and] the last two to clinical work in medicine, surgery, and obstetrics."[40]

The CME and Flexner surveys produced the criteria for determining whether a particular medical school was "reputable," the word used in the West Virginia law and many other state statutes. By making licensure contingent on graduation from a reputable medical school, state medical boards effectively enforced the standards that the CME and Flexner had established.

From the publication of the CME's findings in 1906 to the issuance of the Flexner report in 1910, thirty-one schools, most of them proprietary, closed. Between 1910 and 1922, after the publication of the Flexner report, another fifty schools shut down.[41] Standards for admission to the more elite schools climbed in the process. Fewer persons went on to obtain a medical degree following these major reforms. "[A]ttendance at the regular schools [in 1906] show[ed] a decrease of 1,003 below [1905], a decrease of 546 below 1904 and a decrease of 1,814 below 1903," the AMA reported.[42]

STATUS AND SPECIALIZATION

More stringent admission requirements, a four-year course of study, and enhanced laboratory instruction greatly increased the time and expense of becoming a doctor. By raising the bar appreciably higher than it had been, educational reformers excluded prospective students of modest means who, more often than not, came from small towns and rural areas.[43] Yet when legislators in Virginia attempted to subsidize the costs of medical education, many persons opposed it. "[W]e object, out and out, to the proposal to make doctors at the expense of the State treasury ... [T]here is no sound principle on which the State should be called upon to give gratuitous professional education in the so-called learned professions," an 1884 editorial in the Lynchburg Virginian declared.[44] For its part, the AMA called the Virginia proposal "positively vicious."[45]

The situation was very different in Europe. European governments supported schools that trained rural practitioners and persons of lower social status. Examples included the "secondary schools" of Germany and France, and the "practical schools" of Britain.[46] After reforms to medical education occurred in these countries, governments made efforts to accommodate students from rural areas and lower classes. Rather than reduce enrollments, as occurred in the United States, the French and German governments expanded them, opening new medical schools, hiring new faculty, and extending "capital outlays and operating costs" for laboratory equipment and facilities.[47] Though government was less active in Britain, multiple sources of licensure – the medical corporations and the universities – secured a place for general practitioners in the new pecking order.[48] "The nineteenth century surgeon-apothecary became the twentieth-century general practitioner; the old physician and surgeon became today's specialist consultants," Rosemary Stevens observed.[49]

While medical educators in Europe sought to accommodate class distinctions, medical educators in America sought to obliterate them. Decrying the "heterogeneous state" of US schools, AMA leaders complained: "We have colleges for the uneducated and for the educated student; colleges for the would-be doctor fresh from the plow-handle; colleges in which the pupil may patch up his educational defects – to the satisfaction of himself and the faculty."[50] Rising standards protected the public from poor practitioners, but the failure of government or the medical profession to consider the needs of aspiring practitioners of modest means fostered a medical elite in America. "[T]he drive to make medicine more scientific and comprehensive ... had a profound effect on the student population," Bonner stated. "[S]teeply rising requirements in medicine, along with the closing of the least expensive schools, narrowed the social differences among medical students and brought sharp complaints from the less advantaged," he noted.[51] "The profession grew more uniform in its social composition," sociologist Paul Starr maintained.[52] "The high costs of medical education and more stringent requirements limited the entry of students from the lower and working classes," Starr wrote.[53]

Specialization was an important by-product of the US approach to medical education. The emerging group of medical students – often "older, better educated, more schooled in science" than their predecessors – were less interested in general practice.[54] Many chose to specialize.[55] Specialism is an inevitable result of increasing medical and scientific knowledge, something "we must accept as fact," Boston surgeon F. C. Shattuck contended in a speech in 1900.[56] "The growth of specialism is coincident with the growth of education, and in medicine, as in any other field of knowledge, progress is dependent upon the degree to which special investigation is carried," Shattuck continued.[57] It is in the university setting "that the pursuit of original research on the part of the professors and selected students, the investigation of new discoveries and new phases of medical learning and the possible enlargement of the practical scope of pure science" occurs, the dean of Denver's medical school proclaimed in a 1903 address before the American Academy of Medicine.[58]

The growing emphasis on specialization in medical school education diminished the status of the general practitioner.[59] "Fifty years ago ... [s]pecialism was almost unknown and was limited to the special senses, as the eye or the ear," a GP lamented in a 1915 posting in the *Boston Journal* (now the *New England Journal of Medicine*). "Gradually," he observed, "specialties have increased ... until now their divisions and subdivisions are so minute as to be bounded by a single organ."[60] "The general practitioner, the general medical reader, is in a state of intellectual dyspnea," another GP professed in 1910.[61] "The hard routine of his daily round and the collecting of fees is exhausting enough, but he is asked in addition to keep elaborate bedside notes, to execute numerous laboratory tests, to consult specialists, to subscribe to a half dozen medical journals and compendiums of practice, and to buy new books," he said.[62] "The field of medical practice has grown so large that no ordinary person can successfully traverse it all," a 1901 editorial in the *Journal of the American Medical Association* (now *JAMA*) stated.[63]

As their numbers began to increase, specialists became more assertive, increasingly questioning GPs' qualifications to treat certain body parts and medical conditions.[64] "The untrained physician has no business to do eye work," a New York ophthalmologist warned in 1911. "I have seen some retracting just as poor, if not poorer, coming out of the offices of untrained physicians, as out of the offices of the optometrists. I am unalterably opposed to their doing this work," he stated.[65] General practitioners should refer patients to medical specialists and not attempt to perform procedures they were not trained to perform, specialists often asserted. "The idea here is ... to bring it home to the general practitioner that it is to [specialists] that his patients should be referred," a Colorado specialist stated.[66]

General practitioners bridled at such claims of superiority. "[W]e are confronted with a pseudo-aristocracy whose besetting sin is a selfishness that forgets old-fashioned courtesy," a Boston GP complained.[67] "Divisions into the specialties, and sub-divisions into the branches of the specialties, have resulted in a chaotic mass of antagonistic smaller bodies that seem to have nothing in common but contempt for the man in the ranks," he observed.[68] "Get your practitioner, in whom you believe, ... and trust him above all others," a New York GP admonished patients.[69] "He is, and must be, the final consultant, and is the wisest, probably, of them all," he claimed.[70] GPs are in a better position than specialists to treat patients with chronic conditions, Massachusetts doctor Elliott Joslin maintained. "Diabetes is a disease for the general practitioner to treat," Joslin offered by way of example. "The treatment of the disease broadens the point of view of the one who is responsible for controlling it, because ... its complications embrace all those of childhood and adult life extending into the zones of pediatrics, obstetrics, surgery, neurology and the various branches of medicine concerned with the ears, nose, throat, eyes, and skin," he wrote. "I deprecate any attempt to treat diabetes as an entity apart from association with general medicine," he stated.[71]

THE AMA AND THE SPECIALTY SOCIETIES

The growing rift between GPs and specialists jeopardized the AMA's efforts to unify Regular physicians under its banner. Medical specialty societies had formed in ophthalmology, neurology, gynecology, dermatology, laryngology, surgery, and pediatrics in the second half of the nineteenth century.[72] "The AMA was faced with the dilemma of unifying the general practice of medicine through common entry and educational standards at the very time that specialist interests were demanding a new fragmentation," Rosemary Stevens wrote.[73]

The main point of contention between the AMA and the specialty societies was postgraduate education. In 1913, the AMA Council on Medical Education began to consider the need to extend medical training into the specialty areas. Though it had led the effort to upgrade standards for basic medical education, the AMA was not the only organization interested in formulating standards. Several specialty societites and their examining boards emerged to claim a role.[74] These included the American College of Surgeons (ACS), formed in 1913; the American College of Physicians (ACP), formed in 1915; and the American Board for Ophthalmic Examinations (later changed to the American Board of Ophthalmology), founded in 1916.[75]

Following a lengthy political contest, the AMA and the specialty societies reached an agreement, creating the Advisory Board for Medical Specialties in 1934, an independent body.[76] Specialty recognition through specialty board certification would be a joint undertaking.[77] Physicians would continue to receive their basic education and internship training in the university setting; doctors who wanted to specialize would enter a three-year residency program at an AMA-approved hospital; those seeking specialty certification would then have to pass an examination administered by a specialty board.[78] AMA president Charles Gordon Heyd summarized the process and the reasons why the AMA would oversee it:

Specialism ... cannot be a thing apart from the field of medicine and must fit into the general pattern of medical services. Primarily, the growth of specialism both individually and collectively must rest on a broad foundation of general medical training. The assumption of specialist training by any practitioner of medicine without first being willing to submit his credentials as to his special training is incompatible with his responsibility to society. The technical qualification of the specialist may be determined by tests of examinations, tests of ability, competence of experience and hospital training. These tests must be made and the results appraised and passed on only by men of special training and experience. From its inception the American Medical Association has been concerned with medical education and it could not fail to take cognizance of the rising tide of criticisms against the so-called self-anointed specialists, pseudospecialists and the masquerading specialists.[79]

Although discussions had taken place in the past about the possibility of extending the medical license into specialty areas, these discussions never reached fruition.[80] The rapprochement between the AMA and the specialty societies put an end to such discussions. State licensing boards would be cut out of the process, Heyd said, in order to avoid "confusion and probable divergent requirements."[81] The AMA "represents all the states. It is a federation with all the scientific points of view," he asserted.[82] That the AMA was a unifying force, not only for the profession, but for the whole country, was the message that Heyd delivered.

While the new arrangement helped to resolve the growing friction between the AMA and the specialty societies, it did not augur well for general practitioners. The creation of an educational and credentialing scheme that any medical student could pursue notwithstanding their background and pedigree undermined the role and standing of the general practitioner. "AMA sponsorship of a caste system, however educationally justifiable ... would run up against the GPs' interests," Stevens contended. "There was a danger that a two-class system might develop," she stated.[83]

Many AMA members hoped that more stringent training standards for specialty certification would reduce the number of specialists. Just the opposite occurred. Continuing advancements in medical science combined with entrenched political, economic, and societal forces enhanced the urge to specialize. Gaining board certification became an incentive for many doctors, a means of distinction, in America's competitive market for medical services.[84]

THE RULES OF PROFESSIONAL COMPETITION

From 1870 to 1920, GPs' competitive position in the medical marketplace transitioned from one end of the spectrum to the other, from interprofessional competition with homeopaths, eclectics, and other health care providers to intraprofessional competition with specialists. The institutionally structured relationships common in European countries, GPs as community-based practitioners and specialists as hospital-based consultants, failed to transpire.[85] Hospital affiliation was open to all medical practitioners in the United States, while a closed medical staff was the norm in Europe.[86] US physicians separately billed for their services for the work they performed in hospitals, while European specialists often were salaried hospital employees.[87] Patients could choose any specialist they wanted to see in America, while in Europe patients often needed a referral from a generalist in order to see a specialist.[88]

Absent restrictions on access to patients, competition between generalists and specialists in the United States was keen.[89] GPs competed with specialists, not so much on price, which the profession regulated, but on quality.[90] What, if any, rules governed competition among physicians? Were these rules the same ones that applied to business and commerce or were they different? Could doctors form or join groups, corporations, or hospitals to gain a competitive advantage? Could they advertise? Did the rules favor generalists, specialists, or neither?

In the absence of federal government intervention, which did not occur until many years later, the AMA formulated and enforced the rules of professional competition. The principal vehicle was the AMA Code of Medical Ethics (the "Code"), which appeared for the first time in 1847.[91] The Code contained the basic principles, while the AMA's Judicial Council formed in 1873 interpreted the Code and recommended any changes to it.[92] Achieving economic advantage over medicine's competitors was the main reason for enacting the Code in the first place. Though rival competition diminished in succeeding years, economic interests remained central as the following 1936 AMA pamphlet demonstrates:

Nearly every system of economics is built on an expressed or implied system of ethics. Nowhere is this relation between ethics and economics closer than in medicine ... The present position and future development of the medical group depends quite largely on the way in which that group adjusts itself to present and future economic conditions. The method of that adjustment will depend in a high degree on the relations between medical ethics and the economics which govern the industrial, commercial and financial transactions of today. It is impossible to discuss the questions involved in such adjustments without some explanation of the relations of present day economics to medical ethics.[93]

Though professional groups in other countries also had codes of ethics, ethical rules did not substitute for government policies concerning health care organization and delivery. In Britain, for example, the General Medical Council, an arm of the government, oversaw professional advertising.[94] In the United States, on the other hand, the profession alone regulated advertising and many other competitive practices.

There have been few revisions to the original 1847 Code – in 1903, 1912, 1949, 1957, and 1980. Each Code revision closely tracked important events or changes bearing on economic affairs. Though short and brief, the 1903 and 1912 revisions were huge in substance. They comprised rules on consultations, referrals, advertising, billing, employment practices, and organizational arrangements. These Code revisions and the events surrounding them provide important insights into the early formation of America's health care industry.

Consultations and Referrals

Referrals between GPs and nonphysician providers frequently occurred. Family doctors such as Elliott Joslin in Massachusetts consulted chiropodists in cases involving diabetes, for example.[95] It was not uncommon, moreover, for GPs to consult dentists and optometrists when headaches were severe and the causes were unknown.[96] GPs complained loudly, however, when specialists gained referrals from homeopaths and eclectics.[97] Though the Supreme Court in the *Dent* case had sided with Regular physicians, it did not rule out professional licensing of homeopaths and eclectics if state laws allowed. Not all states followed West Virginia's lead. New York was one of those states; it licensed homeopaths.[98]

New York's licensing of homeopathic physicians led to a confrontation between generalists and specialists over a provision contained in the 1847 Code that barred physicians from "consult[ing with those] whose practice is based on an exclusive dogma."[99] Regular physicians who adhered to a strict medical orthodoxy viewed homeopathy as an "exclusive dogma." Several medical specialists – among them, ophthalmologists, dermatologists, and pediatricians – who practiced in New York City saw things differently. They received patient referrals from homeopaths.[100] These New York specialists opposed the 1847 prohibition.

The dispute over the "consultation clause," as it was known, was so divisive that the New York State medical society withdrew from the AMA, and the AMA, in turn, excluded certain New York physicians from its membership.[101] The rift pitted hard-liners, proponents of medical orthodoxy, against a rising vanguard of specialists and those who trained them. "Rank-and-file general practitioners, and especially ... older professional leaders who remembered the battles they had waged to establish the ideals and institutions of orthodoxy," believed that the New York City specialists "had betrayed orthodoxy for a lucrative alliance with homeopaths," wrote historian John Harley Warner.[102] Younger physicians with science-based training, which generally characterized the New York City specialists, heartily disagreed. Their "argument against the consultation clause was that science was the ultimate touchstone of clinical propriety and had rendered distinctions between competing beliefs and practices ... meaningless," Warner stated.[103]

Prompted by the ever-present William Welch, the AMA removed the consultation clause from the Code in 1903.[104] New York physicians eventually resolved their differences as the older generation gave way to the new. At the fifty-second annual meeting of the AMA in 1901, the association's president, Charles Reed, captured the growing sentiment when he declared: "I proclaim, events proclaim, the existence of a new school of medicine. It is as distinct from the schools of fifty years ago as is the Christian dispensation from its pagan antecedents. It is the product of convergent influences of diverse antecedent origin. It acknowledges no distinctive title, it heralds no shibboleth. It is a school of human tolerance, of personal independence, of scientific honesty."[105] In the view of Reed and many others, the consultation clause was an anachronism, a relic from the past.[106]

Advertising

Because of the many controversies surrounding it, the AMA's prohibition on advertising may be its best-known ethics provision. In 1977, the US Supreme Court, in *Bates v. Arizona State Bar Association*,[107] stuck down blanket restrictions on professional advertising on First Amendment grounds. Until this occurred, however, the AMA rule against advertising was the subject of constant scrutiny, interpretation, review, and revision. Though frequently employed against practitioners who advertised secret nostrums, patent medicines, and cures, much of the debate in the late 1800s centered on the use of business cards, handbills, signs, and other means to designate a specialty area.[108]

The 1847 Code stated that "[i]t is derogatory to the dignity of the profession, to resort to public advertisements or private cards or handbills, inviting the attention of individuals affected with particular diseases."[109] Questions arose over the meaning of these words. Specialists

often claimed that designations such as "Ophthalmologist" or "Gynecologist" on signs and in announcements did not violate the Code.[110]
Before 1903, the AMA disagreed. Delegates to the AMA's annual con-
ventions in 1869 and 1874 passed resolutions stating that doctors were
free to limit their practice to a particular area but could not represent
themselves "by special or qualifying titles, such as *oculist, gynecologist,*
etc."[111] Nathan Smith Davis, the AMA's founder and *JAMA*'s first
editor, wrote in 1883 that "no one is prohibited from publishing or using
a professional card as freely as he likes, simply announcing himself as a
Doctor of Medicine, and giving his residence, office, and office hours. But
if a physician puts upon his card ... that he is an oculist, gynecologist,
etc., he ... asserts a superiority over the general practitioner."[112]

Twenty years after Davis's sharp retort, a 1903 Code revision moder-
ated the AMA's position. The Judicial Council deleted the phrase "inviting the attention of individuals affected with particular diseases" from the
Code and replaced it with the statement that "ordinary simple business
cards [were] not *per se* improper" so long as they conformed to "local
custom."[113] The shift in stance reflected specialists' growing influence
within the medical profession. Whereas one in thirty physicians was a
specialist in 1885, one in nine doctors was a specialist by 1905.[114] Articles
appearing in *JAMA* showed a softening of positions. "The use of such
announcements in certain places and under certain circumstances may be
indiscreet, but does not call for formal condemnation," a 1909 missive
read.[115] More leeway now would be given to those seeking to announce
their expertise. Local societies could still take action if generalists complained, but it was unlikely that they would.

Fee-Splitting

Fee-splitting was added to the list of prohibited practices in 1903. As
originally conceived in the 1890s, "fee-splitting" ("kickback" in the
current vernacular) involved the payment of money from businesses to
doctors for prescribing their products.[116] By the early 1900s, fee-splitting
took on a new meaning. The term now implied a payment or commission
from one doctor to another for referring a patient. A 1903 Code addition
captured the change. It was "derogatory to professional character for
physicians ... to pay commissions [and] for physicians to solicit or receive
such commissions," the new provision read.[117] The prohibition against

fee-splitting also covered certain billing practices. "[M]any physicians doubtless engage in ... combined billing without realizing that they're considered unethical," an article offering guidance on fee-splitting said.[118]

The addition of fee-splitting to the 1903 Code was closely linked to the advancement of surgery. Before the widespread use of antiseptic techniques in the 1890s, such as the sterilization of equipment and the donning of surgical gloves and masks, mortality rates from surgery were almost 50 percent, mostly due to infection.[119] When famed surgeon William Halsted arrived at Johns Hopkins in 1889, no other doctor at the hospital performed surgery. "So little surgery was being performed," Halsted's biographer Gerald Imber noted, "that there were fewer than ten physicians in the United States whose practices were restricted to surgery."[120] Halsted had "no staff, no assistants, no dedicated surgery ward, no specialized operating room, and no residents. Indeed, there was no such thing as a resident," wrote Imber.[121]

By 1920, surgery had gone through a rapid transformation becoming "a dominant force in medical advancement," according to health scholar Atul Gawande.[122] New surgical techniques included the suturing of blood vessels, the care and treatment of wounds, and the grafting of human tissue. These advancements made it possible for surgeons to operate on many of the body's major organs, such as the heart, and in certain locations, such as the abdomen, where bleeding during surgery often was profuse and hard to contain. None of these achievements could have taken place without discoveries and improvements in anesthesia, antiseptics, and blood typing.[123]

Concurrent with advances in surgery, hospitals gained a prominent role in health care delivery. "By the mid-1920s, practitioners in large centers such as New York and Chicago were spending up to 30 percent of their time in hospitals and clinics," historian George Rosen observed.[124] The source of funds for hospital operations changed from mostly charitable gifts to payments for services rendered. In contrast to London's hospitals, which in 1911 received 90 percent of their income from gifts and investments, US hospitals received the majority of their income, upward of 70 percent, from patients.[125] This shift in the source of funding empowered surgeons who proceeded to impose their own rules. Upon its founding in 1913, the American College of Surgeons required its members to sign a pledge stating that they would not split fees.[126] Four years later, when the ACS launched a program of hospital standardization, the ban on fee-splitting became a criterion for ACS certification.[127]

The prohibition on fee-splitting made it more difficult for general practitioners to receive fair pay for their work. "Everyone now realizes that the general practitioner who makes the diagnosis and who is primarily responsible for the care of the patient deserves a much greater percentage of what the patient is able to pay," a *JAMA* editorial observed.[128] Many physicians, even specialists, sympathized with GPs' plight. "If he bills for $10.00 – attendance at operation – he may get it with scowl," one such specialist stated. "Suppose he had devoted half a practice day to hanging around that hospital, and bills $25.00. Does he get it? He does, but not $25.00. He gets the door, and he gets it promptly," he wrote.[129]

In an apparent attempt to mollify GPs' concerns, the Judicial Council qualified the provision on fee-splitting in the 1912 Code. The revised provision now said that it was "unprofessional ... to divide a fee ... *unless the patient or his next friend is fully informed as to the terms of the transaction.*"[130] Yet the ban itself remained in place, largely due to surgeons' growing influence and the staunch opposition of the ACS to fee splitting. When Harold Hays, president of the Association of Private Hospitals, attempted to address the inequity by proposing a 15 percent standard allocation of the specialist's fee to the referring GP, state medical societies in Massachusetts and New York objected. "[E]ven if there is no secrecy in the distribution of this fifteen per cent, there may be grounds for suspicion of possible irregularities inherent in any form of fee-splitting, which might be unjust to the patient," the state medical societies contended.[131]

Free Choice of Physician

Perhaps the most important Code provision was "free choice of physician," which meant that patients should be able to see any doctor they wanted, whether a specialist or a generalist. The free choice principle garnered widespread support among physicians, significantly influencing the future course of health care delivery in America. The principle was so closely associated with the United States that German physicians, seeking to stem a government takeover of health care in their country at the turn of the twentieth century, advocated free choice of physician, calling it the "American plan."[132]

Deeply embedded in custom and practice, the free choice principle was not included in the Code before 1912. The 1912 addition stated that "A physician is free to choose whom he will serve." Though the 1912 wording made free choice a doctor's prerogative, Code drafters later stated that physician free choice and patient free choice were inter-changeable, "mere counterparts."[133]

The 1912 provision was added around the time that the United States and other countries were considering government financing of medical services in order to increase access to care. The earliest effort, which debuted in Germany in 1883, targeted the poor. Plans enacted shortly after World War I, such as the one in France, increased access beyond persons of low income.[134] In the United States, several state legislatures took up compulsory sickness insurance in 1916.[135] During the course of the debate, an AMA committee was formed to examine the various proposals. As related in the next chapter, the AMA committee issued several reports advocating compulsory health insurance.[136] There was one important caveat contained in the committee reports. Free choice of physician, the committee said, was required for any government plan.[137]

A second Code revision concerning the free choice principle occurred in 1934. This time the drafters used the phrase "free choice of physician" rather than "physician choice of patient." As on the first occasion, exter-nal events prompted the change. While the AMA added the 1912 provi-sion during the debate over compulsory health insurance, it added the second during discussions over ways to organize health care delivery, to make it more efficient and affordable. British efforts to organize health care delivery took the form of government planning. Dawson's model emphasizing the benefits of "hierarchical regionalism" became official government policy in 1929.[138]

Though a majority of US physicians did not want government to intervene, many prominent doctors acknowledged that there was need for improvement.[139] Among these doctors was Hugh Cabot, a professor of surgery at Massachusetts General Hospital and later of the Mayo Clinic. In an address before the Mississippi Valley Medical Association in 1915, Cabot touted physician group practice. "There can be no ques-tion as to the efficiency ... of 'group medicine' in arriving at an accurate diagnosis," he asserted.[140] Many other physicians agreed with Cabot's assessment. "The custom of group practice is spreading rapidly and is destined to partially answer the question as to how the patient of moder-ate means can secure the services of the specialists his case may demand," physician Ernest Hunt said in a 1921 speech before the Worcester District Medical Society.[141]

Proponents of group practice often saw it as the natural progression of medical specialization.[142] "Group practice, co-operative practice, or any form of associated effort among individual specialists has arisen partly in recognition of this tendency in specialization," wrote physician William Mason.[143] "The next step in the direction of group practice was observed in the development of the specialties," physician Philemon Truesdale affirmed.[144] Truesdale, the founder of a hospital in Fall River, Massachusetts, bearing his name, was particularly impressed by the Mayo Clinic, which began as a physician group practice in the late 1800s. "It was not until the adoption of the Mayo Clinic as a teaching foundation by the University of Minnesota in 1915 that a mass of evidence was made available, demonstrating beyond question the superiority of an organization such as theirs over the individualistic system," Truesdale professed.[145]

Proponents also believed that specialty groups should be located near hospitals.[146] "In its most finished form the medical group is represented by a hospital with medical and surgical chiefs, chiefs of special departments," wrote Cabot.[147] "Generally speaking, hospitals as organized at present offer their patients a similar type of co-operative diagnosis and treatment, although the various units constituting the whole are likely to be less well co-ordinated than is the organized group," Mason added.[148] *"The collecting of group medicine around a hospital center is,* I think, the best solution of the problem; first, because centralization appears to make for better doctoring; and second, because a hospital offers a logical center, both from the doctor's and the public's viewpoint – a condition not brought about by voluntary grouping," a prominent physician from Massachusetts explained.[149]

The proposition that specialists or groups of specialists should align themselves with hospitals, closely tracked the Dawson Report. But proponents of specialty group practice departed from Dawson when it came to the general practitioner, who was the first point of contact in Britain.[150] To Cabot and other prominent specialists, the GP was no longer needed. His "death knell ... has sounded," Cabot insisted.[151] "The day of the general practitioner ... is nearly at an end," proclaimed H. G. Bonney, the dean at Denver's school of medicine.[152]

While generalists balked at these assertions, they also rejected the notion common to European systems that they should refer patients to specialists for hospital-based care. "Country doctors" should treat patients in hospitals close to them, physician Nathaniel Faxon retorted. "The habit of turning troublesome problems of diagnosis or treatment over to someone else leads to slackness," Faxon wrote.[153] "Rather a small, imperfect hospital in my own town than a modern model of medical and surgical perfection 20 miles away. A local hospital centralizes the health organization of the community. It naturally becomes the head-quarters and general meeting-place of all the physicians of the town," he proclaimed.[154]

Though system-wide integration on the scale that the Dawson Report envisioned did not occur in the United States until almost a full century later (and then only in certain areas of the country), specialty group practice gained ground, creating divisions within organized medicine.[155] The 1934 free choice provision was one of many ways that AMA members, most of them generalists at the time, voiced their opposition not only to government and corporate planning but also to specialty group practice. Indeed, the 1934 provision was added soon after the Committee on the Costs of Medical Care (CCMC), a private entity comprising leading experts from the health care community, endorsed group practice. The AMA adamantly opposed the CCMC's recommendation, stating: "Medical relations cannot be between an oculist and an eye, a corporation and a broken leg, a hospital and a disease, a laboratory and a blood specimen or an insurance company and a compensation case."[156]

CONCLUSION

The successes of America's academic physicians and specialists in teaching, research, and the application of medical and surgical techniques helped them gain a prominent voice in medical affairs from about 1870 to 1918. Under the banner of medical science, the US medical profession expanded its reach economically, politically, and socially. Universities became centers of medical research and learning; hospitals became places where doctors cured illness and disease; and medical societies became locations for the exchange of knowledge and the conduct of professional matters. These three institutions – medical schools, medical societies, and hospitals – formed the core of the professional arena. So long as doctors oversaw these three institutions, the medical profession would be in charge of health care delivery.

The American medical profession was still in the process of constructing the professional arena in 1918. From 1870 to 1918, professional leaders made great strides in medical education and professional organization. Toward the end of this period, professional leaders turned much of their attention to hospitals. It was in hospitals that several different groups and interests both inside and outside the medical profession intersected – generalists, specialists, administrators, philanthropists, and community leaders. As hospital expenses increased to the point that average citizens, those in America's burgeoning middle class, could not afford to pay the full costs of hospital care, calls grew for some form of financial assistance. The form of financial assistance and the means for compensating doctors and hospitals would occupy the attention of policy-makers for the next several decades, eventually expanding the political conflict beyond the professional arena.

3

Group Medical Practice and Group Insurance,
1919–1945

The years following World War I marked a turning point in AMA policy and political strategy. In the aftermath of the Great War, the AMA's leadership changed. Unlike their predecessors, few of the association's new leaders came from the educational ranks. Fewer still were progressive in their political and social leanings. Keenly aware of events occurring in Europe, these new leaders strongly opposed state-sponsored sickness insurance that European countries were enacting and many US politicians were endorsing. In their fight against "socialized medicine," a term used to disparage most anything from government health care to the group practice of medicine, the AMA's new vanguard claimed to stand for general practitioners. Bring back the GP, they said.[1] Though seeking to avoid direct confrontation with specialists and their associations, the new generation professed that the AMA "must not be operated exclusively for [specialists] and should address itself to the necessities of a majority of our medical men."[2]

This chapter covers the period from 1919 to 1945, from the end of World War I to the end of World War II. The central focus is the intense turmoil during this period over collective forms of finance and delivery, from sickness insurance to prepaid group practice, from contract practice to the corporate practice of medicine. AMA leaders opposed all collective forms of finance and delivery that failed to follow the rules of professional competition contained in the AMA Code of Medical Ethics. Claiming that these "experiments in medical practice" would diminish the quality of medical services, organized medicine mounted an aggressive campaign against "unauthorized" forms of health care delivery and anyone who promoted them.[3]

By the mid-1930s, the AMA's bold tactics had attracted the attention of the news media and the Roosevelt administration. Employing the antitrust laws, the federal government entered the health care arena, not as a financier of medical services, but as a proponent of prepaid group practice.[4] The Roosevelt administration's lawsuit against the AMA for violating the Sherman Antitrust Act, which this chapter details, laid the foundation for the group practice of medicine in its various forms, from tightly managed organizations such as Kaiser Permanente to more loosely integrated forms.

ALEXANDER LAMBERT'S SCHEME FOR THE ORGANIZATION OF US HEALTH CARE DELIVERY

As related in Chapter 2, the American medical profession rose to prominence during the years 1870–1918, becoming a leader in science and politics, not only in America, but on the world stage. Many AMA leaders during this period came from the educational, research, and public health ranks. They included Frank Billings, William Welch, the Mayo brothers, Charles and William, and William Gorgas, who spearheaded the fight against yellow fever during the building of the Panama Canal.[5] These prominent physicians were progressive in many respects. They were willing to experiment, not only in research and education, but also in the social and economic arenas. Alexander Lambert would be among the last in this long line of AMA leaders who urged the association to pursue comprehensive reform.

Lambert's credentials included professor of clinical medicine at Cornell University and attending physician at Bellevue Hospital. He served as a trustee of the United Hospital Fund of New York and as AMA president from 1919 to 1920. A prolific writer on the addictive effects of narcotics and alcohol, Lambert was an influential proponent of the Harrison Narcotics Act of 1914, the first in a series of laws that regulated the marketing, dispensing, and prescribing of opioids and narcotics. Perhaps Lambert's most notable role was as personal physician to President Theodore Roosevelt, with whom Lambert shared an ideological predisposition.[6]

In 1916, the AMA established a committee on social insurance with Lambert as its chair. During the period that Lambert chaired the committee on social insurance, he also advised the American Association for Labor Legislation (AALL), a progressive organization that was promoting compulsory health insurance. The work of the AALL and Lambert's committee overlapped; indeed, the two groups had offices in the same building in New York City.[7] Under Lambert's direction, the committee on social insurance studied insurance schemes in other countries and issued a lengthy report touting the advantages of "governmental systems."[8] Based on its findings, the committee concluded that achieving "the best economic . . . value" required a "change in the method by which medical service can be obtained."[9]

The committee's work, contained in several reports to the AMA Council on Health and Public Instruction, the body that created it, was bold and sweeping.[10] An article that Lambert wrote for *JAMA* in 1917 proposed an elaborate scheme for reforming both health care finance and its delivery.[11] Lambert's proposal incorporated many of the views of AALL members and advisors, particularly those of I. M. Rubinow, a leading theorist on social insurance, and Michael Davis, director of the Boston Dispensary.[12] Davis's advocacy of dispensaries "for the sick poor" and "for those of moderate means" greatly influenced Lambert.[13] In 1916, there were about 2,300 dispensaries in the United States; by 1918, there were approximately 3,000 dispensaries, 40 percent of them located in New York, Massachusetts, and Pennsylvania.[14]

In his 1917 *JAMA* article, Lambert set forth a plan of compulsory sickness insurance. Rather than propose "a state fund or any generalized corporate carrier," Lambert backed "a local mutual benefit fund, the directorate of which is composed equally of employers and workmen, with a state representative." Each of these local funds, he said, would distribute cash and medical benefits to individuals located in a particular "district" – "none of which shall contain less than 5,000 persons who are subject to compulsory health insurance."[15]

Lambert's proposal also called for the organization of health care delivery along a continuum from primary to secondary to tertiary care. His approach was not all that different from the one that Dawson was pursuing in England. The first step in Lambert's scheme was for patients to choose their doctors from a "panel or list of physicians willing to do health insurance work." The doctors chosen "must give the sick adequate care for ordinary needs," he wrote. The second step was for panel physicians to send their patients to dispensaries for consults or specialty care if needed. "[D]ispensaries would be places for group medicine, that is, for the gathering together of all specialists, and consulting opinions in general medicine and surgery." The third step involved the hospital. "There must be ample hospital accommodations for patients who need hospital care," Lambert stated.[16]

Inspired by Davis and others, Lambert's proposal advanced several important changes to the existing configuration. It proffered a distinct role for the general practitioner, that of a panel physician. It viewed dispensaries as strategically located group practices that provided mostly specialty care outside the hospital setting. It saw GPs as gatekeepers who referred patients to dispensaries where they would "obtain special treatment or an opinion on some special condition."[17] And it provided that specialists for the most part would work in dispensaries or hospitals.

Lambert and Dawson articulated their proposals about the same time. The common thread between the two visionaries was their experience with military medicine in World War I. According to Daniel Fox, Dawson based his approach on "the military system he had helped to organize in France."[18] So did Lambert, who served in France as medical director of the American Red Cross.[19] The organization of health care delivery that Lambert and Dawson formulated reflected the systematic arrangements called for during times of war – the need to triage the wounded and move them along by level of care.

Still, the two proposals deviated from each other in two important respects. First, Lambert did not favor the English method of compensation, known as "straight capitation," which meant that "the doctor is paid so much per patient per year." "This is the scheme ... of the ordinary lodge practice and club practice, as seen in this country," Lambert wrote.[20] Second, Lambert placed greater emphasis on group medicine and hospitals than Dawson did. Lambert agreed with Richard Cabot, a prominent physician and brother of Hugh Cabot, that "the great fault of English and German systems of sickness insurance is that they do not center themselves around organized groups of physicians, that is, around hospitals."[21]

Before America entered World War I, there was every indication that the AMA would support some type of health insurance plan at the state or federal level. The minutes from the AMA's annual meetings from 1916 to 1919 showed that the House of Delegates generally supported the work of Lambert's committee.[22] "It is of utmost importance to the medical profession ... that we give this question the most careful, painstaking, patient and disinterested study," the AMA minutes from 1919 read.[23] Yet in 1920, the AMA reversed course, moving from qualified approval of sickness insurance to unqualified rejection.

Historical accounts largely attribute the shift to America's entry into World War I, which suspended the committee's work and allowed opposing views to coalesce.[24] It did not help that Lambert's committee touted certain features of the German plan of sickness insurance inaugurated under Chancellor Otto von Bismarck in 1883. Lambert sought to ameliorate any concerns. "It is useless to discard the German experience in health insurance simply because at the present moment we have a prejudice against that nation," he wrote. "The [German plan] existed during the period of Germany's tremendous expansion and development," he noted. "Those sent over to study" events in Germany were generally "favorable to the insurance principles involved and the practical application thereof."[25]

Too much has been made of the war's role in undercutting AMA support for a government plan. No doubt the war interrupted some of the progress the committee was making, but fierce opposition to compulsory health insurance already had existed in America. It was not just government insurance that AMA delegates rejected, moreover; it was also the sweeping changes to the organization of health care delivery that Lambert recommended. The AMA's rank-and-file – mostly independent, fee-for-service practitioners – opposed clinics, dispensaries, and group forms of health care delivery, whether publicly or privately owned and administered.[26] Cries "to get Lambert" at the AMA's 1920 convention in New Orleans suggested that emotions were running high, that Lambert's proposal to reorganize health care delivery had stoked their fears.[27]

THE TWIN COMPLAINTS: THE CONTRACT AND CORPORATE PRACTICE OF MEDICINE

Issues concerning social insurance, group practice, and specialization were closely linked. Many leading specialists and academics supported group practice in the belief that medicine's increasing complexity demanded it.[28] Generalists, on the other hand, viewed group practice with alarm.[29] They perceived that specialists gained a competitive advantage when they worked together.[30] Their opposition to group practice gained legitimacy and acceptance when attached to the twin scourges of the contract and corporate practice of medicine.[31]

Contract and corporate practice, though often conflated, were different in one important respect. Contract practice concerned physicians who provided medical services on behalf of an organization for a salary or a fixed fee. The type of organization that employed doctors did not really matter. It could be a hospital, a clinic, a fraternal society, or a railroad. Corporate practice, on the other hand, referred to entities that were in the business of providing health care to a general population, and employed doctors to help them do it. Organizations such as hospitals or clinics were engaged in the corporate practice of medicine if doctors worked for them.

The medical profession's main argument against both forms was that they undermined the doctor–patient relationship. Doctors might not act in their patients' best interest, spokespersons for medical societies contended, if patients did not pay them directly for their services.[32] While medical societies could prohibit contract practice and punish physicians for violating professional ethics, their powers did not extend to the organizations that hired them. But that did not stop medical societies from lobbying courts and state legislatures to make corporate practice unlawful. Indeed, several state courts and legislatures did.[33] Many courts, for instance, held that corporate practice was against public policy, that it undermined the doctor–patient relationship. Judges also ruled that medical licensing laws did not authorize corporations to practice medicine, that corporations could not circumvent licensing laws by hiring physicians to do it for them.[34]

Letters and editorials condemning contract practice frequently appeared in medical journals such as *JAMA* in the late 1800s and early 1900s. A common theme was that corporations were exploiting doctors. "Medical societies at various points throughout the country are condemning contract practice ... by which certain organizations exploit the medical profession," a 1906 opinion piece in *JAMA* asserted.[35] "It is not the legitimate contract practice that is to be feared, but the organizations that are gotten up for the purpose of buying a physician's services at wholesale and selling them at retail," another missive read.[36] "Contract-practice ... is the most far-reaching evil at work in lowering the dignity and prestige of medical men and their work," a physician wrote from El Paso, Texas.[37]

The editorial pages of leading medical journals frequently associated contract practice with government or state-sponsored medicine. "The insurance examination question is related very closely to that of contract practice," a 1906 *JAMA* editorial stated.[38] "Like every other socialistic plan, [contract practice] involves a general leveling down, which will be unprofitable in the end for both the profession and its patrons," a 1904 editorial read.[39] "The evils of contract practice [require] eternal vigilance on the part of the profession to prevent the installation of a condition of affairs in this country similar to those existing in other lands, like Britain, Germany and Australia," another opinion piece from 1904 forewarned.[40] "I do not favor compulsory health insurance because it is nothing more or less than lodge or contract practice on a universal scale, and this has proved by experience to be an unmitigated evil; unsatisfactory from the standpoint of both physician and patient," a New Jersey doctor wrote in 1917.[41] "Sickness societies" in Germany, the "panel system" in England, and contract practice in America have many features in common, a 1928 article appearing in the *New England Journal of Medicine* proclaimed.[42]

A popular refrain was that the combination of government insurance and contract practice would degrade the quality of medicine. "The physician who puts himself at the beck and call of any one who pays a dollar a year cheapens himself and degrades his profession, and professional non-recognition is only his desert," claimed one writer.[43] "[C]heapening medical services means lowering its quality," asserted another. "[C]ompulsory health insurance does not in Europe, and cannot here, prevent disease or accident or drive a lazy, malingering or chronically sick individual to work."[44]

Notwithstanding strong opposition against it, contract practice gained ground in the 1920s and 1930s as health care costs became unaffordable for many Americans. While the AMA did not strongly object to companies that employed doctors to care for their injured workers – "for instance, when large numbers of workmen are employed remote from urban centers, as in some mining or logging camps" – it opposed "new schemes to compete with regularly established medical practice."[45] Among the new schemes that the AMA targeted were organizations that, in the words of AMA spokesperson R. G. Leland, "are merely the business offices of groups having medical contracts for sale."[46] "These 'associations'," Leland claimed, "usually have a few staff physicians on salary, but most of the physicians who care for the contract cases are paid on a 'piece work' basis."[47]

Leland's remarks came at the height of the controversy pitting the AMA against the aforementioned Committee on the Costs of Medical Care, which called for sweeping reforms to health care delivery. Leland was in charge of the AMA's Bureau of Medical Economics (BME) when the CCMC issued its final report in 1932. The BME's main task under Leland was to assemble information and data in support of the AMA's opposition to contract, group, and corporate practice. The BME sought to counter the findings of the CCMC.[48]

THE CHANGING OF THE GUARD AT THE AMA AND THE RISE OF MORRIS FISHBEIN

Between 1920 and 1924, many who gave even tacit approval to the reports coming out of Lambert's committee on social insurance either left the AMA or retracted their former positions. Frederick Green resigned as secretary of the Council on Health and Public Instruction in 1922, leaving the AMA to work for another organization.[49] George Simmons retired under pressure in 1924 after a lengthy tenure as *JAMA*'s editor.[50] Frank Billings, former AMA president and member of the Board of Trustees, changed his stance after coming under attack in 1921 for past statements favoring government insurance. At the association's annual session in 1921, Billings stated: "I am charged ... with writing articles and working for the legal enactment of compulsory health insurance and of state medicine ... while saying to you ... that I am opposed to it."[51] I. M. Rubinow, who resigned from Lambert's committee in 1918, incurred much of the blame for what opponents of compulsory health insurance labeled Rubinow's "propaganda."[52] Rubinow was called out for his connections with the AALL, whose members previously had worked with many in the AMA, including Lambert. After his stint as AMA president was over in 1920, Lambert never again held a prominent position within the association.[53]

By 1924, the purge was complete and new leadership was in place. The full-time staff at the AMA now included Olin West, secretary and general manager; Will C. Braun, business manager; and Morris Fishbein, *JAMA*'s new editor. West began working for the AMA in 1922 after serving as secretary of the Tennessee State Medical Association. As the AMA's secretary and general manager, West exercised daily operational responsibilities, including oversight of councils, committees, departments, and bureaus.[54] Braun, the only one of the three who was not a physician, started at the AMA in 1891, advancing from advertising clerk to business manager. He had a prominent role in the AMA's early financial successes, helping to boost *JAMA*'s advertising revenues from less than $10,000 in 1898 to $1,750,000 by 1946.[55] Fishbein began his career with the AMA in 1913, serving as assistant to George Simmons. Fishbein would become the AMA's chief spokesperson, lobbyist, political insider, and policy-maker. Two years before his departure from the AMA in 1949, *Time* magazine called Fishbein "the nation's most ubiquitous, the most widely maligned, and perhaps most influential medico."[56]

Fishbein, West, and Braun oversaw the inner workings of the AMA for almost twenty-five years, from about 1924 to 1949. Their ability to control and influence the AMA's internal affairs derived in large part from the AMA's substantial growth in membership following its 1901 reorganization. Revisions to the AMA constitution in 1901changed the representation in the House of Delegates to include elected members from the state medical societies and the scientific sections.[57] After its reorganization, the AMA was a formidable force. Political power and authority flowed from the local medical societies to the state societies, and then to the AMA.[58]

In 1901, the AMA had 11,121 members, or about 10 percent of the nation's physicians.[59] By 1920, the association had 82,994 members or about 57 percent of all physicians.[60] This enormous growth in membership in a relatively short period of time strained the organization's operational capabilities. Small size meant that physicians holding high office, such as AMA president, could exercise managerial oversight and still practice medicine. But an organization representing well over half of the nation's doctors was too much for a practicing physician to oversee on a daily basis. While the AMA sought to place policymaking authority in its elected leaders, creating a nine-person (later six-person) Board of Trustees in 1901 and a three-person Executive Committee in 1919, responsibility for the association's daily affairs moved to its full-time staff.[61]

JAMA 's central importance in recruiting new members, securing AMA revenue, and communicating political and policy positions was also a big factor. The editor of *JAMA* arguably held the most important position within the AMA. The choice in 1883 of Nathan Smith Davis, the AMA's founder, to become *JAMA* 's first editor was a clear indication that many physicians foresaw the position's importance and potential. With the appointment of Davis, AMA members hoped that *JAMA* would rise to the level of the *British Medical Journal*, generally regarded at the time as "the foremost publication in medicine."[62] Their hopes and expectations soon would be realized. From 1900 to 1919, subscription and advertising revenues substantially increased. In 1900, *JAMA* 's circulation was about 13,000; by 1919, it was more than 67,000.[63] Revenue from advertising in 1919 was $312,440, a considerable sum at the time.[64] Upon becoming *JAMA* 's editor in 1924, Fishbein not only gained control over the association's principal publication, he also became the AMA's chief fundraiser.

Though scientific articles were a central feature of *JAMA* at its inception, Nathan Smith Davis frequently wrote editorials about medical affairs, provoking debate and reaction in letters to the editor.[65] After Davis stepped down in 1888, the Journal experienced a period of turnover until George Simmons took over. During Simmons's twenty-five-year tenure from 1899 to 1924, *JAMA* refined and standardized its format while maintaining a mix of scientific articles and editorials that appealed to a broad audience. "Under Dr. Simmons' editorship, [*JAMA*] began to assume more definite form and departmentalization," Fishbein recounted. "The interest of the members is shown in many letters published as correspondence to the editor. The space devoted to society proceedings was greatly elaborated, as was also the space devoted to editorials and comments," wrote Fishbein.[66]

In 1912, AMA president William Welch began touting the need for a "small medical journal" devoted to the general practitioner. Many readers, Welch indicated, had complained that *JAMA* had become "too advanced and too technical for many practitioners."[67] Rather than develop a journal for GPs as Welch had suggested, however, AMA leadership pursued the publication of specialty journals. Specialty societies such as the American College of Surgeons, which had its own journal, the *Annals of Surgery*, opposed the new venture. The ensuing dispute delayed until 1920 the AMA's publication of the *Archives of Surgery* (today's *JAMA Surgery*).[68]

The selection of Fishbein as editor signaled that *JAMA* would continue its appeal to a broad readership. Fishbein referred many technical submissions to the specialty sections and published editorials, comments, and correspondence to elicit discussion on topics of general interest. Few likely foresaw the extent to which Fishbein would use his position as editor to steer, direct, and announce AMA policy on a wide range of topics. "Doctors traditionally avoid publicity," Milton Mayer, a writer for the *Chicago Tribune*, related. "Fishbein saved them the trouble. His books, articles, columns, speeches, debates, and press releases consolidated his position as the spokesman, and the only spokesman, of American medicine. His aptitude for the sensational – and for sensationalizing the scientific – monopolized the popular press for him. He and his ghostly coterie of assistants wrote the official addresses, made the official announcements, and coached the official witnesses."[69]

In his autobiography, Fishbein later confirmed Mayer's assessment. "When the press asked for an interview I gave them one; when they asked a question, I gave them an answer. When a feature writer came to prepare an article about the American Medical Association and its work, he was at liberty to interview anyone he wished, but he usually started and ended with me simply because many of the others in the headquarters office referred him to me with questions which they perhaps did not wish to answer."[70]

Though the taciturn Olin West was the AMA's general manager, he exercised no authority over Fishbein.[71] According to Mayer, "[t]he general manager was Fishbein's nominal superior at Chicago headquarters, but Fishbein generally managed."[72] Fishbein reported directly to the

Board of Trustees and regularly attended its meetings. "He became an imposing figure, the almost permanent nature of his presence there adding weight to the vigorously argued opinions he had to offer," wrote the AMA's biographer Frank Campion.[73] "[T]here was hardly an important decision made in which he did not participate ... and make strong recommendations," Ernest B. Howard, a prominent AMA executive who worked with Fishbein, stated.[74] "He [was] definitely the most dynamic, the most vocal, the most capable in terms of myth-making and business management," political scientist Oliver Garceau reported.[75] He was "the czar of the industry, the boss of the machine," at a time when the AMA was politically the most dominant interest group in America.[76]

"BETWEEN THE DEVIL AND THE DEEP BLUE SEA"

One of the initiatives that Fishbein favored was support for the general practitioner. To Fishbein and others in the new vanguard of AMA leaders, the organizational changes that Lambert and others had proposed were unnecessary and detrimental. Relatively few illnesses required specialty care and hospitalization, Fishbein asserted.[77] The vast majority involved complaints and diseases "that any good general practitioner can diagnose and [treat]," he said.[78] In denouncing group practice in a 1936 article, Fishbein questioned the need to reorganize when "85 per cent of the conditions for which people consult their doctors can be treated by a good medical practitioner with the equipment he can carry in a handbag."[79]

Fishbein echoed the thoughts and beliefs of Hubert Work, a prominent AMA member, who preceded Fishbein's rise to power. "The primary function of a physician, to cure the sick, is submerged by the scientific ambition to diagnose rare diseases or a few ailments," Work announced at the AMA's 1919 convention.[80] Work believed that medical schools were overemphasizing specialty care. "Failure to gain practical knowledge of the simple things in medicine tremendously depreciates recent graduates," Work declared. "[T]he average medical college curriculum costs so much time and money that only the rich can attain it," he said.[81] "The general practitioner ... must come back. Otherwise the crossroads communities will soon have no qualified physician, and from necessity will revert to the opportunist and the midwife."[82]

Work was operating in a different environment than Fishbein ten years later. Fishbein's comments concerning GP's capabilities occurred against the backdrop of the Great Depression. "Some of the old order" is being restored because of "the economic depression," AMA president Dean Lewis wrote in 1934. General practitioners were "faring better than specialist[s]" because they "treated [patients] in their homes," at lower cost, Lewis observed.[83] Increased competition between generalists and specialists for patients and fees during the Great Depression inflamed long-standing tensions. Fishbein fanned these flames. His assertion that GPs could handle 85 percent of all cases squarely challenged the specialists. Specialists took the bait. Speaking for specialists, Hugh Cabot said: "I cannot assent to the dogma that the general practitioner can today deal satisfactorily with the problems of diagnosis and treatment of 85 per cent of the conditions with which he is faced. Such omniscience seems to me quite beyond the average or even the extraordinary human mind."[84]

Yet GPs themselves were split over the nature and extent of medical procedures they felt equipped to undertake. The biggest question involved surgery. Joseph Cobb, a family doctor from New England, raised the matter at the annual meeting of the New Hampshire Medical Society in 1928. Cobb believed that GPs must be prepared to do emergency surgery "and properly treat all accidents incident to the industrial occupations and to the country life."[85] Physician Homer Marks, who attended Cobb's presentation, agreed: "[G]eneral practitioners ... should devote an increasingly longer time to major surgery ... Today it is possible for the general practitioner by frequent excursions to the metropolitan centers and by other means at his disposal to equip himself to do this class of work."[86] But physician David Parker, who also attended Cobb's lecture, dissented. He warned that many GPs lacked sufficient training to perform surgery. "I think the important factor in this question is not whether or not the so-called general practitioner should do surgery, but whether this particular practitioner has had sufficient preliminary surgical education, training, and experience to enable him to have an accurate knowledge of living pathology and to develop surgical judgment as well as technique," Parker stated.[87]

In addition to surgery, there were many other tasks and procedures that raised concerns about the GP's capabilities. Specialization was progressing, not only by disease and body part, but also by age, treatments, and technologies. Certain nonsurgical or medical specialties, such as pediatrics, dermatology, radiology, urology, and anesthesiology, were contemplating or establishing specialty boards in the early 1930s.[88] The practice of medicine was becoming so complex, John Peters of Yale Medical School suggested, that "[a]lthough the general practitioner is and must remain the fundamental unit in any medical system, the mere distribution of medical attention, exposure of patients to physicians, cannot be interpreted as the provision of adequate care."[89] Health systems in other countries were relying too much on the GP, Peters contended. "It is the greatest weakness of national health insurance systems that [exposure to physicians] has hitherto been almost their sole objective," Peters stated. "Undoubtedly they have bettered the general health of the people somewhat by bringing more persons into contact with physicians." But "[i]n this day ... a practitioner with only stethoscope and prescription pad can offer but a small part of the benefits which medicine has to contribute," he professed.[90]

GPs no doubt were at a crossroads. Addressing the members of the New England Surgical Society in 1935, Peer Johnson, chief of surgery at a small community hospital captured the dilemma that GPs faced: "At present the general practitioner finds himself between the devil and the deep blue sea. By some he is told that he should be able to diagnose and care for from eighty to ninety per cent of all illness; while by others that his incapacity is so great that he must give way to a new order."[91]

THE CCMC REPORT OF 1932

In truth, Fishbein's support for general practitioners masked his true intent. Just as corporate practice and other collective forms of health care delivery threatened the AMA, which was built on independent practitioners working through their local societies, so did group practice. Fishbein feared purveyors of group practice to the same extent he feared proponents of socialized medicine. The Mayo Clinic was a common focus of Fishbein's attacks. "These experiments have involved the development of groups, such as the Mayo Clinic, and several hundred replicas thereof on a smaller scale, throughout the country," he professed.[92]

The divide between leading specialists, such as Peters and Cabot, and leading AMA spokespersons, such as Fishbein, over group payment and group practice spilled over into the public arena in the 1930s. The trigger was the 1932 report of the Committee on the Costs of Medical Care. Before 1932, much of the disagreement occurred behind the scenes, in medical journals, at professional meetings, and at academic conferences. After the CCMC issued its report, this largely obscure debate involving leading members of the health care community quickly became an acrimonious affair. The biggest loser in the end would be the GP.

The CCMC was, in many respects, a spin-off from Lambert's committee on social insurance. Prominent AMA members, alarmed by the AMA's

this we offer medical care furnished by the individual physician ... with groups and clinics organized only where the nature of the situation" determines.[99]

The AMA's reaction to the CCMC's final report was largely antagonistic. Its adverse responses took the form of resolutions, new or revised ethical standards, and enforcement activities. Characteristically, Fishbein was hyperbolic. "The alignment is clear," he wrote in *JAMA*. "On the one side the forces representing the great foundations, public health officialdom, social theory – even socialism and communism – inciting to revolution; on the other side, the organized medical profession of this country urging an orderly evolution ... which will observe the principles that have been found through the centuries to be necessary to the sound practice of medicine."[100]

In 1933, the House of Delegates adopted a resolution claiming that the "organization of groups around hospitals or otherwise" could lead to "state medicine."[101] About a year later, the House issued what it called the "Ten Principles," perhaps the clearest formulation of the AMA's rules for health care delivery. The most important principles were as follows:

- *First*: All features of medical service in any method of medical practice should be under the control of the medical profession. No other body or individual is legally or educationally equipped to exercise such control.
- *Second*: No third party must be permitted to come between the patient and his physician in any medical relation. All responsibility for the character of medical services must be borne by the profession.
- *Third*: Patients must have absolute freedom to choose a legally qualified doctor of medicine who will serve them from among all those qualified to practice and who are willing to give service ...
- *Fifth*: All medical phases of all institutions involved in medical services should be under professional control, it being understood that hospital service and medical service should be considered separately ...[102]

In addition to the Ten Principles, the Judicial Council revised the Code of Medical Ethics in 1934.[103] For the first time, the AMA defined contract practice to mean "the carrying out of an agreement between a physician *or* a group of physicians, as principals or agents, and a corporation, organization or individual, to furnish partial or full medical services to a group or class of individuals for a definite sum or fixed rate per capita."[104] The Bureau of Medical Economics provided further perspective. Adherence to the Code precluded any form of "third party intervention for profit in the confidential relations of a physician and a patient," the BME stated.[105]

In 1936, the House of Delegates passed a resolution that strongly reinforced the ability of local medical societies to enforce Code violations. The resolution stated that hospitals should deny privileges to physicians who were not members of their local medical societies.[106] Known as the Mundt Resolution, for the Illinois doctor who proposed it, the decree had its greatest effect on hospitals that trained medical interns. Should a hospital grant privileges to a doctor who lacked local society membership (engaging in contract practice, for instance), the AMA could remove the hospital from its list of approved locations for internship training.[107]

The Mundt Resolution was a significant step, one that the House of Delegates took after a period of lengthy deliberation.[108] Attempts to regulate the nature and quality of medical training for interns and residents seemed well within the AMA's purview. Indeed, Justice Field, who authored the Supreme Court's opinion in the *Dent* case, wrote that the "subtle and mysterious" nature of medical practice meant that "comparatively few can judge" a physician's qualifications.[109] But to claim, as the AMA had done in its Mundt Resolution, that certain forms of payment and delivery were forbidden expanded the profession's regulatory powers beyond anything the Court in the *Dent* case intended. What happened next significantly affected the course of US health care delivery. The AMA's boldfaced assertion of regulatory authority in Mundt ran headlong into a presidential administration that opposed AMA efforts to rein in group practice.

GROUP HEALTH ASSOCIATION

One of the philanthropic organizations that supported the CCMC was the Twentieth Century Fund, established in 1919 by department-store mogul Edward A. Filene, a strong proponent of reorganizing the health care system to make it more efficient.[110] Filene favored the majority report and, under the auspices of the Twentieth Century Fund, backed the formation of several group payment plans designed in accordance with the report's recommendations. By 1936, the year that the AMA House of Delegates passed the Mundt Resolution, twelve such plans were in existence and nine more were under consideration. "[S]ubstantial progress has been made in the promotion of voluntary, cooperative, group payment medical service organizations," the Fund reported.[111]

On February 19, 1937, the Fund announced the formation of the Group Health Association, a Washington, DC, cooperative that employed doctors to care for and treat federal workers. In March 1937, the Home Owners' Loan Corporation, a New Deal agency, transferred more than $40,000 in public funds to the fledgling organization, most of it for the purchase of medical equipment.[112] Fishbein immediately denounced the transfer, claiming that public funds had been improperly diverted to a private entity. "Why should government employees be subsidized by the American government; they ought to pay for medical care out of their wages, exactly the same as anybody else does," he contended.[113] Adept at public relations, Fishbein solicited and gained support from the media. "What is this sacred thing, the Group Health Association?" the *Arizona Republic* queried. "If a membership list of the Group Health Association were obtainable, we think we would find it was largely made up of adherents of the New Deal."[114] Though Congress cancelled the transfer, the loss of $40,000 in start-up funds did not stop the plan's forward progress.[115]

Group Health faced two additional hurdles, both legal in nature. The first was a claim by the US Attorney for the District of Columbia that Group Health was "illegally engaged in the practice of medicine."[116] The second was a claim by DC's Superintendent of Insurance that Group Health was "engaged in the business of insurance in violation of the law."[117] When combined, the two assertions placed Group Health in a double bind, a Catch-22. If Washington, DC, laws forbid the corporate practice of medicine, as many states did, then Group Health might not be able to employ or otherwise engage physicians to provide medical services to its members. On the other hand, if Group Health was not practicing medicine, then it might be functioning as an insurer for its members. That would require compliance with DC insurance laws and regulations. Either way, Group Health might not be able to continue.

Rather than wait for the US Attorney and the DC Superintendent to file their claims (the US Attorney threatened an injunction or an involuntary dissolution of Group Health), Group Health sued for declaratory relief in the federal district court in Washington, DC. In a 1938 decision, the district court ruled in favor of Group Health, side-stepping the insurance issue on a technicality.[118] As to the contention that Group Health was illegally engaged in the corporate practice of medicine, the court disagreed, holding that Group Health physicians were "in the position of independent contractors" because the cooperative did not "undertake to control the manner in which they attend or prescribe for their patients."

This was a bit of a stretch, since Group Health paid its physicians a salary. But the relationship between Group Health and its doctors was not the central reason for the court's ruling. The main reason was that Group Health "was not in the business of making money by furnishing medical services to anyone who may come along." That Group Health did not operate as a for-profit entity, in other words, was the court's central consideration.[119]

Having averted the legal crisis, Group Health faced a series of attempts by the AMA and the local medical society in Washington, DC (the D.C. Society) to obstruct its operations. These included actions and threatened actions against Group Health doctors and those who aided them – expulsions from local medical societies and the termination of staff privileges at hospitals with residency programs. The first of these tactics (expulsions from medical societies) had been used before, specifically against group plans and clinics in Los Angeles, Milwaukee, Chicago, and Elk City, Oklahoma.[120] But the second tactic, the coercion of hospitals, was a new strategy grounded in the Mundt Resolution. In advancing this new tactic, the D.C. Society circulated a "white list" that included only those doctors it deemed eligible for hospital privileges .[121]

While expulsion from professional associations could damage a physician's practice and reputation, lack of hospital privileges was career-ending, "professional suicide" in the words of one commentator, "partial revocation of licensure to practice medicine" in the words of another. [122] "Conceivably the association might have functioned without medical society doctors and without the benefit of their consultations," the US Department of Justice (DOJ) asserted in the forthcoming legal proceedings against the AMA and the D.C. Society for antitrust violations. "But under present-day conditions," the DOJ maintained, Group Health "could not offer provisions for health services of value, without [access to] hospitals."[123] Invoking the Mundt Resolution was a very effective tactic. After expelling one Group Health physician from the D.C. Society's membership rolls, another doctor resigned from Group Health in order to avoid sanctions.[124] In one documented instance, a Group Health patient with a serious heart condition could not secure a specialty consultation because DC-area specialists feared disciplinary action.[125]

THE GROUP HEALTH CASE BEGINS

The Department of Justice first gained knowledge of Group Health's plight from Hugh Cabot. In November 1937, the journal *Science* reported that Cabot was among a group of 430 doctors who had signed and widely distributed a petition calling for "a national public health policy."[126] Affronted by the Committee's "manifesto," a label that Fishbein must have given the petition, the AMA Board of Trustees rebuked the doctors for their public announcement. Apparently, the board believed that the doctors could not issue such a statement without their approval. "Until ... the regularly chosen representatives of the 106,000 physicians who constitute the membership of the [AMA] ... determine, after due consideration, that some fundamental change or revolution in the nature of ... medical service in the United States is necessary, physicians will do well to abide by the principles which the House of Delegates has established," the board admonished.[127]

The rebuke must have deeply offended Cabot.[128] In a speech before Group Health members in Washington, DC, on May 4, 1938, Cabot blasted the AMA. "This is pure Fascism of the Italian type," he asserted.[129] Almost three weeks later, on May 23, Cabot wrote to Thurman Arnold, the head of the DOJ's antitrust division, detailing the AMA's attempts to destroy Group Health.[130] Cabot could not have chosen a better time to complain, or a better person to solicit. Unable to get Congress to pursue a plan of compulsory health insurance largely because of AMA opposition, the Roosevelt administration was seeking other ways to increase access to health care services.[131] Group Health offered an opportunity. Arnold, a seasoned litigator who had a history of using the antitrust laws to reform entire industries, was just the person to lead the effort. "Within a day of receiving Cabot's letter," historian Patricia Spain Ward recounted, "Justice Department officials indicated to [Group Health] their willingness to investigate its difficulties."[132]

On July 30, 1938, Arnold announced the results of the DOJ's investigation into the anticompetitive activities of the AMA and the D.C. Society.[133] "The close relationship existing between the [D.C. Society] and the principal hospitals in Washington has resulted in denial to Group Health Association's physicians of access to hospital facilities in the District of Columbia," Arnold stated. "Not even in emergency cases are doctors allowed to attend to their patients," he alleged.[134] Such findings supported a criminal indictment for violating Section 3 of the Sherman Antitrust Act of 1890. "No combination or conspiracy can be allowed to limit a doctor's freedom to arrange his practice as he chooses, so long as by therapeutic standards his methods are approved and do not violate the law," Arnold proclaimed.[135]

Though few seriously contested the government's findings, the prospect of a criminal indictment against the AMA for violating the Sherman

Act created a firestorm of negative publicity. As the *Chicago Tribune* editorialized three days after Arnold's announcement, the law itself was hardly settled. "It is not necessary to go into the merits of [the] controversy," the *Tribune* asserted. "The worst that can be said of the medical societies – and it has been said often – is that they have been following trade union practices." Yet trade unions, the *Tribune* pointed out, "are specifically exempt from the operations of the anti-trust laws." This was "doubly curious," the newspaper added, "because of all the trade unions ever known the medical association is the one which has been the least selfish, the most public spirited."[136]

Several newspapers shared the *Tribune*'s perspective. "[W]hen Congress years ago passed the antitrust laws it never dreamed that they would or could be applied to such conditions as Mr. Arnold is now attacking," the St. Louis *Daily Globe-Democrat* stated.[137] "In proceeding against professional nonprofit organizations, which are not concerned with prices or commodities and in the ordinary sense are incapable of operating in restraint of trade, the Department of Justice has entered a field commonly regarded as outside the scope of the antitrust laws," the *Philadelphia Inquirer* remarked.[138] "Arnold thinks that the antitrust laws apply to the offering of services as well as to the production of goods. That, if we are not mistaken, is a new interpretation," the *Chicago Daily News* observed.[139]

Arnold was undeterred, however. He had weathered similar attacks in other cases. According to Edward Kearney, one of Arnold's biographers, Arnold "utilized grand jury investigations and criminal indictments in such a way as to achieve a dramatic as well as a practical effect." He "would choose a certain industry ... and launch a massive investigation," Kearney stated.[140] Arnold's penchant for publicity and his belief that "the only thing that would make businessman behave was the threat of indictment" embodied his approach to antitrust enforcement, wrote Spencer Waller, another Arnold biographer.[141] "Far from shying away from investigating or attacking the sacred cows of the economy, Arnold seemed to delight in tormenting them," wrote Waller.[142]

Labor unions, automobile manufacturers, motion picture producers, and oil company executives were among the organizations, companies, and individuals that Arnold targeted for their monopolistic practices.[143] Arnold had even gone against America's big three automakers, charging them with the unlawful coercion of automobile dealers. Fearing an adverse jury verdict, two of them, Ford and Chrysler, signed consent decrees in order to avoid going to trial.[144]

Though Arnold denied that he was using the Group Health case to initiate broad-ranging changes to the health care industry, his pretrial rhetoric appeared to be contradictory.[145] In his July 30 announcement, for instance, Arnold stated that he "selected [the Group Health case] because its importance is nation-wide and its value as a precedent is of far-reaching consequence on one of our most pressing problems." "[C]ooperative health associations," such as Group Health, were good public policy, he declared.[146]

Few in the press believed Arnold when he said that he was not attempting to "solve the problems of medical economics."[147] The looming criminal indictment was an attempt to "extort a consent decree" from the AMA that would "settle the complex issues centering around medical care," the *New York Herald Tribune* asserted.[148] "The government's charges evidently were designed to intimidate the medical profession into acceptance of the socialistic spending contemplated by the New Deal health program," the *Indianapolis Star* professed.[149] "This is not a criminal indictment in the usual sense of the word but rather an effort to change the point of view of organized American medicine on a much-debated issue," the normally pro-administration *New York Times* contended.[150] "The grand jury investigation of the opposition to group medicine is a coup almost deserving the overworked adjective sensational," the *Philadelphia Evening Bulletin* protested.[151]

But if Arnold thought he could settle the matter before trial, he was mistaken. There would be no consent order, no settlement agreement, in the Group Health case. Fishbein would not compromise or capitulate. If necessary, the AMA would take the case all the way to the Supreme Court, he threatened. To Fishbein, this was a matter of principle. The "maintenance of a free medical profession [is] fundamental to the life of the American people and of the American democracy," he proclaimed.[152]

ORGANIZED MEDICINE ON TRIAL

On December 20, 1938, the DOJ indicted the AMA and several codefendants, including the D.C. Society, certain Washington-area hospitals, and several individuals, Fishbein and Olin West among them.[153] Because Group Health was located in Washington, DC, the federal government had jurisdiction. DOJ did not have to show that defendants' actions crossed state lines, that they involved interstate commerce. Group Health presented Arnold with a rare opportunity.

Press criticism of Arnold's actions remained consistent throughout the proceeding. Many newspapers across the country stridently opposed the criminal indictment. "[T]he premise upon which the indictment is based is absurd," the Atlanta *Constitution* protested.[154] "We have in this rough-shod procedure one of the best examples yet produced of the New Deal's reckless and ill-considered methods of achieving its ends," the Springfield, Massachusetts, *Union* contended.[155] "[W]e think that medicine, of all occupations, is least motivated by the acquisitive impulse," the New York *World-Telegram* asserted.[156] "The government had everything to gain and nothing to lose by the star chamber inquiry," a columnist for the *Washington Post* stated.[157] "Such a dictator is this Thurman Arnold, who has used his power to indict as a tyrant's club to force the [AMA] to alter a position taken by the democratic action of its members," New York's *Daily Mirror* objected.[158]

The paramount legal issue in the case concerned the application of the Sherman Antitrust Act to professional associations. The resolution of this issue hinged on the meaning of the word "trade" in Section 3 of Sherman. Section 3 prohibited contracts, combinations, and conspiracies "in restraint of trade or commerce in any Territory of the United States or of the District of Columbia."[159] The AMA and the D.C. Society contended that Section 3 did not apply to them because the medical profession was not a "trade" and thus could not be involved in "trade or commerce."

The initial hearing on the "trade" issue occurred in the federal district court for the District of Columbia. In his written opinion, the district judge held for the AMA, finding that the meaning of the word "trade" did not include "the learned professions" – medicine, law, dentistry, etc.[160] There was some support for the notion that "learned professions," such as medicine, were not trades in the commercial sense. In a 1834 Supreme Court ruling, Justice Joseph Story wrote that "[w]henever any occupation, employment, or business is carried on for the purpose of profit, or gain, or a livelihood, not in the liberal arts or in the learned professions, it is constantly called a trade."[161] Succeeding Supreme Court opinions, the district judge determined, reinforced Justice Story's interpretation.[162] But the federal appellate court for the District of Columbia disagreed, reversing the district judge's decision, and holding that "the common law governing restraints of trade has not been confined ... to the field of commercial activity ... but embraces as well the field of the medical profession."[163]

Having settled the trade issue, at least for the time being, the Group Health case proceeded to trial more than two years after the indictment had issued. Rather than contest the facts, defense attorneys cast their clients as underdogs who were simply acting in the public interest.[164] These attempts apparently failed to impress the jury. Though the trial lasted two months and produced a mountain of evidence, the jury took only eleven hours to reach its verdict. It found the AMA and the D.C. Society guilty of violating the Sherman Act, but exonerated Fishbein, Olin West, and the remaining codefendants.[165] Despite the jury's quick and demonstrative decision, the district judge imposed meager sanctions. He fined the AMA $2,500 and the D.C. Society $1,500, "bare token payments compared to the more than half million dollars which the AMA estimated it had spent in legal costs," Patricia Ward protested.[166]

Notwithstanding the small fines, the AMA and the D.C. Society appealed the verdicts against them. They could not allow the DC Court of Appeals ruling to stand on the trade issue. Before the case could be heard in the Supreme Court, however, defendants had to return to the appellate court for another hearing. Though the appellate court once again ruled against them, this time it provided a different, narrower reason for its decision, one that saved the learned profession's exemption or, at the very least, rendered its future uncertain. Rather than hold that the practice of medicine constituted a "trade" under Sherman, the appeals court grounded its second decision in the commercial activities of the Group Health Association. It did not matter, the court said, whether medicine was a "trade" under Sherman. What mattered was that defendants had restrained the business of Group Health, a commercial entity.[167]

The case now went to the US Supreme Court where, on January 18, 1943, the Court affirmed the guilty verdicts. Though the Justices had asked the parties to consider "whether a physician's practice of his profession constitutes a trade" under Sherman, they also sidestepped the trade issue. "As the Court of Appeals properly remarked," the Justices concluded, "the calling or occupation of the individual physicians charged as defendants is immaterial if the purpose and effect of their conspiracy was [the] obstruction and restraint of the business of Group Health." Thus, "we need not consider or decide ... whether a physician's practice of his profession constitutes a trade under Section 3 of the Sherman Act."[168]

AFTERMATH

By failing to decide that doctors' economic activities fell under Sherman, the Supreme Court left open many questions, such as anticompetitive conduct between or among physicians. Yet the DOJ's action and the Supreme Court decision sent a big message – the AMA and its umbrella state and local medical societies did not have carte blanche to police the health care industry. The AMA's coercive tactics, the Ten Principles, the Mundt Resolution, and some of the provisions contained in the Code of Medical Ethics could face outside scrutiny. Physician group practices, group payment plans, and other collective forms of health care delivery were protected forms of competition. The professional arena that organized medicine had constructed did not extend to all facets of health care delivery.

But the Group Health decision did not incur widespread change, at least not immediately. Absent significant financial incentives of the type that the Medicare and Medicaid programs introduced years later, the market forces that Group Health sought to unleash remained quiescent. Several group practices and group payment plans emerged in the years following the Group Health case (Kaiser Permanente in 1945, Group Health of Puget Sound in 1947, and the Health Insurance Plan of Greater New York (HIP) in 1947), but these systems were confined to discrete parts of the country. The health care industry was not yet ready for systemic change; nor was the AMA going to let that happen. Though many doctors continued to support compulsory health insurance, their advocacy was driven more by ideology than by economics.[169] Physicians who practiced medicine on a contract or salary basis at the start of the Group Health litigation (about 22,000, or one-seventh of the total number of doctors in the United States)[170] still faced many challenges, but at least the Supreme Court had validated their standing.

The caustic rhetoric that Fishbein had employed against group practice diminished, and with it, accusations of "socialized medicine."[171] Subsequent battles between the AMA and presidential administrations over health care reform did not incur widespread denunciations of contract practice. In the midst of the battle with the Truman administration over a national health plan, the AMA even argued that "voluntary medical prepayment plans ... would accomplish the [Truman plan's] major objectives with far less expense and give the public the highest quality of medical care, without regimentation."[172]

CONCLUSION

The period from 1919 to 1943 was a tumultuous time in the United States and the rest of the world. Two world wars and an economic depression exhausted the resources of Britain, France, and Germany. For the US health care industry, these dates have special significance. In 1919, the AMA began to turn away from the scientific spirit that had fostered its hegemonic rise in the previous two decades. By the mid-1930s, this shift was complete. The association embraced a set of principles that were inconsistent with medicine's forward progress. In 1943, the US Supreme Court in the Group Health case announced that the AMA had over-stepped its authority, that certain principles bearing on economic affairs were against public policy.

Underlying many of the events from 1919 to 1943 was a core tension. This was the contest between generalists and specialists over the proper approach to health care delivery in the face of increasing demand and task complexity. Many leading specialists and academic physicians promoted group practice and group payment plans. A majority of physicians, on the other hand, favored independent, fee-for-service, practice. Rather than strive for a designated role in an integrated delivery system (as was occurring in many European countries), generalists sought a level playing field. They did not want to be part of a tiered delivery system that excluded them from the hospital setting.

The hardening of positions created new alliances when reformers such as Hugh Cabot turned to the Roosevelt administration for assistance. But the principles of business competition that Thurman Arnold proposed were no more suitable to Cabot and other apostate physicians than the rigid ethical principles that the AMA had promulgated. A new, younger breed of doctors entering medical practice worked to fashion a strategy that would maintain the profession's standing in a rapidly changing environment. Their approach sought to bring hospitals, insurers, and accrediting bodies under the rules and guidelines of the professional arena.

4

The Hospital as Community Health Center, 1946–1964

Though the AMA's membership comprised mostly office-based private practitioners, many of them generalists located in rural communities, small towns, and small cities, the association could not resist the trend toward urban specialization and hospital-based care. If the AMA was to represent all physicians, as it claimed to do, then it would have to accommodate the interests of doctors who did much of their work in hospitals, such as surgeons, pathologists, and radiologists, as well as a new breed of dynamic and vocal hospital administrators who had developed their own political base of support.

The approach that took hold during this time frame conflated the interests of generalists, specialists, and hospital administrators. In this approach, the hospital, not the doctor's office, clinic, or dispensary, became the central location or focus of health care delivery in the United States. Most of the hospitals that provided acute care were privately owned and nonprofit – "voluntary" hospitals, which were independent and community-based. Government-owned hospitals, which claimed the majority of patient beds, typically provided long-term or chronic care to patients with tuberculosis or mental illnesses. Medical staff organizations (MSOs) comprising physicians with hospital privileges were responsible for treating patients in voluntary hospitals, despite the fact that few if any such doctors were hospital employees. Instead, most were "attending" physicians with private offices in close proximity to the hospitals in which they worked.

The convergence of physicians around the hospital in the United States gained momentum in the decades following World War II. This chapter traces this convergence and examines the unique political, economic, social, and legal conditions for its occurrence. Why did hospitals take the lead over health centers, dispensaries, and public health departments in providing community-based care? What effect did the ascendance of voluntary hospitals have on general practitioners? What effect did they have on group practice? Why did government planning, initiated in the 1940s and 1950s, fail to gain traction? Which individuals and organizations were the main proponents of a hospital-centered model in the United States and what were their reasons for promoting it?

FROM HEALTH CENTERS TO HOSPITALS

The notion that general practitioners should offer primary and preventive care appealed to American public health workers in the early twentieth century. Among the leading advocates was Charles Wilinsky, Boston's longtime deputy health commissioner who years later would become president of the American Public Health Association. In his remarks before the Greater Boston Medical Society in 1925, Wilinsky professed the need for GPs to take a more active role in public health and preventive medicine. They had not been doing that, he said. Instead, most of their work involved treating and curing disease. "[A] great deal has been said and much has been written about the general practitioner being an important and necessary factor in [preventive care]. Yet nothing has really been done to thoroughly interest and arouse in him a strong desire to participate in the preventive program," Wilinsky said.[1] Though GPs "frequently function[ed] on the staffs of dispensaries, health centers, and baby conference stations," Wilinsky noted, they were "doing nothing to develop these same services in their own offices for their own patients."[2]

Absent GPs' active involvement in preventive care, community health centers emerged to fill the gap. Writing in 1927, Wilinsky stated that "in more recent years we have seen the birth, growth and development in the health and welfare field of an institution which has aptly been called the 'department store of health,' but technically described as the 'health center.'"[3] "The term 'health center,'" Wilinsky advised, "covers a variety of types of institutions varying in scope of activities. Some are institutions for the dissemination of health education only, while others may conduct baby conferences or venereal disease clinics. Some may carry on the many functions of the health department while others are miniature dispensaries."[4]

More than a thousand health centers were "scattered throughout" the United States in 1927.[5] Rather than view health centers as partners in patient care, however, GPs saw them as competitors that took patients from them. GPs' main complaint was that health centers were treating and curing disease. They wanted health centers to stick to prevention and diagnosis, and they lobbied state legislatures to restrict funding for health centers that failed to comply. Health centers could not win this battle. Medical societies had too much political clout for supporters of health centers to overcome. Perhaps the most prominent example involved Hermann Biggs, New York State's health commissioner. Biggs had to restrict his plans for a network of rural health centers after the state legislature curtailed funds.[6]

Recognizing the political risks involved, Wilinsky endeavored to draw a fine line. "In order to promote properly the principles of preventive medicine it is important that only such services as are truly prophylactic shall be a part of the health center, leaving the curative field to the practitioner, hospital and existing dispensaries," he wrote.[7] But this was easier said than done. Separating prevention from cure proved to be difficult. Public health initiatives (sanitation and chlorination of water supplies) and advances in medical science (vaccines for prevention and antibacterial drugs for treatment) were leading to the eradication or control of many infectious diseases such as rabies, typhoid, cholera, plague, diphtheria, pertussis, tetanus, and tuberculosis.[8] Between 1900 and 1950, life expectancy markedly increased from about fifty to seventy years.[9] As life expectancy increased, so did chronic diseases such as cancer and diabetes.[10] The consequences were profound. "This radical shift in the leading causes of death ... compels careful readjustments of facilities to meet the future needs of an increasingly aging population," Wilinsky wrote in 1954.[11] Yet it was hospitals, not clinics, dispensaries, or community health centers, which took the lead in the treatment of chronic diseases.[12]

It made sense, of course, that modern hospitals should become prominent locations for handling life-threatening and acute conditions that required surgery, complex treatments, and close monitoring for short periods. Advances in medical technology in the decades before and after World War II included cardiac catheterization, echocardiography, kidney dialysis, and the iron lung.[13] These and other new technologies were expensive and often took much space. They required trained personnel to operate them, specialists who knew how to use them, and nurses and medical residents to monitor and provide postoperative care.

But the notion that almost all hospitals, from large to small, should own the latest in medical technology and become central hubs for community health care was uniquely American.[14] The implications were profound. Rather than serve primarily as the end stage in a tiered delivery system, US hospitals evolved to treat patients at all levels of the care continuum – beginning, middle, and end. Rather than bottom-up, US health care delivery evolved to become top-down. All parts of the delivery system would coalesce around hospitals, from emergency care to ambulatory care, from laboratories to X-ray facilities, and from clinics to doctors' private offices.

Most all members of America's health care community endorsed this arrangement, even proponents of public health. In a joint statement issued in 1948, the American Hospital Association and the American Public Health Association called for the "integration of hospitals and health departments."[15] Integration, the joint statement conveyed, involved "joint housing," "common use of laboratory and clinical facilities," and, in some cases, "the appointment of a single administrator for both organizations." Of the two, moreover, hospitals would have the dominant role. "Not only has the hospital developed during the past few decades into the basic institution providing the technical facilities for adequate health appraisal and modern diagnosis and treatment of disease, but it has also become an indispensable workshop for the practicing physician," the statement read.[16]

The widespread view that the hospital should be the centerpiece of health care delivery shaped US health policy to a significant degree. Congress appropriated funds in 1946 under the Hill-Burton Act for the construction of hospitals in small towns and cities across the United States; Blue Cross plans and commercial indemnity insurers became lucrative sources of hospital revenue in the 1940s and 1950s; and most initiatives concerning health quality promoted in-patient over out-patient care.

A HOSPITAL IN EVERY SMALL TOWN AND CITY ACROSS THE UNITED STATES

Despite continued resistance from organized medicine, supporters of the CCMC's recommendations – physicians, social scientists, planners, and policy experts – continued their quest to reform health care delivery. Their ideas appeared to gain some traction when Congress passed the Hospital Survey and Construction Act, known as the Hill-Burton Act, in 1946.[17] The law's main purposes, the legislation's sponsor Senator Lester Hill said, were twofold: (1) "to make a careful state-wide survey of the hospitals and health facilities," in order to determine "where additional facilities [and federal funding for construction] are needed," and (2) "to encourage the States to correlate and integrate their hospital and public-health services and plan additions so that all parts of the country would be adequately served."[18]

The new law gave the US Surgeon General the authority to determine which projects should receive federal funding. Though the law contemplated the construction of several different types of health care facilities, the vast majority of program grants supported the building or expansion of voluntary hospitals.[19] From 1947 to 1971, "short term hospitals" accounted for 54 percent of all projects and 71 percent of all funds; "long-term care hospitals," including nursing homes and chronic disease hospitals, garnered 16 percent of the projects and 14 percent of the funds; "outpatient facilities" accounted for only 10 percent of the projects and 6 percent of the funds; and public health centers received 12 percent of the projects and 3 percent of the funds.

The Surgeon General favored the construction of small (50 beds or less) and medium-sized (50–100 beds) hospitals over large ones (100 beds or more).[20] Sixty-eight percent of the hospitals approved for construction in the first four years of program had fewer than 50 beds, while 89 percent had less than 100 beds. Small towns and small cities were the principal benefactors. Localities with populations of 5,000 persons or fewer accounted for over 71 percent of new construction projects, while localities with populations of 10,000 or more comprised just over 12 percent of new projects. By the end of 1948, 643 projects had been approved; by the end of 1949, 1,019 projects; and by the end of 1950, 1,145 projects were in progress.[21]

In addition to promoting small- and medium-sized hospitals in small towns and small cities, the Surgeon General gave preference to nonprofit ones. The percentage allocation in the first four years of the program was about 54 percent nonprofit to 46 percent public.[22] These figures were somewhat misleading, however, because they were aggregated across regions. Almost all projects which the Surgeon General approved in the New England and Mid-Atlantic states went to nonprofit facilities, 97 percent and 83 percent, respectively. In certain western and southern states, on the other hand, the majority of the funds went toward the construction of public, often county-owned, hospitals.[23]

Early evaluations of the Hill-Burton program indicated that spending allocations were in line with congressional intent despite the emphasis on voluntary hospitals over other types of facilities. "[T]he program is tending to place hospitals in the smaller population centers, where they will service predominantly rural people," the authors of a 1950 report for the Public Health Service said. "This is precisely the purpose for which the program is designed, for the law specifies that the program shall build hospitals where they are most needed, with special emphasis given to rural places and places of low per capita income," they wrote.[24]

A second evaluation covering the years 1948–1954 confirmed the earlier findings. "The Hill-Burton formula gave a much larger share of money to the low income states where hospital and health facilities were much less adequate than to high income states," the authors of the second evaluation wrote. "Statistics show the lower income states constructed more hospital facilities per person during this period than the high income states," they said.[25] Though the second evaluation found that the Surgeon General was directing funds as intended when Hill-Burton was enacted in 1946, it warned that building small hospitals in rural areas might not be the best approach. "One danger" from "channel[ing] [money] into rural areas," evaluators wrote, was that "rural areas have been losing population for a number of years. Hospital facilities needed today may not be needed in the future." [26]

By the early 1970s, this warning had fully resonated. According to a 1974 study, the conditions that had fostered a government policy to advance funds for the construction of general hospitals in small towns and cities no longer existed. "In the twenty-seven years since the 1946 act establishing the program, the financial climate for voluntary hospitals has undergone major change," the 1974 study stated. "Third-party financing of hospital care, such as Blue Cross, Medicare, and Medicaid, has become the dominant source of hospital revenue, and hospitals have become enormously expensive, in terms of both construction and operating costs. Whatever goals were set for the Hill-Burton program in 1946," the situation in 1974 was "very different," the authors of the study wrote.[27]

An unintended consequence of building hospitals in small towns was that it made it more difficult to rationalize health care delivery. Hill-Burton funds were fueling the hospital-centered model that organized medicine favored, rather than a broader spectrum of facilities offering out-patient as well as in-patient care.[28] To reiterate what Senator Hill said in launching the program, states were to survey "hospitals and health facilities" and attempt to "integrate their hospital and public-health services ... so that all parts of the country would be adequately served." Program implementation, however, focused almost entirely on building stand-alone hospitals, not "health facilities" that provided basic, primary care. This would have important implications for physician practice patterns and, more specifically, access to primary care physicians for the prevention and treatment of chronic diseases.

Those who implemented Hill-Burton appeared to overlook studies showing that hospitals were drawing all types of doctors, GPs as well as specialists, in the years after World War II.[29] The main reason was the hospital emergency room. Emergency rooms, postoperative recovery rooms, and intensive care units (ICUs) appeared in the 1940s and 1950s, becoming standard fare in US hospitals by the early 1960s. By putting new life-saving and life-sustaining technology and the personnel who could use it in one location, and by making it available to the public any day of the week and any time of the day, voluntary hospitals had become irresistible draws not only for patients, but also for busy GPs.[30] The lack of gatekeeping in the United States meant that all varieties of attending physicians could oversee hospital-based care.

Research undertaken at Hartford Hospital in Connecticut in 1956 found that there was a 400 percent increase in the use of hospital emergency rooms between 1945 and 1955.[31] Though automobile accidents, insurance coverage, and overall population gains undoubtedly accounted for some of the increase, these factors alone could not explain the fourfold gain. What the Hartford Hospital researchers discovered was that patients often went to the ER either because their doctors told them to go there or because their doctors were unavailable. Based on these findings, the researchers concluded that the nature of medical practice itself was changing, that "a shifting pattern in patient care" was occurring. This "shifting pattern," they said, reflected:

... physician acceptance of the emergency room as a location preferable to his office or the patient's home for the treatment of injuries and acute illness, probably owing to the fact that he is more likely to be in or near the hospital at the time he is called and that such a facility places at his command a wide variety of services (laboratory, x-ray, operating and so forth) that he may need; public need for the facility because of increase in possibly needed services available in such a facility ...; increase in likelihood of finding a physician and of obtaining prompt attention ...; public acceptance of the hospital as the center of the community; convenience (the patient need not call one to several physicians seeking aid); and third-party coverage.[32]

The findings of the Hartford Hospital study were not unique or isolated to a particular area or region of the country. Many doctors were sending their patients to the ER for nonurgent care and treatment in the 1940s and 1950s.[33] Summarizing the research, historian Beatrix Hoffman wrote: "The percentage of ER visits classified as 'nonurgent' or 'nonemergency' in the 1950s and 1960s was substantial ... Hospitals reported rates of nonemergency visits ranging from forty-two percent to as high as seventy percent of their total caseloads."[34]

Hill-Burton was not simply a driver of new hospital construction. Hill-Burton funds helped to fuel a shift in patient care in which doctors used emergency rooms for treating a large variety of illnesses and conditions. Free and open access to emergency rooms with sophisticated medical technology, nurses, and other highly trained personnel deterred physician group formation, regional integration, hierarchy, and geographic outreach. The economics of the situation were such that general practitioners were less likely to combine their resources or refer their patients to specialists if their offices were in close proximity to hospitals that provided outpatient care.

HOSPITALS AND HEALTH INSURANCE

Hill-Burton furnished funds for new hospital construction and renovation of existing facilities at a time when such funds were scarce and needed. But the one-third of construction costs that Hill-Burton provided was insufficient to renovate and expand most hospitals unless revenues from other sources were included. In Britain, the government took over voluntary hospitals in 1948 to keep them from "disappearing" because of their poor financial condition.[35] In the United States, on the other hand, voluntary hospitals gained a reliable source of revenue through the private sector.

After World War II, Blue Cross plans and commercial indemnity insurers became the principal sources of hospital revenue. In 1940, there were 20,662,000 persons with health insurance in the United States; by 1960, the number of individuals with health insurance stood at 142,334,000, an increase of almost 700 percent.[36] A fortuitous series of events accounted for the surge in health insurance in a relatively short period. The first of these was the 1943 wartime freeze on wages, which spurred employers and their employees to seek other forms of compensation. Soon after the wage freeze took effect, the National War Labor Board announced that wage and price controls did not apply to fringe benefits, including the premiums that employers paid for health insurance. Then in 1949, the US Supreme Court upheld a National Labor Relations Board ruling that employee benefit and pension plans could be included in collective bargaining. Finally, in 1954, the Internal Revenue Service determined that the premiums that employers paid on behalf of their employees were tax exempt.[37]

Once it became clear that the provision of health insurance benefited all interests – labor, management, and insurers – the most important question that remained was the type of health insurance plan that management and labor wanted. Management did not have to search very far. Large commercial carriers, such as Equitable, Metropolitan, and New York Life, which sold multiple product lines, were willing to "tailor" their health insurance plans in order to satisfy employers.[38] "Employers could decide which hospital services would be covered, the percentage of reimbursement, and the amount of an employee's contribution," historian Jennifer Klein remarked. In addition, "employers could decide whether specialists would be included, whether benefits for physicians' care covered visits to the physician's office or only treatment in the hospital, and whether payments would start with the first visit," Klein wrote.[39]

Employees often were dissatisfied with company plans. Indemnity coverage, which most commercial carriers sold, reimbursed the employee or subscriber, not the hospital or the doctor who submitted the bill, exposing the employee to additional and often substantial out-of-pocket costs.[40] Commercial insurers rarely covered employees' families, preexisting conditions, or diagnostic services, moreover; nor did they provide "conversion privileges," that is, discounted individual rates for workers who left group plans. By contrast, Blue Cross paid hospitals directly. In addition, Blue Cross often covered family members, preexisting conditions, and diagnostic care.[41] Not surprisingly, most employees preferred Blue Cross.

Blue Cross traced its origins to a "hospital plan" devised at Baylor University Hospital in 1929. What was unique about the Baylor plan and other hospital plans that soon succeeded it was their focus on service benefits. Though physicians liked the comprehensive coverage that Baylor and other hospital plans offered, they opposed certain features.[42] Such plans did not cover all hospitals in a particular area, and they often combined hospital and physician services for billing purposes. Medical societies complained that restricting the number of hospitals violated "free choice of physician" and that combining doctors' fees with hospital expenses promoted the corporate practice of medicine.[43]

The person who would bridge the divide between doctors and the hospital plans was C. Rufus Rorem, an influential voice at the American Hospital Association (AHA) from 1937 to 1946. Rorem had begun as early as 1933 to devise a set of principles for hospital plans. The principles he formulated were threefold: (1) plans "[should] be limited to hospital services"; (2) plans "should involve participation by all hospitals of standing in the community"; and (3) plans "should be promoted on a noncommercial basis." By reimbursing hospital costs only, Blue Cross plans largely side-stepped the controversy with physicians over separate billing arrangements (Blue Shield, which lagged behind Blue Cross by several years, would reimburse doctors). By requiring the participation of all community hospitals, plans satisfied "free choice of physician." And by operating as nonprofits, plans received tax-exempt status, enhancing the AHA's membership.[44] In 1939, Rorem's principles became the key criteria for AHA approval of Blue Cross plans.

Blue Cross plans enjoyed a surge in popularity in the late 1930s due in part to Rorem's efforts. By 1940, Blue Cross plans had 6 million subscribers, while commercial insurers had 3.7 million.[45] Commercial insurers steadily gained on Blue Cross, however, overtaking the nonprofit insurer in total enrollments by 1951. Blue Cross plans had 40.9 million subscribers in 1951, while commercial carriers combined for 41.5 million. After 1951, commercial carriers steadily increased their market share relative to that of Blue Cross.[46]

The expansion of insurance coverage, whether through Blue Cross or commercial carriers, greatly stimulated hospital admissions.[47] Total admissions climbed from 9,838,289 in 1945 to 14,691,482 in 1953, a 67 percent increase in only eight years.[48] Economist Milton Roemer devised a formula that showed the link between the two. Roemer calculated that "hospitalization insurance tends to increase the likelihood of hospital admission in a particular year by 56 per cent, ... [from] 90 per 1,000 for noninsured persons ... [to] about 140 admissions per 1,000 per year."[49]

Insurance coverage also meant higher reimbursement rates for hospitals and physicians. While physician pay increased 94.6 percent from 1940 to 1960, hospital reimbursements grew an astonishing 343.7 percent.[50] Payroll expenses accounted for a large part of the increase. Average payroll costs per patient in 1945 were $4.48; in 1960, they were $20.56.[51] Ten hospitals in New York City's Federation Hospital System[52] documented a six-fold increase in expenditures, from just under $8 million to almost $48 million between 1942 and 1959.[53] During that same period, the average cost per patient day grew from $6.81 to $27.90 for payroll, food, and supplies.[54]

Those principally responsible for paying the bills – employers, unions, workers, and insurers – raised concerns about rising hospital rates. Blue Cross, in particular, was affected because its premiums were closely tied to hospital charges. Though Blue Cross received discounted rates under state laws, premiums still had to increase, sometimes substantially, in order to cover the higher costs. "By broadening its benefits to attract subscribers, Blue Cross ... drummed up business for the hospitals. But it could sustain the strategy only if the hospitals agreed to the corollary, holding down premium increases," historian Lawrence Brown wrote. "By the early 1960s (indeed by the late 1950s) cooperation [between Blue Cross and hospitals] was badly strained," Brown said. "A new conventional wisdom was taking hold in the partner's environment. Perhaps enthroning the hospital as the center of community care was not such a good idea after all," he remarked.[55]

HOSPITAL STANDARDIZATION AND MEDICAL STAFF ORGANIZATION

Many hospitals were undeniably deficient in the quality of care they provided in the early decades of the twentieth century. Poor recordkeeping, inadequate laboratory and X-ray facilities, and a disorganized medical staff were common deficiencies. The American College of Surgeons was determined to improve the situation. In 1918, the ACS began an inspection tour of several of the nation's hospitals, just as the AMA had done for medical schools twelve years earlier. ACS surveyors found that 89 out of 692 hospitals, or only 13 percent, passed inspection.[56] The majority of deficiencies, surveyors discovered, stemmed from inadequately trained doctors. The solution, they said, was to raise the standards for hospital privileges. "It was the free-wheeling, 'open-staff' voluntary hospital in the rapidly expanding American environment that presented the problems and induced the reforms," economists Roemer and Jay Friedman wrote.[57]

Open rather than closed staffing marked a big difference between American and European hospitals. Most European hospitals had closed medical staffs comprised of salaried specialists. "In Great Britain and Sweden, nearly all medical and surgical services in the hospitals are rendered by organized staffs of salaried specialists," Roemer related. "In France and Switzerland, this is not the general rule, although a growing proportion of in-patient care in the governmental general hospitals is performed by salaried men," he noted. "Only a small percentage of physicians have any direct access to hospitals, either governmental or voluntary. The patient is cared for by the physician who is 'on service' at the time," he conveyed.[58]

An important figure in the ACS's standardizing campaign was Canadian doctor and former hospital administrator Malcolm MacEachern.

Called "Mr. Hospital" by many of his colleagues, MacEachern served as president of the American Hospital Association from 1924 to 1925, director of hospital administration at Northwestern University from 1943 to 1956, and director of hospital activities at the ACS from 1923 to 1951.[59] Two years after MacEachern's arrival, the ACS published its first *Manual of Hospital Standardization*. The 1926 Manual and its subsequent editions contained the requirements for hospitals seeking ACS accreditation. MacEachern's stern leadership and unwavering efforts while at the ACS helped to bring about solid improvement in hospital performance. By 1945, 81 percent of the 3,938 hospitals that the ACS surveyed were approved, a huge advance since 1918.[60]

MacEachern's views on hospital standardization were set forth in his lengthy textbook, *Hospital Organization and Management*.[61] After its initial publication in 1935 (there were several reprint editions), the book quickly became "a classic in the field."[62] MacEachern favored closed staffing and said so: "An efficient medical staff organization can be developed more readily and the clinical work kept under better control in a closed hospital, inasmuch as the medical staff consists of a relatively small group of selected physicians who are directly responsible for the professional work on their respective services."[63] Open staffing, he believed, was "beset with difficulties because a large number of physicians working therein have no direct interest in the hospital except as a facility for the care of their patients."[64]

MacEachern's solution for the open staffing problem involved detailed standards for the formation and composition of medical staff organizations. So long as MSOs satisfied ACS standards, MacEachern believed that hospitals with open staffing could be accredited. MacEachern advised that membership in "the local medical society, and practicing in the community or within reasonable distance of the hospital" should be among the basic qualifications for medical staff appointment.[65] Staff members did not have to be board-certified specialists, he allowed, but the process for their selection should be rigorous. "While in practically all hospitals it would be unreasonable to demand that the members be exclusive specialists, it is reasonable that they be of proven ability," he wrote.[66]

But questions surrounding the criteria for hospital privileges remained, particularly those concerning the GP. GPs had to find a specialty department that would accept them, a big obstacle for many.[67] Some hospitals required board certification for staff membership, even though the ACS did not mandate it.[68] Specialty board certification as a litmus test for staff membership drew a sharp retort from the AMA. "Such a policy is contrary to the principles of the [Council of Medical Education and Hospitals],” the association maintained.[69] “Hospital staff appointments should depend on the qualifications of physicians to render proper care to patients as judged by the professional staff of the hospital and not on certification or special society membership.”[70]

Hospital privileges would be a constant source of friction among generalists and specialists until managed care, many years later, took hold in the United States. So long as independent practitioners benefited financially from access to voluntary hospitals and could send their patients to them for nonurgent care, the conflict concerning medical staff appointments would remain.

THE CREATION OF THE JOINT COMMISSION

A new controversy now emerged. Facing financial difficulties and MacEachern’s pending retirement, the ACS decided to stop surveying hospitals after 1950.[71] This raised a whole new set of challenges as the AMA, the specialty societies, and the AHA maneuvered to gain control over the hospital accrediting process. The AHA and its executive director, George Bugbee, were the first to take action.

Bugbee was in the forefront of a talented group of hospital administrators who influenced the trajectory of the health care industry. Born in 1904, Bugbee was superintendent of Cleveland’s City Hospital before becoming the AHA’s first nonphysician CEO in 1943.[72] One of Bugbee’s first moves as the AHA’s executive director was to take over the position of editor of *Hospitals*, the association’s flagship journal. In an interview he gave for the AHA’s “Oral History” project in 1984, Bugbee said that his reason for doing so was to circumvent a power struggle: “The model I wanted to avoid was Dr. Olin West and Dr. Morris Fishbein at the AMA where the editor of [*JAMA*], Dr. Fishbein, was more powerful than the Executive Secretary,” he recounted. “I also insisted that the director of the Washington Service Bureau, as we called the Washington office [the AHA’s main office was in Chicago], report to me rather than to the Council on Government Relations. If I were going to run the Association, I was going to try to do it.”[73]

Bugbee’s decisive management style would prove to be an important factor in the formation of the Joint Commission on Accreditation of Hospitals, known today as the Joint Commission. After learning that the ACS was relinquishing its role as hospital accreditor, Bugbee approached his board of trustees about continuing the program under

AHA auspices. At Bugbee's prodding, the AHA's House of Delegates voted to assume control of the hospital accreditation process.[74]

AMA leaders were upset. They threatened action if the AHA took further steps. "The medical profession will not allow professional staffs of hospitals to fall under the complete control and domination of hospital trustees and administrators," they said. "If the American Hospital Association proceeds to usurp the rights of professional groups to determine the best medical standards, it can expect, to say the least, some very interesting developments."[75] Though it was not entirely clear what AMA leaders meant by "some very interesting developments," the message had its intended effect. "One could say the fat was in the fire," Bugbee said.[76]

The principal antagonists now came to the bargaining table. Much of the controversy centered on the composition of the new entity. Following a year of negotiation, during which AMA representatives complained that they "encountered discouraging problems," the parties reached an agreement on membership.[77] They decided that the AMA would appoint six members to the new entity, the AHA six, the ACS three, and the American College of Physicians three. An invitation was extended to the Canadian Medical Association to appoint one member. In 1959, the Canadian Medical Association withdrew to form its own organization.[78]

As subsequent events would demonstrate, the AMA and the AHA would continue to clash over hospital policy, leading to some heated exchanges.[79] By establishing the Joint Commission, however, doctors and hospitals contained the political discord between them. Doing their best to make it appear that all interests had come together, the authors of a 1951 *JAMA* editorial stated: "That the plan has become a reality is a testament to those men representing the medical profession and the field of hospital administration who sat through long hours of discussion and debate to reach agreement on points that had seemed to be irreconcilable."[80]

Not long after its formation, the Joint Commission adopted most of the ACS's preexisting standards, including those on medical staff organizations.[81] Bugbee was not particularly happy about this. He decried the lack of "organizational unity" that an autonomous medical staff presented. "It may well be that the voluntary hospitals, with their desire to facilitate the work of physicians, have gone too far in releasing them from an important share of the responsibility for making the hospital itself operate at optimum," he wrote in a 1959 article. "Nothing comparable to the dichotomy in hospital organization is to be found in [other] industr [ies]," he observed. "The present hospital organization works partly because of the importance of the effort, partly because of the training and dedication of a large part of the personnel. However, the organization with its division of authority, does nothing to ensure adequate communication between physician and hospital personnel."[82]

As with many other aspects of health care in America, the Joint Commission was an American invention, a US anomaly. No other country had anything comparable.[83] The Joint Commission was not the result of a public debate involving elected officials, political parties, or contrasting ideologies. Deliberations concerning its formation took place in private, in meetings among representatives from medical and hospital associations, in committees formed to explore various proposals. The powerful coalition that comprised the Joint Commission presented a formidable obstacle to future health care reformers and government planners. Upon enacting the Medicare and Medicaid programs in 1965, the federal government not only adopted but institutionalized the traditional pattern of health care delivery that the Joint Commission protected.[84]

FROM GENERAL PRACTITIONERS TO PRIMARY CARE PHYSICIANS

In 1949, general practitioners represented 50.1 percent of all practicing physicians; by 1970, GPs represented only 18.6 percent.[85] Table 4.1 captures this downward trend. The reasons for this were largely twofold. First, GPs failed to develop a distinct role of their own in outpatient care. Instead, as indicated, GPs came to rely on hospitals as extensions of their private practices. Second, hospitals garnered the majority of funds needed for the purchase of equipment and the employment of nurses and other

TABLE 4.1 *Percentage of primary care physicians among all active doctors of medicine in the United States, 1949–2000*

Primary Care Generalists	1949	1960	1970	1980	1990	2000
General/Family Practice	50.1	35.6	18.6	14.5	12.9	12.0
General Internal Medicine	6.5	10.6	12.8	14.1	13.9	13.9
General Pediatrics	2.5	4.5	5.8	6.6	6.7	7.0
Total	59.1	50.7	37.3	35.2	33.5	32.9

Source: National Center for Health Statistics, *Health, United States, 2004 with Chartbook on Trends in the Health of Americans* (Hyattsville, MD, 2004): 311.
Note: Includes Puerto Rico, US Virgin Islands, and US Pacific Islands.

support personnel. Public funding for health centers and clinics for primary care was minimal in the United States, and private insurance was either nonexistent or inadequate to support their development.

Those who worked in hospitals gained a big advantage over those who worked outside them. "During the past 20 years the incentives available to physicians have been greatest for doctors who concentrate to a considerable degree on the care of hospitalized patients," physician Glen Garrison wrote in a 1970 editorial for the *New England Journal of Medicine*. These incentives include the "exclusive use of operating rooms" and "medical personnel that are provided at public expense." Under the circumstances, Garrison observed, "it is easy to understand why physicians have gravitated to subspecialty medical practice and away from primary medical care."[86]

Seeking to bolster the number and status of general practitioners, the AMA in 1946 "approved a resolution encouraging hospitals to establish general practitioner services."[87] The move was seen as a prelude to GPs gaining a specialty board of their own. Several years would pass, however, before this would occur.[88] Many in the older generation of GPs did not want a specialty board, and their principal organization, the American Academy of General Practice (AAGP), reflected their position. It was not until about the mid-1960s that the AAGP's position changed as a new generation of physicians who called themselves family practitioners emerged.[89] Once the AAGP altered course, those advocating specialization moved expeditiously to establish an examining board. Three years later, in 1969, the AMA officially endorsed a specialization in family medicine.[90]

Not everyone believed that a new specialty board was the answer to declining numbers of physicians entering general practice, however. In 1963, the AMA formed a commission under the leadership of John Millis, president of Western Reserve University, to delve further into the situation. Following a three-year investigation, the Millis Commission determined that the GP was becoming obsolete, that increasing medical complexity and the growth of chronic diseases called for a "new type of physician."[91] In its final report, released in 1966, the Millis Commision called this new type of doctor a "primary physician."[92]

Primary physicians, the report recommended, should provide "comprehensive and continuing health care, including not only the diagnosis and treatment of illness but also its prevention and rehabilita[tion]."[93] They should not limit their practice to a specific body part or disease, and they should help patients navigate the health care system. "When a patient needs hospitalization, the services of other medical specialists, or other medical or paramedical assistance, the primary physician will see that the necessary arrangements are made, giving such responsibility to others as is appropriate, and retaining his own continuing and comprehensive responsibilities," the report envisioned.[94] At a press conference announcing the issuance of the commission's report, Millis remarked that the primary physician "might in some ways be comparable to that of a quarterback of a football team."[95]

So that primary physicians could satisfy these new obligations, the Millis Commission advised a course of training that "would include the medical counterparts of ecology, evolution, and fundamental theory rather than the specifics of molecular biology, virology, or the physiology of individual organs."[96] This additional training would not be limited to a specific area of medical specialization. Indeed, the commissioners did not want to usurp the traditional role of the specialty boards. Rather, the recommended designation constituted a category of physicians who performed the functions included in the report. Primary physicians could be internists, pediatricians, or family practitioners, so long as they were generalists.[97]

Though the AMA Board of Trustees and the House of Delegates voted to approve the Millis Report, the report's recommendations concerning primary physicians were controversial.[98] AMA members had difficulty reaching consensus on the definition of primary care and the type of physician who could provide it.[99] Many members balked at the primary physician's gatekeeping function, the coordinating and quarterbacking role that Millis had suggested.[100] While gatekeeping gained some traction in America in the 1950s and 1960s, in part because of rising costs and union demands, none of the big insurers, commercial indemnity carriers or the nonprofit Blue Cross/Blue Shield plans, pursued it.[101] Gatekeeping was a "radical" concept in the United States at this time, one that the AMA and other professional associations adamantly resisted.[102]

None of these efforts, neither the new specialty board in family medicine nor the Millis Report, mitigated GPs' downward trajectory.[103] In 1964, two years before the Millis Commission released its findings, medical school professor Kerr White wrote that "the available data do not appear to support the view that pediatricians and internists are being produced in adequate numbers to meet the demand for physicians to give primary continuing medical care." "This is especially true," White stated, "in the smaller metropolitan and semi-rural areas of the country where more than a third of the population still lives." Rather than become general internists or general pediatricians, recent medical school graduates are subspecializing, he related.[104]

Subsequent studies confirmed White's findings. Studies undertaken in the early 1980s revealed, for instance, that there was a "remarkable increase in subspecialty training [after] 1971."[105] One such study projected a growth rate of 205 percent for subspecialists, but only 77 percent for general internists for the twenty-year period from 1978 to 1998.[106] As for the new specialty in family medicine, the situation was also discouraging. While the overall percentage of physicians entering primary care stabilized in the 1970s, the percentage of family practitioners continued to decline.

THE SLOW GROWTH OF PREPAID PHYSICIAN GROUP PRACTICE

Notwithstanding hospitals' allure, there was at least one alternative that was increasing in popularity. This was prepaid physician group practice. Prepaid group plans in which doctors worked in groups or clinics and offered comprehensive services made some modest gains in the years after World War II largely because of labor unions.[107] Unions touted the cost savings and the comprehensive care that such plans delivered. Speaking on behalf of the unions, labor activist Nelson Cruickshank observed that Kaiser Permanente "was so financially successful that it generated surpluses," while Blue Cross and commercial insurers "struggled unsuccessfully to control costs."[108] Acting on its own initiative, the United Mine Workers established group practice clinics in Appalachia in the 1950s and 1960s.[109] These group clinics provided preventive and primary care.

Despite the US Supreme Court's landmark 1943 decision in the Group Health case chastising the AMA for its anticompetitive practices, resistance to group practice remained strong among independent practitioners. Medical societies searched for ways to evade the Supreme Court's Group Health decision. Their resistance took two forms. One strategy called for societies to establish their own prepaid health plans with the intention of putting rival plans out of business. The second strategy called for societies to gain state legislative authority to review and approve the formation of group practice plans under an exception to the federal antitrust laws known as "state action immunity."[110]

Medical societies in Washington and Oregon pursued the first approach. In 1946, leaders of various granges, labor unions, and consumer organizations established Group Health Cooperative of Puget

Sound (the "Cooperative") to provide health care to dues-paying members and their families. Seeking to crush the Cooperative, the King County Medical Society (King County encompassed the city of Seattle and the surrounding area) employed several tactics. As in the Group Health case, these tactics included exclusion of Cooperative doctors from medical society membership, area hospitals, and specialty consultations. But King County physicians did not stop there. In addition, they organized their own health plan for low-wage industrial workers, resolving that any doctor "who engage[d] in any competing industrial contract practice" would be "dropped from [plan] membership."[111]

In 1949, the Cooperative and its physicians brought suit in the Washington State courts seeking to enjoin the anticompetitive practices of the King County Society. Two years later, Washington's supreme court ruled in favor of the Cooperative. The court's decision hinged in part on evidence that the King County Society had attempted to destroy contract practice. "[T]here is reason to believe that the purpose of the Society in restraining competition extends to the ultimate extermination of all contract practice by the Cooperative," the court determined.[112]

A similar situation transpired in Oregon. When Oregon's hospital associations established prepaid group plans in the 1930s, state and local medical societies threatened doctors who joined such plans with expulsion. But in 1941, the medical societies reversed course. They abandoned efforts to punish doctors and instead established their own prepaid health plan, which they called Oregon Physicians Service (OPS) (OPS changed its name to Oregon Blue Shield in 1946). Within two years of its formation, OPS gained a 60 percent share of Oregon's health insurance market, while capturing 85 percent of the state's licensed doctors.[113]

In 1948, the Department of Justice took action to save the group plans that the hospital associations had created. This time, however, the DOJ was on the losing side. The federal district court that heard the case ruled in favor of the medical societies, and the US Supreme Court, in a 1952 opinion, affirmed the lower court's decision. The Supreme Court was not convinced that DOJ had proven its case, given the testimony of "apparently reputable, credible, and informed professional men" that "no attempts [had been] made to prevent individual doctors from cooperating with them." This could have ended the matter, but the Court proceeded to offer the following advice: "We might observe in passing," the Court remarked, "that there are ethical considerations where the historic direct relationship between patient and physician is involved which are quite different than the usual considerations prevailing in ordinary commercial matters. This Court has recognized that forms of competition usual in the business world may be demoralizing to the ethical standards of a profession."[114]

While the Court's "passing" observation suggested a departure from its earlier ruling in the Group Health case, this was more perception than reality. Based solely on the facts and legal principles involved in the Oregon case, its 1943 Group Health decision was unaffected. OPS doctors had abandoned the draconian tactics that the AMA and the D.C. Society had employed in Group Health. Moreover, the Court's comment in the Oregon case was dictum (superfluous advice). Yet the Court's dictum signaled that it was not ready to move beyond the Group Health decision, that organized medicine remained in charge of its customary sphere of operation.

The second strategy pursued by medical societies was state legislative authority to regulate group practice plans. Between 1939 and 1950, twenty-six states passed legislation designed to curtail such plans; in seventeen of those states, medical societies could refuse to certify closed-panel practices.[115] The approach stemmed from an exception to the federal antitrust laws that the US Supreme Court had created.[116] Under the exception, known as "state action immunity," a state legislature could delegate authority to a private organization, such as a state medical society, to regulate a specific activity. The approach was not all that different from what had transpired in the *Dent* case.[117] As had occurred in *Dent*, state medical societies sought immunity from liability to regulate the practice of medicine.[118]

But this time, proponents of group plans were larger in number and better organized. They fought back, successfully challenging medical societies in state courts in California and New Jersey.[119] In Kentucky, moreover, proponents thwarted legislation that would have stripped doctors of their medical license if they worked for a union plan.[120] These results showed increasing support for group practice plans.[121] "Attitudes have changed somewhat over the years," an article in the *New England Journal of Medicine* acknowledged.[122]

In 1954, the AMA formed an ad hoc commission to determine the extent of group practice plans across the country. The AMA's Board of Trustees selected one of its own, Leonard Larson, to chair the commission.[123] Like many other members of his generation, Larson did not share the views of Morris Fishbein, Olin West, and other former AMA leaders who opposed physician group practice.[124] Indeed, Larson had been a pathologist with the Quain and Ramstad Clinic in Bismarck, North Dakota, where he practiced with other doctors.[125]

The Larson Commission proceeded to inventory group practice plans, eventually accumulating data on 206 of them. Of the 206 plans it identified, the commission found that 128 were "closed panel plans," 64 were "cash indemnity, service (full payment) or a combination of both," and 14 "were a combination of cash indemnity/full payment and closed panel plans." Closed-panel plans, the commission reported, had a combined enrollment of 2,386,789 persons, "constitut[ing] a little less than half (48 percent) of the enrollment in all [206] plans."[126] Though Blue Shield plans, by comparison, exceeded these enrollments by a wide margin – there were 116 Blue Shield plans at the end of 1954 with combined enrollments of 34 million for surgical benefits and 25 million for regular medical benefits[127] – the commission could not ignore the fact that closed-panel arrangements were proliferating.

Following a four-year investigation, the Larson Commission in 1959 released its findings. After reviewing the commission's findings, the Board of Trustees and the House of Delegates voted to loosen the AMA's restrictions on closed panel plans.[128] The AMA's revised policy was as follows: "Each individual should be accorded the privilege to select and change his physician at will or to select his preferred system of medical care." [129] The revised policy marked an important shift in the AMA's unwavering adherence to free choice of physician. Characterizing the new policy as a "most significant action," AMA president Louis Orr declared: "While the policy reaffirms our fundamental faith in the principle of freedom of choice, it also recognizes the patient's right to select the type of medical care plan he wants – including a closed panel plan."[130]

Though the AMA's acceptance of group practice plans was significant, the policy shift did not immediately affect the existing configuration, which still comprised mostly independent practitioners and free-standing community hospitals. Group practice had developed too slowly and too late to displace the hospital and "establish tailored health service schemes" in the European framework, Rosemary Stevens indicated.[131] Moreover, the multispecialty form of group practice that the CCMC had touted was not in the offing. America's version of group practice did not mirror European clinics, which comprised mostly general practitioners. As Stevens's data showed, single-specialty groups surpassed multispecialty groups during the 1960s. Many of these single-specialty groups did not include primary care physicians.[132]

DOCTORS, HOSPITALS, AND THE LIMITATIONS OF
GOVERNMENT PLANNING

The concerted focus on hospitals in the United States stifled the development of alternative locations for patient care and treatment. By the early 1960s, the adverse effects were apparent. Some leading members of the health care community began to voice their concerns, among them Ray E. Brown, a widely respected hospital administrator and professor of health administration. In a lecture at Harvard's School of Public Health in 1963, Brown observed that patients were admitted to hospitals because there were few other options:

The failure to provide suitable alternatives to staying in the hospital has made it an all-or-none proposition if the patient is to have satisfactory access to the community's medical facilities. The failure to develop a comprehensive system of care forces the patient to go to bed in the acute facilities. In general, there are no organized outpatient services for the private ambulatory patient, no organized home-care programs as an integral part of the hospital's operations for the pay patient and not very many long-term facilities integrated with the services of the general hospital for either the free or pay patient.[133]

While the dearth of outpatient facilities adversely affected all patients, those living in rural areas and urban centers suffered disproportionately. Examining the practice patterns of Boston-area doctors from 1940 to 1961, Joseph Dorsey, the director of medical planning for Harvard Community Health Plan, found that physicians who subspecialized in internal medicine and pediatrics "have almost totally avoided the poor areas in our community."[134] "Only 9.8 per cent of all [general internists, pediatricians, and obstetrician–gynecologists] were located in the lowest three [1960] census tracts [based on income, education, and occupation], which contained 60 per cent of the overall population," he related.[135] Dorsey's findings tracked those in other urban centers.[136]

Hospitals, moreover, were not the best locations for managing chronic diseases, which were proliferating. Whereas voluntary hospitals were equipped to deal with episodic events, they did not offer preventive or long-term care and rehabilitative services. In a 1947 joint statement, the AMA and other prominent associations observed that keeping "the long term patient in the acute general hospital is wasteful," while calling for "a new orientation which places major emphasis on the early stages of chronic illness with a view to preventing or at least delaying the progress of the disease process."[137]

persons. Rather, neighborhood health centers were established to fill a gap in the system; they were patchworks or safety-net providers that targeted low-income and uninsured individuals. "They never became more than a marginal alternative," Paul Starr remarked.[145] Though federal dollars were allocated to neighborhood health centers in the early and mid-1960s, the amount was small compared with that spent on teaching hospitals.[146] "Americans frequently acted as if scientific progress, coupled with economic growth, would promote equity," Daniel Fox commented. "The British," on the other hand, "emphasized the role of efficient administration, which could be independent of science, in the equitable distribution of resources," he noted.[147]

CONCLUSION

By 1965, the principal component in US health care delivery was the voluntary hospital that provided the highest, the most intense, and the most expensive level of care, not the doctor's office, the clinic, or the dispensary. Despite differences between medical associations and hospitals, their interests were closely aligned. The series of events from 1946 to 1964 strengthened their ties. Medical education and training focused almost exclusively on hospitalized patients, profoundly influencing doctors' career choices. Compensation arrangements favored inpatient care. Increasing specialization in medical diagnosis and treatment placed a premium on access to expensive technology.

By placing hospitals at the center of health care delivery, America's health care community undercut efforts to rationalize the system, to organize services regionally along a continuum of ever-increasing task complexity. What transpired made sense considering the economic, professional, and social incentives existing at this time. Why should doctors forgo private practice if they could treat their patients in hospitals and independently bill for their services? Why should doctors establish clinics or form group practices for the purchase of equipment and supplies if they could use what hospitals had acquired? Why should doctors locate their offices in communities or rural areas if there were no hospitals nearby?

US health policy in the post–World War II period demonstrated the inherent weaknesses and contradictions of government planning in a delivery system in which private interests dominated. But more than the opposition of special interests was involved. Resistance to government planning of any form was deeply ingrained in American society.

The principles and institutions that had created and fostered the 1960s' health care landscape, from free choice of physician to professional self-regulation and from medical schools to autonomous medical staff organizations, anchored the entire system. Some type of cataclysmic event or series of events would have to occur in order to change the existing arrangement, something that augured a new approach to health care delivery that satisfied long-standing norms and traditions.

5

The Turn to Market Competition, 1965–1995

The enactment of the Medicare and Medicaid programs in 1965 marked the beginning of a thirty-year transition to the current type of corporate health care systems that have been forming in the past couple decades. During this thirty-year transition, several events occurred that changed the configuration of US health care delivery from a cottage industry grounded in professional norms and ethics that medical societies devised and enforced to a business enterprise based on rules of competition that courts and federal agencies interpreted and imposed.

This chapter details the complex series of events that laid the groundwork for the current corporate landscape, from public financing of health care for the aged and poor to accelerating costs and efforts to control them; from the rejection of anticompetitive rules and ethics bolstering the medical monopoly to the creation of a health care market featuring new forms of service delivery; and from tightly integrated health maintenance organizations (HMOs) emphasizing prepaid group practice and gatekeeping to loosely integrated corporate health plans comprising large physician networks.

MEDICARE, MEDICAID, AND HEALTH CARE DELIVERY

The US government's enactment of Medicare for the aged and Medicaid for the poor in 1965 marked a turning point in the financing of health care. America was joining other nations of the world in making health care available to large segments of the population, and it was using public programs to do it. Almost overnight, the federal government became a major player, inserting itself into the health care community alongside hospitals, physicians, and private insurers. The federal government's entry was sure to alter the political dynamics – the formation of new alliances, the development of new institutions, and the creation of new incentives. Change was in the offing, but few could foresee its future direction to any degree of certainty.

While the AMA officially opposed Medicare and Medicaid, its leaders worked behind the scenes with the Johnson administration to ensure that free choice of physician, fee-for-service payment, and professional autonomy remained in place. "At the meeting of the AMA [in June 1965], when Medicare was already part way through Congress, the mood of the delegates was defiant," Frank Campion reported.[1] "But beneath the pugnacious rhetoric, some voices of political reality could also be heard. From the floor [of the AMA House of Delegates], Russell B. Roth suggested that if the Medicare bill passed, which seemed likely, the board or the Council of Medical Service should be authorized to work out the regulations with HEW [Department of Health, Education, and Welfare]."[2]

Seeking to smooth the transition to government-financed health care, the Johnson administration gave organized medicine a prominent voice in formulating the program's new regulations.[3] The end result was that Medicare and Medicaid codified not only the medical profession's principal tenets for providing medical services, but also long-standing payment practices. "The Great Society programs served the new logic of increasing access for underserved groups, but did not directly challenge the previously existing professional logic stressing quality of care as defined by professional standards," policy analysts Richard Scott and colleagues observed.[4]

Patients would have free choice of physician. There would be no gatekeeping, no emphasis on primary, first-contact care. Fee-for-service would be the dominant form of payment. "Fiscal intermediaries," not government agencies, would reimburse physicians for their services. There would be separate funding streams for hospitals and physicians: Medicare Part A would finance hospital costs from a payroll tax, while Medicare Part B would pay doctors' bills out of general tax revenues and monthly premiums. Hospital and physician services would not appear on the same bill. Medicare Parts A and B would "mimic" Blue Cross and Blue Shield.[5]

In further deference to the medical profession, a provision in the Medicare statute called the "noninterference principle" was included. The provision stated that the new legislation should not "be construed to authorize any Federal officer or employee to exercise any supervision or control over the practice of medicine or the manner in which medical services are provided ... or to exercise any supervision or control over the administration or operation of any ... institution, agency, or person."[6] These were not simply words intended to mollify doctors. They reflected continuing support for professional control over health care delivery. To ensure compliance with this provision, Congress gave the Joint Commission the power to accredit or certify that hospitals receiving Medicare dollars met Commission standards. Joint Commission accreditation, in other words, would be a prerequisite for Medicare reimbursement.[7]

Unfortunately, the new legislation failed to establish constraints on spending. Not long after the law went into effect, hospitals and doctors increased the volume and price of their services in response to the enhanced demand that the new government programs created. Few in the health care community seemed surprised when costs rose far beyond what Congress had projected.[8] Though Congress had forecast that Medicare's total expenditures (Parts A and B combined) would be $1.3 billion for 1967, the program's first full year of operation, the actual costs were $4.6 billion. Congress also had projected that Part A expenditures would be $3.1 billion in 1970 and $4.2 billion in 1975. The true costs instead were $7.1 billion and $15.6 billion, respectively.[9]

COST CONTROL AND MARKET COMPETITION

The federal government instituted several measures in the early 1970s in an effort to control rising costs. In 1972, Congress established Professional Standards Review Organizations (PSROs) to monitor and approve Medicare payments, and, in 1974, Congress mandated health planning at the state and local levels. The 1974 law created "a new generation of state and local planning bodies," known as Health Systems Agencies, and required states to pass Certificate-of-Need (CON) laws to help facilitate the planning efforts.[10] CON laws forced hospitals and other health care facilities to seek government approval before building, expanding, or acquiring expensive medical technology.[11]

When these efforts failed to produce the desired results, policymakers turned to market competition to contain costs. Market theory, frequently associated with Milton Friedman, was sweeping economic departments at universities across the country in the mid-1970s. Market theory gained adherents because inflation was high and government efforts to control it, such as wage and price controls, had aggravated the situation. Friedman's followers maintained that government itself was the problem, that regulation inhibited free markets, and that if left alone markets would self-correct.[12] Friedman's ideas had fully resonated by the late 1970s when the Carter administration moved to deregulate the airlines, trucking, and telecommunications industries.

The health care industry presented a different set of problems, however. Unlike the transportation and telecommunications industries, the health care market was not constrained by government regulation; instead, the main culprit was organized medicine. Market proponents, such as economist Mancur Olson, contended that ending the medical profession's ethical rules and constraints on economic activity would be similar to removing government restrictions in other industries.[13] Olson's contention stemmed from the notion of "market failure," an economic term that referred to certain market imperfections that skewed demand and supply. In the case of health care, insurance coverage increased demand for services beyond what might be necessary because someone else, some third party, paid the bills. The problem was exacerbated when those providing the services, doctors in this case, also advised patients which services to use and whether to use them.

Olson claimed that fee-for-service payments to physicians were fueling the rise in health care costs. He argued that, by incorporating fee-for-service, the Medicare and Medicaid programs "were designed and administered in such a way as to generate vastly increased incomes for physicians and some relatively well-to-do providers."[14] By removing the medical profession's ethical constraints on certain forms of competition, market proponents such as Olson sought to encourage the rise of new and innovative forms. These new and innovative forms could include pre-paid group plans that monitored demand and supply using capitated payments, utilization review, and gatekeeping.

The use of the federal antitrust laws to stimulate market competition called for the fusion of legal and economic theory. Its chief proponent was law professor Clark Havighurst. Testifying before a US Senate subcommittee in 1974, Havighurst excoriated organized medicine for using what he claimed were anticompetitive tactics (he used the 1952 Oregon physicians' case as an example) to defeat prepaid group plans.[15] Havighurst argued that a big reason why PSROs had been unproductive was because they were comprised of physicians with close ties to their local medical societies.[16] He sought to persuade federal courts and agencies to strike down the learned professions exemption to the antitrust laws, which allowed medical societies to continue to stifle market competition.

"[An] antitrust victory against the medical profession would be one of the most fortunate developments that could occur in trying to get the health care services marketplace in order," he declared.[17]

The Department of Justice and the Federal Trade Commission followed Havighurst's advice. They finished the work that Thurman Arnold and the Roosevelt administration had begun forty years earlier. The seminal case was initiated by Lewis Goldfarb, an FTC employee, who claimed that minimum fees that lawyers charged for title examination in Fairfax County, Virginia, were a form of price fixing. The Supreme Court agreed, striking down the learned professions exemption in finding for Goldfarb.[18] Six months later, the Federal Trade Commission moved against the AMA, targeting ethical restrictions on advertising, solicitation, and contract practice. The FTC's 1978 ruling against the AMA and certain state and local medical societies for breaching the antitrust laws opened the health care industry to market competition.[19]

Next came the 1983 case of *Arizona v. Maricopa County Medical Society*. Similar to what had transpired in Oregon more than three decades earlier, medical societies in Arizona had established certain foundations for medical care (FMCs) comprising independent practitioners. Insurance companies or self-insured employers needed FMC approval if they wanted to engage the services of an FMC doctor. Approval came with an important contingency attached. Health plans had to accept the maximum fee schedules that FMCs had adopted.[20]

Arizona's attorney general sued the local medical societies and their FMCs, claiming that the maximum fee schedules served to stabilize and increase physicians' income. Holding that the fee schedules were illegal per se, the Supreme Court observed that the FMCs were "not analogous to partnerships or other joint arrangements in which persons who would otherwise be competitors pool their capital and share the risks of loss as well as the opportunities for profit." Because FMCs comprised "hundreds of competing doctors," the Court's opinion stated, the maximum fee schedules were a form of price fixing. Doctors had to find another way of organizing, one that integrated service delivery, if they wanted to compete as a single entity.[21]

Taken together, the FTC's ruling against the AMA and the Supreme Court's decisions in *Goldfarb* and *Maricopa* helped to end organized medicine's domination of the health care industry. By outlawing restrictive rules and ethics and by targeting anticompetitive activities of state and local medical societies, federal courts and agencies opened the health care industry to new forms of competition, new ways of organizing, and new ways of delivering health care services.

ESTABLISHING A HEALTH CARE MARKET

Abolishing professional restrictions would prove to be the easy part, however. Encouraging market behavior that fostered reformers' goals would be more difficult. For much of the twentieth century, reformers often touted group practice arrangements, such as the Group Health Association, for controlling costs and delivering both primary and specialty care. Whether it was big labor, the DOJ, or the CCMC, the multispecialty group practice was the preferred form. Kaiser Permanente became the gold standard.

Enacted into law in 1973, health maintenance organizations (HMOs) were the 1970s version of prepaid group plans. According to Lawrence Brown, HMOs marked "the transition between the benefit- and government-expanding public philosophy of the 1960s and the cost- and government-containing philosophy of the 1970s."[22] On the one hand, HMOs were the fusion of finance and delivery in a single organization for the purpose of achieving certain ends – the "maintenance" of health and the control of spending. On the other hand, HMOs were jerry-rigged, the result of a political compromise between opposing camps. While some favored traditional forms of prepaid group practice - Kaiser-types that either employed their own doctors (staff-model HMOs) or entered into contracts with one or more medical groups (group-model HMOs), others wanted HMOs to include loose networks of self-employed doctors, known as Independent Practice Associations (IPAs).[23] In the end, Congress allowed all three types of HMOs to form: staff models, group models, and IPA models.[24]

To help HMOs get started, the federal government provided financial assistance if they met certain requirements – community rating, open enrollment, and standard benefit packages.[25] Following almost three years of poor performance (only four HMOs had qualified for federal aid by 1975), Congress lowered the bar for obtaining financial assistance.[26] Still, the results were disappointing. While the number of qualified plans increased to almost 300 by 1981, this was far short of 1,300 that the Nixon administration originally had projected.[27]

By the mid-1980s, HMOs began to gain traction. The main reason for their success had little to do with amendments to the 1973 legislation, however. Instead, the stimulus was skyrocketing premiums under traditional indemnity insurance, forcing employers to search for alternative plans. An important precipitating event leading to high premiums was the Reagan administration's action to reign in hospital spending in 1983.

Facing potential insolvency of the Medicare Part A trust fund, members of Congress and the Reagan administration adopted a new payment scheme.[28] The new approach, the prospective payment system (PPS), paid hospitals for their services in advance based on the average costs associated with a particular patient's diagnosis. The brainchild of researchers at Yale University in the 1970s, diagnosis-related groups (DRGs) were the mechanisms or categories for determining what a particular diagnosis and its treatment on average should cost. As policy analysts Rick Mayes and Robert Berenson explained: "[T]he new system established predetermined payment amounts for 467 different diagnosis-related groups ... If the hospital managed to treat the Medicare patient for less than the DRG allotted, it kept the 'savings' as profit. Conversely, if the hospital incurred more costs than the DRG allotted, it had to absorb the difference as a loss."[29]

Rather than lose money, as some might have expected, hospitals did quite well in prospective payment's immediate aftermath. Hospitals' annual profit margins doubled to 6.2 percent from 1984 to 1985, largely because initial payments were based on preexisting hospital expenditures.[30] By reducing the length of patient stays, hospitals received a windfall profit, the resulting spread between payments and actual expenses incurred. But that would soon be the end of it. Politicians viewed high profit margins as an opportunity in 1986 to lower the annual percentage increases in DRG payments. Seeking to maintain their profit margins, hospitals increased their rates to private pay patients, an approach known as "cost shifting."[31]

Cost-shifting had a domino effect. Insurers reacted by raising their premiums to cover the increase in hospital rates. Unable to afford the higher premiums, small employers either dropped or reduced insurance coverage. Large employers, on other hand, pressed their insurers to provide alternatives to costly indemnity plans.[32] Commercial insurers responded, as they had in the 1940s and 1950s, by tailoring their plans.[33] Formed in 1982, the Cigna Insurance Company was the first to respond when it developed and sold a "managed health and dental care program" to Allied-Signal Corporation in 1987. The plan covered 37,000 salaried and nonunion employees.[34] Cigna's contract with Allied-Signal began the shift from traditional indemnity insurance to managed care plans. At the end of 1988, 73 percent of covered employees across the United States were in indemnity plans, while 27 percent were in managed care plans.[35] By 1995, the percentages stood at 27 percent and 73 percent, a complete reversal from eight years earlier.[36]

Unlike the early HMOs, which typically employed or contracted with small numbers of doctors and hospitals in local or regional areas, the one that Cigna developed for Allied-Signal comprised a nationwide network of free-standing hospitals and independent physicians.[37] Remarking on the reasons for choosing Cigna, Allied-Signal's corporate director of human resources said: "Cigna had a health care network in place across the United States, almost in a pattern that paralleled our major locations, so it was easier for them to adapt to our needs."[38] Other commercial insurers followed Cigna's lead.[39] In their haste to capture market share, commercial carriers did one of three things. They entered into contracts with office-based physicians and hospitals of their choosing; they purchased a preexisting network; or they rented access to one.[40]

Physician networks ran the gamut from tightly integrated groups of doctors (staff- and group-model HMOs) to ones that included independent practitioners (IPA-HMOs); from plans that used primary care physicians as gatekeepers (most HMOs) to those that allowed patients to choose any doctor from a preferred list of providers (preferred provider organizations [PPOs]).[41] Most insurers preferred the IPA model over staff and group models because it gave them more flexibility to customize their plans.[42] The transition to loosely integrated networks was rather swift. From 1985 to 1995, IPA-HMOs almost doubled from 168 to 326, while the number of staff- and group-model HMOs increased by only 15 percent. Whereas IPAs represented 44 percent of the total number of HMOs in 1985, they comprised 57 percent of the total by 1995.[43]

THE CONSOLIDATION OF THE HEALTH INSURANCE INDUSTRY

In order to meet large employers' specifications, carriers like Cigna had to do two things – they had to offer a broad range of plans and they had to keep costs down. While loosely integrated physician networks allowed carriers to accomplish the first objective, they did not guarantee the second. Because doctors and hospitals operated locally, insurers needed to gain a significant share of local markets if they wanted to control spending.[44] Carriers' share of the national insurance market was not the main factor; it was their bargaining leverage over doctors and hospitals in the local market for health care services that really mattered.

The quest for significant market share prompted insurance company mergers and acquisitions. Before the early 1990s, much of the merger activity involved small for-profit HMOs (fewer than 100,000 members).[45] In or around 1993, however, national commercial carriers and certain Blue Cross plans became more active, merging among themselves and acquiring smaller plans in local markets. Five major acquisitions involving publicly traded managed care organizations (MCOs) occurred in 1993, twelve in 1994, and fourteen in 1995.[46] By the late 1990s, the turmoil in the insurance industry had run its course. "The consolidation of commercial carriers is nearly complete, with only CIGNA and Aetna showing staying power for the long run," health economist James Robinson wrote.[47]

To the AMA and many of its members, the merger activity of insurers was threatening. They wanted the federal authorities to take action, to treat insurance companies as they had been treated.[48] For at least two reasons, however, the federal antitrust agencies were less likely to take action against insurers than against physicians. First, mergers among national insurers frequently did not reduce competition in most local markets.[49] One study, for instance, found that market concentration fell in 162 markets after mergers occurred, "largely [because of] the entry of new HMOs."[50] Second, courts typically viewed those who paid for health care more favorably than those who provided it. "In theory, antitrust law is concerned about monopsony [the market power of buyers] as well as monopoly [the market power of sellers], since both can depress output and impair allocative efficiency," antitrust experts Peter Hammer and William Sage explained. But "[i]n practice, monopsony is seldom the subject of antitrust scrutiny . . . in health care markets, because courts traditionally assumed that payer activism enhanced price competition, benefitting insured patients," they wrote.[51]

Doctors were slow to respond to insurance company consolidations by forming groups and organizations to enhance their bargaining position.[52] The desire to be independent, to spurn group practice and corporate medicine, remained strong among physicians. Becoming a doctor was a lengthy process involving years of medical education, training, and socialization. Most physicians (about two-thirds) were still self-employed in 1995. "[T]here has been some movement of physicians into corporations, but . . . the extent to which this has occurred . . . has been quite limited," health scholar Lawrence Casalino reported.[53]

Professional customs, norms, and values would have to change significantly before corporate medicine could gain widespread acceptance. Rather than consolidate, physicians seeking bargaining leverage gravitated toward independent practice associations. IPAs allowed doctors to remain in solo office practice and receive fee-for-service compensation.[54] These forms were the closest physicians could come to duplicating the FMCs that medical societies established and the Supreme Court struck down in the *Maricopa* case.[55]

The pressures that hospitals faced were different from those of physicians, and they responded differently in kind. Two big challenges loomed: increased competition from hospitals outside their local area, and the growing emphasis on outpatient care. The first of these, increased competition, occurred when preexisting markets or boundary lines expanded, either because HMOs referred patients to lesser-expensive hospitals outside a particular area or because nationwide hospital systems, such as Columbia/HCA, entered the local market. The second of these, greater focus on outpatient care, stemmed from the need to reduce the length of hospital stays following the switch to prospective payment under Medicare Part A. During the 1990s, competition between hospitals and specialists in the outpatient market became quite intense, as the next chapter details.

Like insurers, hospitals were corporate entities, which meant that their employees, their subsidiaries, and any of the organizations they acquired and owned, such as clinics or nursing homes, were component parts of the same legal entity. Yet when hospitals merged or acquired other hospitals, the federal antitrust agencies often intervened, citing potentially adverse effects on local markets.[56] Before 1995, the federal courts supported DOJ and FTC actions; after 1995, the federal courts more often disagreed with the antitrust agencies, reversing several decisions. The reasons for court reversals had more to do with "the importance of hospitals as social institutions" than adherence to antitrust doctrine, wrote Hammer and Sage. "The courtroom dynamic of nonprofit hospital merger[s] ... reflects an unusual feature of hospital markets," they observed.[57]

PRESIDENT CLINTON'S HEALTH PLAN AND THE FAILURE OF MANAGED COMPETITION

Reformers who hoped that managed care would rekindle efforts to rationalize health care delivery were discouraged by the course of events.[58] The 1980s were no more receptive to prepaid group practice than the previous decades had been. The widely held notion that managed care plans would engage in "health maintenance" was a "misnomer," health economist Uwe Reinhardt maintained. "The theory behind

HMOs – that coordinated care could treat acute episodes and improve patients' health during their lifetimes while controlling costs – remain[ed] just that," he said.[59] Physician Paul Ellwood, the architect of the HMO model, recanted after initially calling for the inclusion of IPA-HMOs in the 1973 legislation. "Political expediency in the initial plan designed to promote HMO growth led to the inclusion of three mistakes: for-profit plans, independent practice associations, and the failure to include outcome accountability," he lamented.[60]

Increasing awareness that health insurers and health care providers were drifting apart prompted President Bill Clinton's ill-fated health plan. Announced in 1993, the Clinton plan adopted an approach known as "managed competition" to bridge the divide among doctors, hospitals, and insurers. Managed competition was an idea that Alain Enthoven, a Stanford business professor, had formulated. Observing that competition in the health care industry was far from perfect, Enthoven argued that government needed to adjust the rules of competition so that purchasers, payers, and providers would organize more efficiently and effectively. Health plans should not be rewarded "for selecting good risks, segmenting markets, or otherwise defeating the goals of managed competition," he maintained. Doctors and hospitals should encourage providers to "develop efficient delivery systems," he said.[61]

The mechanisms that Enthoven proposed for redirecting the behavior of insurers and providers were twofold. In the case of insurers, Enthoven recommended the creation of "collective purchasing agents" for "large group[s] of subscribers." "Armed with data and expert advice," these agents or "sponsors," as Enthoven called them, would select among various private carriers and then "serve as the single point of entry to all participating health plans." Sponsors, Enthoven indicated, could include large employers, unions, the Medicare program, or health insurance purchasing cooperatives (HIPCs) formed to represent "small employers and individuals in a geographic area."[62]

In the case of providers, Enthoven touted "organized systems of care." Though he clearly favored "multispecialty group practices that ... provide a comprehensive set of health care services in exchange for a periodic per capita payment set in advance," Enthoven was not wedded to them.[63] "Successful large-scale HMOs based on individual practice styles [which] have emerged in recent years" might be suitable candidates, he said.[64] Seeking to assure politicians that his proposal "[did] not depend ... on the steady growth of existing prepaid group practices" in order to succeed, Enthoven made a bold prediction.

He proclaimed that if his scheme became law "thousands of hospitals and their medical staffs could quickly form integrated organizations and begin accepting capitation contracts."[65]

Those opposed to managed competition echoed earlier concerns about government interference. "Systems incorporating both insurance and delivery are to be found more frequently in health policy proposals than in the managed care marketplace," James Robinson observed. "The administrative, information, and clinical competencies required for an organization that actually delivers health care are quite distinct from those of an organization that develops, markets, and monitors contractual networks," he noted.[66]

Congress's failure to enact President Clinton's health plan ended legislative efforts to introduce managed competition. Yet the failure of the Clinton plan did not erase the signature pieces of managed competition from the reform agenda; rather, the setback delayed their introduction. Health insurance purchasing cooperatives and integrated systems of delivery would resurface as state insurance exchanges and accountable care organizations in President Barak Obama's Affordable Care Act of 2010.

PHYSICIAN WORKFORCE POLICY AND MANAGED CARE

In an effort to meet growing demand for medical services following enactment of Medicare and Medicaid, the US government sought to increase physician supply through federal aid to medical education. Between 1965 and 1980, the number of medical schools expanded from 88 to 126, and the number of medical school graduates more than doubled from 7,409 to 15,135.[67] Rather than enter primary care, however, most new graduates specialized.

US policymakers were slow to perceive that corrective action would be needed to promote primary care once government dollars began to pay for medical services, creating a fertile ground for capital expansion, technological growth, and physician specialization.[68] In hindsight, the incentives to specialize should have been apparent. "Instead of establishing a fixed fee schedule," Paul Starr related, "Medicare paid doctors according to their 'customary' fees, assuming them to be the 'prevailing' fees in the area." Basing reimbursements on "prevailing" rates favored doctors who provided services in "high-priced areas." In addition, Starr noted that physicians received "higher compensation for services performed in a hospital than for identical services performed in an office."[69]

Managed care's ascendance in the mid- to late 1980s was the stimulus for government action. "Managed care providers ... employ a complement of physicians that is much more heavily dependent on generalists than is the case in nonmanaged care settings," industry experts stressed.[70] Yet there were not enough PCPs to fill the available slots. Studies were showing that managed care plans had trouble recruiting primary care doctors because medical schools and residency programs were geared toward specialty practice.[71] As a result, "many delivery systems now have three times as many specialists, twice as many hospital beds, and yet only about one-half to two-thirds the needed number of primary care physicians," Stephen Shortell and colleagues wrote in 1994.[72]

Tasked by Congress to examine the problem and recommend solutions, the Council on Graduate Medical Education (COGME) in 1992 called for a reduction in the overall supply of physicians and a change in the percentage of generalists to specialists from 30/70 to 50/50.[73] COGME's 50/50 split, or 1:1 ratio between generalists and specialists, was based on the needs of staff- and group-model HMOs. According to COGME's 1992 report, "The most cost-efficient delivery systems within the United States are closed-panel HMOs that employ approximately 50 percent primary care physicians."[74] In addition, the report noted that a 1:1 ratio mirrored those in other countries. "Fifty percent of Canadian physicians and 70 percent of British physicians are general practitioners or family physicians," COGME stated.[75] COGME did not undertake a detailed study to develop or support its recommendation. "Experimental data do not exist," the 1992 report maintained, "to define the ideal proportion of generalists and specialists needed to provide optimal access to primary care services and optimal availability of secondary and tertiary services in the most cost-efficient manner."[76]

Though at least one prominent critic thought the 50/50 goal "excessive,"[77] there was general agreement that rising health care costs were associated with America's highly specialized physician workforce.[78] "[R]esearch supports the view that generalist physicians practice a less resource-intensive style of medicine than specialists and therefore may represent a more economical approach to the provision of primary care," workforce experts Kevin Grumbach and Thomas Bodenheimer declared.[79] Studies showed that requiring patients to have a referral from their PCP in order to see a specialist reduced unnecessary care and lowered costs.[80]

While COGME's 50/50 recommendation appealed to planners and experts, it would be very difficult to achieve even if medical schools and residency programs made substantial and sustained efforts to bring it about. Not only was educating and training a new generation of doctors a lengthy process, but replacing the one that existed also took many years. "One point that is often overlooked is that a physician's projected work life is forty years," Fitzhugh Mullan and colleagues at the federal Bureau of Health Professions wrote in a 1993 article.[81] "Changes in educational outcome, therefore, affect the practice community slowly," they observed. "If residency programs began graduating 50 percent generalists next year, it would take until 2040 for the physician workforce as a whole to reach the 50 percent point," they wrote. "Likewise, it would take until 2004 to reach the goal of 50 percent in general practice if every graduate entered primary care starting this year."[82]

A potential problem was that COGME's recommendation was predicated on the belief that managed care organizations would continue to utilize PCPs as gatekeepers. "[C]losed panel staff or group model" HMOs will prevail in the long run if they "can overcome [their] inherent limitations," COGME indicated.[83] "HMOs with strong utilization controls will dominate," workforce planners at the federal Bureau of Health Professions predicted.[84] "The structure and staffing of tomorrow's managed care arrangements will be similar to those of today's group- and staff-model HMOs," they maintained.[85]

Because it would require sustained efforts over many years to achieve a 50/50 split, the assumption that staff- and group-model HMOs eventually would prevail was crucial to the endeavor. By the end of the 1990s, however, it was apparent that this prediction was far off the mark.[86] Reformers either ignored or failed to see that staff- and group-model HMOs were exceptions to the rule, that important underlying principles and powerful institutions discouraged the formation of staff- and group-model HMOs. The result was that physician workforce policies that COGME and the Bureau of Health Professions promoted became disconnected from market realities. No matter how hard reformers tried, the imbalance between generalists and specialists remained, creating significant challenges for those seeking to expand access to health care in the forthcoming years.[87]

CONCLUSION

The events recounted in this chapter greatly increased the number of actors and interests involved in the policymaking process. The professional arena was no longer the only place where important decisions occurred. A government sector emerged after the implementation of Medicare and

Medicaid comprising congressional committees and subcommittees; federal, state, and local agencies; and related advisory groups. These groups and entities fashioned their own rules, regulations, and guidelines for compensating doctors and hospitals, for building health care facilities, for purchasing expensive medical equipment, and for overseeing the quality of care. Moreover, a market arena arose in the mid- to late 1980s comprising managed care organizations, loosely integrated physician networks, nascent hospital systems, and other early corporate forms. Though many of these entities were nonprofit, their behavior closely tracked those of business firms. Antitrust laws, court decisions, and agency rules and regulations placed some limits on their activities, but these entities were largely free to pursue their own goals.

For reformers, this period was fraught with disappointment. The high point arguably came in 1973 when Congress fused finance and delivery in the HMO form. HMOs reflected a continuation of a government policy favoring prepaid physician group practice, which Thurman Arnold and other reformers had pursued. For several reasons, however, staff- and group-model HMOs lost ground to more loosely integrated forms. Managed care organizations that used gatekeeping to restrict access to specialists encountered increasing resistance.

The period ended in turmoil. The professional arena was in disarray. Membership in the AMA had plummeted; specialty societies were taking the lead. The health care market was still transforming, still trying to find an organizational center or core. Reformers wanted prepaid group practices to succeed, but insurers, doctors, and hospitals were not cooperating, and the Clinton health plan had failed. Similar to what had transpired following World War II, the health care community – politicians, bureaucrats, doctors, and reformers – looked to hospitals to steady the course.

6

The Emergence of Corporate Health Systems, 1996–2015

The year 1996 marked the high point for tightly managed care, for enrollment in HMO plans that emphasized gatekeeping and first-contact primary care.[1] That year was also the one in which employed workers with health insurance steadily moved from HMOs and point-of-service (POS) plans to preferred provider organizations (PPOs), from more restrictive "toward less restrictive forms of managed care."[2] The year 1996 also marked a return to "accelerated premium growth" following six consecutive years of decline.[3] From 1989 to 1990, the annual premium increase was 11.5 percent; from 1995 to 1996, the premium increase was 0.5 percent.[4] But by 2002, premium growth was again in double digits, rising 12.7 percent from 2001 to 2002.[5]

The events depicted in this chapter, from the backlash against managed care to the corresponding rise of entrepreneurial specialism, from the formation of multihospital systems to the use of hospitalists to manage inpatient care, and from decreasing access to health services in rural areas and urban centers to the passage of the Affordable Care Act, were deeply rooted in the past. Yet, most all of these occurrences bore signs of conflict among the professional, government, and market arenas that, by 1996, were fully functioning and striving to set the rules. With few if any exceptions, the current features of the delivery system that emerged from these struggles were unique to the United States.

THE ASCENDANCE OF PREFERRED PROVIDER ORGANIZATIONS

The growing popularity of PPOs was puzzling, perhaps even troubling to some researchers and analysts. "What is curious about the strong popularity of the PPO is that its definition is fairly amorphous, and the industry itself appears to characterize itself less by what the PPO is than by what it is not – namely, an HMO," researchers Robert Hurley and colleagues noted. "Even less clear is what value, if any, the PPO arrangement yields to its customers," they said.[6] Agreeing with this assessment, James Robinson wrote: "PPOs offer choice but not efficiency; a broad network but little coordination; no gatekeeping but high deductibles. [On the other hand,] HMOs offer efficiency and coordination but run counter to the current trend toward consumerism, self-referral, and self-care."[7]

The shift from HMOs to PPOs coincided with declining support for managed care among doctors and patients. During the mid- to late 1990s, a "managed care backlash" occurred. Doctors often railed against constraints on their medical decision-making, such as obtaining preauthorization for certain tests and procedures, waiting for second opinions before undertaking a course of treatment, or restrictions on prescribing and specialty referrals. Patients complained about coverage denials, limitations on specialists and hospitals, and the decreasing amount of time that physicians spent with them. "[T]he managed care industry has not dealt effectively with its shortcomings and this has come to be seen as adversarial to the interests of consumers," market watchers observed.[8]

While many accounts emphasized the roles of consumer organizations, politicians, and the media, the pushback began in the professional ranks, spilling over from there.[9] In 1992, the AMA launched "Medicine in Transition," a public relations initiative that demonized managed care.[10] Included in the initiative were television spots, speakers' bureaus, and "white papers," all of which attributed improper or unethical practices to managed care organizations. A 1995 report of the AMA's Judicial Council, for example, cited "ethical dilemmas" that arose when MCOs provided financial incentives to PCPs for limiting referrals, diagnostic tests, and certain medical procedures.[11]

Gatekeeping, in particular, was the focus of many attacks. "Specialists . . . rebel[led] against the gatekeeper role, viewing PCPs as their competitors rather than their colleagues," Bodenheimer and others remarked.[12] The word "gatekeeper" fell into such disrepute that PCPs often balked when the designation was applied to them.[13] "The widely used term *gatekeeper* (which many physicians find insulting) suggests that the role of the physician in the managed care setting is to limit care, rather than provide it," a primary care doctor penned.[14] Executives at Kaiser Permanente sought to distance their plan from gatekeeping's implications as well. "We don't use the gatekeeper model," a Kaiser spokesperson told the *New York Times*.[15]

Reacting to the growing criticism, state legislators passed hundreds of "consumer protection laws," hoping to mollify their constituents. These laws included "prudent layperson" standards for emergency room use, minimum hospital stays for patients undergoing certain procedures, external review of plan coverage denials, restrictions on provisions such as gag clauses in managed care contracts, and "any-willing-provider" laws that forced HMOs to increase access to doctors.[16] While these laws had some impact, the shift toward "managed care light," toward PPOs, had started before they were implemented. PPOs became the solution, a hybrid form that bridged the gap between the professional and market arenas.

Employers spurred the PPO trend. Given the bad publicity that HMOs had generated, employers offered their workers a wider choice of plans.[17] Once they did this, however, employers could not easily return to plans with restrictive cost controls.[18] When premiums began to rise again in the late 1990s, employers continued to offer PPOs, but found other ways to control costs. They reduced coverage, dropped it altogether, or required employees to pay a greater share. More often than not, employers increased the amount that employees paid.[19]

Low-income workers were hurt the most by these developments.[20] Large disparities in "take-up rates" (employees who stayed on their employer's plan) between low and high wage earners appeared, largely because of cost-sharing.[21] In the bottom wage category, the percentage of workers who accepted their employer's plan slipped from 58 percent in 1996 to 37 percent in 2008. Low-wage workers flooded the growing ranks of uninsured.[22] From 1997 to 2010, the number of uninsured persons increased from 41 to almost 47 million, the "vast majority ... in families with at least one full-time worker."[23]

THE RISE OF ENTREPRENEURIAL SPECIALISM

Concurrently with managed care's demise, physicians began to adjust to the new environment. Specialists in particular became more entrepreneurial, more adept in business affairs. Specialists on the whole were too well entrenched – as administrators, researchers, faculty members, accreditors, and government advisors (rate setters on advisory panels) – for the type of restrictions that HMOs instituted to take hold. Unlike those in European countries, few US specialists were employees of hospitals and clinics.

Most had private offices, considerable autonomy, and lucrative incomes. Those who specialized in traditional areas of primary care, such as internal medicine or pediatrics, often subspecialized. Specialization had a lengthy history in the United States. Closed-panel HMOs with PCP gatekeepers did not.

Specialists' conquest of HMOs and their return to the top of the health care community following a relatively brief hiatus occurred in two phases. During the first phase, from the late 1980s to the mid-1990s, specialists cautiously approached the managed care phenomenon, seeking ways to adjust to the new requirements. Many specialists sought "primary care physician" status or joined large multispecialty groups in order to secure a steady source of referrals.[24] Conflicts between generalists and specialists over gatekeeping were common and intense.[25]

During the second phase, from about 1996 to 2009, specialists became more entrepreneurial, more independent. Advances in medical technology – in anesthesia, in surgical devices, and in medical imaging – allowed specialists to perform many procedures in the outpatient setting where they could bill fee-for-service because prospective payment under Medicare Part A did not apply.[26] The growth of medium to large single-specialty group practices was particularly noteworthy in this second phase.[27] Trends varied by specialty area. Of the "fifty-five specialist groups of ten or more physicians" that Lawrence Casalino and colleagues studied, cardiovascular groups were the most common (17 groups), followed by orthopedic (10), neurology (6), ophthalmology (5), and oncology (5).[28] Several accounts supported their findings.[29]

Just as the number of single-specialty groups increased, so the formation of new multispecialty groups "ceased."[30] Many factors were involved, such as diseconomies of scale, poor management practices, and reduced Medicare payments to HMOs following Congress's enactment of deficit reduction legislation in 1997.[31] As Medicare reimbursements decreased, the need for cost management increased. The higher costs of specialty services became a target of cost containment in multispecialty groups. "[O]verruns can amount to millions of dollars if the use of specialty services is not closely managed," Thomas Bodenheimer stated.[32]

Conflicts between specialists and primary care physicians over cost management and compensation arrangements ensued.[33] California was a bellwether. Large multispecialty groups, both network and IPA models, were more prevalent in California than in most other parts of the country.[34] Managing California's multispecialty practices was challenging.

Between 1996 and 1998, 99 out of 300 groups failed, the California Medical Association reported, several of them in 1998 when the two largest physician practice management companies, FPA Medical Management and MedPartners, ceased operations and sold most of their assets.[35] MedPartners alone comprised "140 group practices and 23 IPAs totaling 4,000 physicians."[36] According to William Osheroff, a family physician and former health plan executive who was closely familiar with the situation in California, "Some of the groups that failed grew too rapidly and had little expertise in management."[37]

The growth of single-specialty group practice signaled the rise of entrepreneurial specialism, doctor-owned ambulatory surgery centers (ASCs), diagnostic imaging centers, and specialty hospitals.[38] Ambulatory surgery centers proliferated in the late 1990s and early 2000s. According to one study, 242 new ASCs formed in 2000 and another 343 in 2001 "compared with an average of 166 annually in the preceding eight years."[39] "The rate of visits to freestanding ambulatory surgery centers increased about 300 percent from 1996 to 2006, while the rate in hospital-based centers was flat," another survey revealed.[40] Advancements in medical technology favored specialists who, by joining together, could achieve economies of scale: ophthalmologists who removed cataracts; cardiologists who implanted coronary stents, pacemakers, and cardioverter defibrillators; and orthopedists who replaced knees and hips. [41]

In addition to ASCs, single-specialty groups established or helped to establish diagnostic testing facilities that housed the latest equipment in medical imaging, computed tomography (CT), magnetic resonance imaging (MRI), and positron emission tomography (PET).[42] Though Medicare fraud-and-abuse legislation (known as Stark II) curtailed referrals that doctors made to imaging centers they owned, the law contained important exceptions. Significantly, there was no ban on "self-referral to ASCs or specialty hospitals, or to services provided within a physician's practice."[43] Taking advantage of the loophole, specialists installed "smaller, less expensive, and easier-to-operate versions of CT and MRI scanners" in their private offices.[44] By 2008, physician ownership of medical imaging equipment was widespread. One survey showed that more than 20 percent of doctors in small-group practices (3–10 doctors), more than 45 percent in medium and large practices (11–50 doctors), and almost 53 percent in very large groups (more than 51 doctors) owned or leased advanced imaging equipment.[45]

Physician-owned specialty hospitals also flourished. Before 2002, fewer than 50 physician-owned specialty hospitals existed; ten years later, there were about 235 of them.[46] "Large single-specialty cardiology or orthopedic medical groups" predominated.[47] Most specialty hospitals, about 74 percent, were for-profit, compared with 20 percent of all general hospitals, according to a 2003 report from the US General Accounting Office.[48]

The term "focused factories" became associated with many of the activities that large specialty groups were undertaking.[49] Coined in 1974, "focused factories" was a concept that business schools promoted to improve industrial productivity. The idea was to narrow or reduce manufacturers' "product mix," to simplify or streamline the production process, to get companies to focus on what they did best.[50] Harvard business school professor Regina Herzlinger initially applied the concept to the health care industry in 1997.[51] Herzlinger argued that the industry was bloated and fragmented, that new organizational approaches were needed to overcome waste and inefficiency, to enhance "value" to consumers. Traditional means – "all-purpose healthcare organizations" and "professional bureaucracies" – had largely failed, she said.[52] A better approach, she stressed, was to concentrate services around a particular procedure, disease, or disability, from "cataract surgery to … cancer."[53]

While "focused factories" or something similar to them enjoyed widespread support, there were many critics.[54] Confusion surrounding the meaning of the term led to wide-ranging and imprecise applications, from cancer clinics to trauma centers, and from specialty hospitals to ambulatory surgery centers.[55] More importantly, by concentrating on a particular disease, the approach diverted attention and resources from primary care, from the prevention, coordination, and management of multiple chronic diseases or comorbidities.

CHRONIC DISEASES AND THE PRIMARY CARE PHYSICIAN

By 2005, almost 44 percent of US citizens, or 133 million people, suffered from at least one chronic condition.[56] The rapid increase in chronic diseases at the end of the twentieth century placed added on stress on America's dwindling primary care workforce. The timing could not have been worse. Generalists, as previously indicated, frequently sent patients to hospitals for care and treatment. All this changed under Medicare prospective payment in 1983. As COGME explained:

When most sick patients were hospitalized, their care was provided under controlled circumstances. The physicians were supported by hospitals' substantial

infrastructure of nurses and consultants. With DRGs, the situation was transformed: many chronically ill patients remained in the ambulatory care setting and
depended solely on the services of the primary care physician and a small office
staff.[57]

Compensation levels for PCPs failed to match increasing patient work-
loads. In 1997, the median income for certain medical and surgical
specialists ranged from $225,000 to $300,000; for primary care physicians, on the other hand, it spanned from $125,000 to $150,000. In
2014, the median compensation for medical and surgical specialists
ranged from $400,000 to almost $600,000; for primary care physicians,
it spanned from $225,000 to $325,000. These large pay disparities made
specialty practice even more enticing. "The percentage of ... U.S. medical
school graduates choosing family medicine decreased from 14 percent in
2000 to 8 percent in 2005," COGME reported.[58]

In 2006, the American College of Physicians warned about an
"impending collapse." "Primary care, the backbone of the nation's health
care system, is at grave risk of collapse due to a dysfunctional healthcare
payment and delivery system," the College announced. If "immediate and
comprehensive reforms" did not occur, ACP declared, "there will not be
enough primary care physicians to take care of an aging population with
increasing incidence of chronic diseases."[59]

Policymakers were in a quandary. Efforts to boost the number of PCPs
based on COGME's 50/50 recommendation had been unsuccessful.[60] Yet
the need for primary care physicians or something like them seemed more
apparent than ever. As several studies were showing, the United States
was spending considerably more on health care than other countries, but
was falling behind on certain measures, such as life expectancy and infant
mortality. America's weak results, experts claimed, stemmed from poor
coordination and management of chronic diseases, as well as inadequate
access to preventive services.[61]

While COGME and the American College of Physicians pushed for
more primary care doctors, others in the health care community looked to
nurse practitioners (NPs) and physician assistants (PAs) to alleviate the
problem. Many clinicians and researchers believed that NPs and PAs were
viable alternatives, that they could provide most primary care services
safely and effectively, obviating the need for more PCPs.[62]

Attempts to give NPs a greater role in patient care and treatment met
considerable resistance from the medical profession, however.[63] In 2009,
the AMA issued a lengthy report questioning the ability of NPs to care for
patients absent physician supervision.[64] The report focused on differences

between NPs and primary care physicians in the length and nature of their education and training. "The limited clinical training required for NPs (it can range from 500 to 720 hours), even with their prior RN experience … [is] not comparable to the two years of inpatient clinical training that medical students undergo during their third and fourth years of medical school, plus the three years of full-time, intensive residency training for physicians in the primary care specialties," the AMA's report stated.[65]

Notwithstanding the AMA's assertions, as well as those of certain other specialty societies, much of the research concerning NPs was positive.[66] As early as 1986, the US Office of Technology Assessment had concluded that "nurse practitioners, physician's assistants, and certified nurse-midwives provide[d] care whose quality is equivalent to that of care provided by physicians."[67] A much-touted 2000 study appearing in *JAMA* found that "patient outcomes were comparable" between primary care physicians and independent nurse practitioners.[68] In 2010, moreover, the Institute of Medicine (IOM) released a report also highlighting the comparable quality of care that NPs provided. "The contention that [advanced practice nurses] are less able than physicians to deliver care that is safe, effective, and efficient is not supported by research that has examined this question," the IOM report stated.[69]

Following release of the IOM report, the momentum increased for expanding nurse practitioners' scope of practice. Medical societies found it increasingly difficult to "hold the line."[70] In 2010, the National Committee on Quality Assurance, the principal accrediting body for health plans in the United States, reversed its earlier refusal to accredit nurse-led primary care practices.[71] By 2012, twenty-seven states no longer required physician involvement in NP diagnosis and testing; nineteen states abandoned physician oversight of NP prescribing.[72]

Another approach that potentially offset declining levels of PCPs was team-based care. Several health systems, including Group Health of Puget Sound, the Mayo Clinic, and the Geisinger Health System in Pennsylvania, had begun experimenting with new delivery models in the late 1990s. Perhaps the best-known design to emerge was the "chronic care model." The chronic care model and its later iteration, "the patient-centered medical home model," emphasized team-based care, "patient-centeredness," and system integration.[73] A team or group of health care professionals, rather than a single physician, shared responsibility for a "patient population" in the chronic care model.[74] The new model quickly gained traction. Government agencies, including the Bureau of Primary Health

Care and the Veterans Administration, in addition to large corporate health systems, adopted many of its features.[75]

Based on these developments, several forecasters maintained that the physician shortage had been overstated.[76] Earlier projections, some said, reflected historical practice patterns, "a traditional model of patients being cared for by a single physician."[77] Team-based care, enhanced use of nurse practitioners and physician assistants, new forms of communication such as telemedicine, and new forms of recordkeeping such as electronic health records were changing the way that health care was organized and provided. "Given the current trends toward adoption of these practices, the widely perceived national primary care physician shortage that has been forecast may, in fact, be greatly overestimated," researchers Linda Green and colleagues concluded.[78]

Efforts to overcome declining numbers of PCPs through substitute providers and team-based delivery models carried some big risks, however. There was no guarantee that nurse practitioners would enter family practice in sufficient numbers. The new models, moreover, called for a sizable infrastructure – a team of health professionals, electronic health records, large data systems, and electronic communication systems including telehealth and telemedicine. Where would the money come from?

CORPORATE-STYLE INTEGRATION

Corporate health systems with the money and resources to support the development of information and communications technology began to form in the late decades of the twentieth century. These systems emerged in conjunction with the rise of the market arena in which the rules of competition prevailed and the incentives for growth closely tracked corporate profits. The formation and evolution of these corporate systems significantly influenced the composition and configuration of generalists, specialists, hospitals, and related health care facilities across the United States. Whereas political, social, and demographic considerations carried great weight in other countries, revenue enhancement principally determined the course of system integration in the United States.

Corporate health systems typically followed the path of "horizontal" and "vertical" integration. "Horizontal integration" referred to the combination or consolidation of similar entities such as hospitals or physician group practices. "Vertical integration," on the other hand, involved the combination or consolidation of dissimilar entities at different stages of the care cycle, from the beginning (primary care) to the end (geriatric or hospice care). When both horizontal and vertical integration occurred in the same health system, the result was called an "integrated delivery system" (IDS). Whether horizontal, vertical, or some combination of the two, the word "integration" entailed an ownership arrangement. It did not encompass contractual or other loose affiliations among providers.[79]

Those who studied the way corporate health systems formed in the United States, many of them organization theorists, used the hospital as their locus or unit of analysis. In the case of vertical integration, researchers started with hospitals or multihospital systems and then moved forward (forward integration) or backward (backward integration) to reconstruct patterns of corporate activity.[80]

Horizontal integration involving hospitals gained momentum following Medicare's shift to prospective payment in 1983. Reduced payment for inpatient services encouraged hospitals to decrease the length of patient stays. Instead of integrating to expand the scope and size of their operations, hospitals merged to reduce excess capacity, to decrease rather than increase the number of hospital beds. According to economists Martin Gaynor and Deborah Haas-Wilson, "From 1985 to 1995, the number of hospitals fell by 9 percent, from 5,762 to 5,194, and the number of hospital beds fell by 9 percent, from 1 million to 873,000."[81]

Vertical integration involving hospitals and doctors accelerated in the late 1980s in the wake of gatekeeping under tightly managed care. Hospitals employed primary care physicians, acquired their practices, or formed physician–hospital organizations to ensure a steady source of referrals.[82] Specialists, for the reasons mentioned, often formed single-specialty groups, many of them small to medium in size.[83] Competition between general hospitals and doctor-owned facilities (ambulatory surgery centers and specialty hospitals) was keen.[84]

When many large multispecialty groups in California and elsewhere failed in the late 1990s, so did some of the larger, often proprietary, hospital chains. But this did not mean the end of multihospital systems. Following another reduction in Medicare payments in 1997 and perceiving less need for PCPs after gatekeeping's demise, many hospital systems shed their physician networks. Corporate management "removed words like 'integrated delivery system' [and] 'group practice without walls'" from their vocabularies.[85] Relationships between doctors and hospital executives deteriorated.

Only a few years later, however, hospitals renewed their acquisition of physician practices. "By late 2002," a prominent trade journal stated, "consultants were again receiving telephone calls from hospitals and health systems in competitive markets indicating that since divesting of or 'pruning' their networks of employed primary care physicians they had lost market share."[86] The location of facilities and doctors was important in this second round. Hospitals pursued "economic integration as an offensive strategy," analysts said. They moved into mostly affluent areas to "neutralize the threat" of entrepreneurial specialists, to "preempt their market entry and [to] prevent the loss of the outpatient market share."[87]

Service volume was a key focus of the new strategy. "Specific parameters for practice acquisition should include ... existing volumes and potential incremental volumes," a 2012 guide from the American Hospital Association advised.[88] "The medical practice 'game' is won or lost on the revenue side of the income statement," a prominent financial consultant to hospitals remarked. "Where there is no volume, there is no value – or at least not enough value to make payroll," he stated.[89]

In order to enhance service volume, multihospital systems targeted certain specialty lines.[90] Cardiology was the most sought-after specialization, followed by orthopedics, general surgery, endocrinology, gastrointestinal, urology, and oncology.[91] Hospitals were attracted to the high volume of procedures these specialists performed. Under the Current Procedural Terminology (CPT) codes, which the AMA had developed, specialists could charge separately for each procedure. The higher the number of pacemakers implanted or knees replaced, the greater the revenue.[92]

Hospitals had another reason, also income enhancing, to acquire specialty practices. In addition to dollars gained from tests run or procedures performed, hospitals could charge "facility fees for office visits and procedures" under Medicare.[93] This was a powerful incentive. Free-standing clinics that physicians owned and operated could not add facility fees to their list of charges. Only hospitals could charge for them. The discrepancy gave hospitals a competitive advantage in the outpatient setting.

The employment of PCPs and the acquisition of their practices was part and parcel of hospitals' volume-based strategy. "[H]ospitals increasingly are hiring primary care physicians to capture referrals for their employed specialists," researchers at the Center for Studying Health System Change reported in 2010.[94] "Smart specialty physicians and wise hospital executives understand that market share and market potential for both specialists and hospitals is a function of establishing and maintaining a strong relationship with primary care physicians," an article appearing in a prominent trade journal advised.[95] Corporate systems were even willing to lose money on PCPs in order to generate more referrals.[96]

THE HOSPITALIST MOVEMENT

While hospitals engaged primary care physicians to treat patients and refer them to specialists for outpatient tests and procedures, they also began to hire PCPs to work within the hospital itself, to help coordinate and manage inpatient care.[97] Writing in 1996, academic physicians Robert Wachter and Lee Goldman coined the word "hospitalist" to denote generalists who worked entirely within the hospital setting.[98] While only a "few hundred" physicians were hospitalists when Wachter and Goldman published their seminal article in 1996, their numbers quickly rose to 20,000 by 2006, and then to 48,000 by 2014.[99]

The hospitalist movement, or some version of it, was not confined to the United States. Many hospitals in other countries also began to engage generalists in the 1990s and early 2000s for reasons similar to those in the United States: complex technology, comorbidities, and rising hospital costs.[100] Unlike the situation in the United States, however, the employment of generalists to act as hospitalists did not fundamentally change existing practice patterns.[101] "The hospitalist movement is a fresh idea for America. But it is old news in Canada North of the border here," a Canadian doctor said. "I have practiced as a hospitalist for almost a decade. And some of my colleagues have been hospitalists well past their 60th birthdays," he remarked.[102]

For the hospitalist movement to gain appeal in the United States, a change in practice patterns involving generalists had to occur. As indicated, PCPs saw their patient volumes increase because of managed care. The introduction of Medicare prospective payment in 1983, moreover, undercut PCPs' ability to send patients with chronic diseases to hospitals for extended treatment and care. In 1978, the typical PCP saw about ten patients on average in the hospital each day; by 2001, the PCP saw only two patients on average each day.[103]

Hospitals had to adjust their workforce not only because of changes in PCPs' daily routines, but also because of the need for more quality control. Keeping up-to-date on the latest procedures and technologies was a growing challenge. "Some physicians . . . find it difficult to maintain inpatient procedural skills," Ohio physician Mark Marinella noted.[104]

In 1999, the Institute of Medicine released its widely acclaimed and influential report, *To Err is Human*, which estimated that 44,000 to 98,000 inpatient deaths occurred annually from preventable medical mistakes.[105] Soon after the report's publication, the Joint Commission instituted new safety standards and began making unannounced hospital inspections. Responding to regulatory pressures, hospitals adopted "quality-improvement and error-reduction programs," which made heavy use of information technology to report errors and track procedures.[106] Certain financial incentives, various "pay-for-performance" initiatives that public and private insurers piloted and introduced in the early 2000s, also spurred hospitals to focus on quality. By 2015, "at least 5.5% of Medicare dollars [were] linked to quality measures ..., including mortality, readmission rates, patient-centered care, and other clinical outcomes," studies showed.[107]

Before the release of the IOM report on preventable medical mistakes, hospitalists struggled to prove their worth. A common belief, which many critics put forth, was that the hospitalist movement was closely tied to corporate interests, that "financial considerations" were largely behind it.[108] Perceptions changed following publication of the Institute's 1999 report. Hospitalists became an integral part of the effort to address medical errors.[109] Quality became their central concern.[110]

Hospitalists received a further boost in 2003 when the Accreditation Council for Graduate Medical Education capped the amount of time that medical residents worked in the hospital at 80 hours a week. Because hospitalists were onsite 24/7, they could fill gaps in patient coverage.[111] Even before the cap was announced, however, hospitalists were involved in teaching and training medical residents and junior doctors. "Academic hospitalists are emerging as core teachers of inpatient medicine," Wachter and Goldman stated.[112] By the mid-2000s, most of the major teaching hospitals had established hospitalist programs.[113]

As the hospitalist movement gained muster, PCPs' ranks grew thinner. While a relatively small number of family physicians were becoming hospitalists (they never exceeded 5 percent of the total number of hospitalists at any point in time), large numbers of general internists were making the switch.[114] Seventy-five percent of all hospitalists were trained in general internal medicine by 1999,[115] 82 percent by 2008,[116] and almost 90 percent by 2010.[117] "The rapidly developing 'hospitalist' movement ... threatens the traditional role of the internist as the caregiver for adults in health and disease," physician James Nolan declared.[118] That hospitalists were "younger, on average, than their counterparts in office-based practice," drove some of this anxiety, he said.[119]

Unless growing numbers of family physicians compensated for the loss of general internists to the hospital setting, US primary care might falter even further.[120] As of 2015, however, there was no clear indication that interest in family medicine was increasing.[121] Family medicine residents, data showed, comprised 10.2 percent of the total number of medical school graduates from 2014 to 2015, almost unchanged over the previous ten years.[122] At the University of Kansas Medical Center and other medical schools where significant rural populations were in close proximity, the dearth of students entering family medicine was of great concern.[123]

ACCESS TO CARE AND THE GROWING RURAL/URBAN DIVIDE

The hospitalist movement was one sign among many of a growing rural/urban divide. Significant numbers of rural hospitals closed in the 1980s and 1990s, creating a bandwagon effect.[124] Sick patients traveled to urban areas in search of doctors and hospitals that could treat them.[125] Doctors and other medical personnel followed, including primary care physicians.[126] Researchers reported "a tremendous impact on acute and emergency room access" in counties where hospitals closed.[127] The lack of nearby facilities disproportionately affected elderly and low-income individuals.[128]

In 1997, Congress took action to address the situation when it authorized the Medicare program to exempt qualifying hospitals (designated "Critical Access Hospitals") from the prospective payment system and reimburse them for costs incurred ("101% of their Medicare allowable costs for inpatient and outpatient care").[129] In order to qualify for the higher payment rate, rural hospitals had to meet certain conditions. They could not exceed 25 acute care beds; they could not be closer than 35 miles from another hospital; they had to maintain an average length of stay of 96 hours or less; and they had to provide 24/7 emergency care.[130]

By 2003, 891 rural hospitals qualified for CAH status, and by 2015, 1,337 hospitals did. The number that qualified for CAH status in 2015 comprised about one-third of all acute care hospitals and almost three-quarters of all rural hospitals across the United States.[131] If not for the increase in Medicare payments, many more rural hospitals would have closed. When questions were raised in 2013 about continuing the program, evaluators concluded that the percentage of rural hospitals under financial stress would markedly increase from about 28 percent to 44 percent should CAH status cease.[132]

Because of their fragile financial condition, low patient census, and distance from urban centers, rural hospitals often were poor candidates for health system integration.[133] By bolstering their financial status, proponents of the 1997 legislation hoped to make network formation more attractive to large corporate systems. But the enticement was not enough.[134] "[O]ur findings suggest that the CAH program ... has not changed rural hospital incentives to participate in a system, nor does CAH-designation necessarily make a hospital a more desirable partner in a system," a study examining data from 2002 to 2012 reported.[135]

Efforts to form rural hospital networks largely had failed long before Congress passed CAH legislation in 1997. One such attempt involved the formation of rural networks comprising both strong and weak hospitals.[136] After an initial burst of activity in the late 1980s, many networks soon disbanded.[137] Those that continued showed few signs of the type of integrative activity that would allow them "to realize short-term economic benefit."[138] Rural hospital networks "should be viewed more as a social experiment than as a foundation on which to rebuild the health care systems serving rural communities," program evaluators for Robert Wood Johnson's Rural Health Care Program stated.[139]

While CAH status may have saved many hospitals, it did little to attract new medical school graduates.[140] Medical schools were producing doctors in record numbers in the 1980s and 1990s (US physicians increased from 467,679 to 813,770 from 1980 to 2000), but the "maldistribution" between rural and metropolitan areas remained.[141] Despite certain state and federal government incentives (loans, grants, and higher reimbursement rates, for example), the lure of big city practice, including the stark differences in money and prestige that most students experienced during residency training, proved difficult to overcome.[142] "Students in a rural MD-granting medical school program who had pre-medical experiences observing or shadowing in an urban hospital were 67 percent less likely to enter family medicine residencies," a Kansas study found.[143] Though many critical access hospitals "offered rural health clinics, obstetric care, and inpatient surgery," these clinics also suffered from a shortage of PCPs.[144]

The 1997 legislation was one more instance in which policymakers sought to patch the gaps in America's fragmented delivery system. Similar to former attempts, the 1997 law treated the symptoms while often neglecting the underlying cause of the disease. Despite research showing that inadequate primary care was strongly associated with preventable hospitalizations for many chronic conditions,[145] policymakers continued to allocate the bulk of resources to acute care.

ACCOUNTABLE CARE ORGANIZATIONS AND THE AFFORDABLE CARE ACT

The last time the federal government had attempted to align finance and delivery was in 1993 when the Clinton health plan failed.[146] Congress and the Obama administration tried once again in 2008. While the measures that Congress adopted to increase insurance coverage under the Affordable Care Act – Medicaid expansion and state insurance exchanges – were topics of frequent debate and discussion, the principal vehicles that the new law chose to achieve clinical integration, accountable care organizations (ACOs), received relatively meager attention. For many reformers, however, ACOs were "vital" to the new law's success.[147]

ACOs were no particular person's brainchild, although Donald Berwick – pediatrician, Harvard Medical School professor, administrator of the Centers for Medicare and Medicaid Services (CMS), and leading member of America's health policy community – arguably was their chief architect.[148] The pieces that comprised the ACO concept had been coming together before Berwick and his colleagues at the Institute for Healthcare Improvement assembled them in a 2008 article.[149] Berwick's plan for ACOs used some of Alain Enthoven's ideas on managed competition, more specifically the formation of "organized systems of care" that would "begin accepting capitation contracts."[150] Berwick, who had served on an advisory commission in the Clinton administration, set out to correct some earlier mistakes.[151]

In Berwick's view, one of the biggest obstacles to getting doctors involved in any prepayment plan was risk, specifically the financial risk that doctors incurred when they agreed to care for a large group of patients for a set fee in advance. Early experiences with risk contracting showed that most doctors were poor risk managers, that in the absence of large organizations or hospitals to support them, few could assume full capitation.[152] Following the managed care backlash in the mid-1990s, the pendulum swung back to fee-for-service, though various "pay-for-performance" incentives emerged in the effort to reduce overutilization.[153]

Berwick and his fellow colleagues designed an approach that they hoped would address the problem of financial loss associated with poor risk management. Their idea was to use ACOs (Berwick called them "integrators" in his 2008 article) to "induce coordinative behavior among health service suppliers."[154] While their ideal candidate was something akin to Kaiser Permanente, they indicated that other forms and entities would suffice.[155] ACOs would span the health care landscape offering inducements to doctors, hospitals, and insurers to work together. Part of the enticement would be additional Medicare payments that participants would receive if by working together they achieved cost savings below a predetermined benchmark. Another enticement was reduced risk for

The rise of entrepreneurial specialism was predictable. Specialization, as Rosemary Stevens has shown, has been a distinctive feature of the American landscape since at least 1870. When market competition took hold in the mid-1980s, specialists dominated both inpatient and outpatient care. Board-certified in areas such as cardiology, orthopedics, and ophthalmology, specialists were in a much better position than generalists to package and promote new health care technologies.

The adverse consequences of America's pronounced emphasis on medical specialization crystallized between 1995 and 2015. Many studies, scholarly works, and government reports have linked weak primary care to America's relatively poor world ranking on measures of overall population health. Attempts to correct the situation using various financial incentives largely have failed. The overproduction of specialists relative to generalists is structural (no designated role for PCPs), institutional (medical education, training, and board certification), and financial (substantial pay disparities).

The hospital systems that emerged in the late 1990s and early decades of the twenty-first century were corporate entities, creatures of the market regime. They lacked any connection to a national health policy in which government dollars were their sole or principal source of payment. Using hospitals as their base, corporate systems expanded horizontally and vertically to enhance market share. Seeking competitive advantage, they purchased the practices of primary care physicians to increase referrals, and they pursued lucrative specialty lines in cardiology, orthopedics, and ophthalmology to increase revenues.

As corporate mergers and acquisitions among doctors and hospitals progressed, researchers and analysts warned that the form of integration taking place bore little if any resemblance to true clinical integration.[163] Few of the purported advantages of clinical integration – combining "structures and systems to coordinate patient care services across people, functions, activities, and sites over time" – were occurring.[164] Private health systems lacked the economic incentives to pursue primary care gatekeeping or to place doctors and clinics in rural and low-income communities. While Americans with comprehensive health insurance had access to many of the world's leading specialists, the overall quality of care, as measured by life expectancy and infant mortality, lagged behind that in other countries despite demonstrably higher per capita expenditures.[165] "Societal goals are clearly not the primary aim of economic integration," Lawton Burns and Ralph Muller wrote. "[R]evenue and income goals of providers seem to be the dominant motivation."[166]

Accountable care organizations, or something like them, may alleviate but cannot overcome the current situation. ACOs are the most recent iteration in a long line of attempts – from prepaid group practice plans to staff- and group-model HMOs, from comprehensive health planning to managed competition – to merge finance and delivery or, at the very least, to decrease the gap between them. Like their forebears, ACOs are stop-gap measures, not comprehensive solutions to rising costs and disproportionate access to high quality primary care.

As stated at the beginning of this book, finance and delivery are interrelated. The two must go hand-in-hand to keep costs under control, make basic services available to all, and improve population health. The current system, while expensive, fragmented, and overspecialized, serves the needs of many individuals, but far from all of them. America's structural deficit in primary care is its biggest weakness, yet federal and state governments allocate substantial public funds to perpetuate the existing arrangement. Policymakers should pause to consider why so many persons, insured and uninsured, use safety-net providers – community health centers, free clinics, and hospital emergency rooms – for their basic health care.[167] Perhaps this is because they really are not safety-net providers after all. Perhaps some of them (community health centers, in particular) are the type and form of health care delivery that a significant portion of the population wants and needs.[168]

Notes

Chapter 1

1 Tomoko Ono, Michael Schoenstein, and James Buchan, "Geographic Imbalances in Doctor Supply and Policy Responses," OECD Health Working Paper No. 69 (OECD Publishing, 2014); OECD, Health at a Glance 2011: OECD Indicators (OECD Publishing, 2011); Valerie Paris, Marion Devaux, and Lihan Wei, "Health Systems Institutional Characteristics: A Survey of 29 OECD Countries," OECD Health Working Paper No. 50 (OECD Publishing, 2010); US General Accounting Office (GAO), "Primary Care Physicians: Managing Supply in Canada, Germany, Sweden, and the United Kingdom," GAO/HEHS, 1994.

2 Where sufficient data are available for comparison, the table and figure compilations in this book will seek to include six countries – Australia, Canada, France, Germany, Britain, and the United States. If a country is not included, it is because sufficient data are not available from a common and generally reliable source. There are several reasons for choosing these six countries for comparison: (1) consistency in data collection and compilation through the Organisation for Economic Co-operation and Development (OECD); (2) shared levels of economic development; (3) shared disease patterns (particularly the timeline for the shift from acute to chronic diseases); (4) shared histories, cultures, and traditions (political, philosophical, legal, institutional); (5) shared levels of scientific progress, inquiry, and diffusion of knowledge (clinical education, training, research, journals, university systems, professional development); and (6) demographic and geographic similarities (rural/urban, immigration patterns, country size, etc.). While the last of these may be problematic, the fact that the United States combines many of the features of the other five countries (size and space, population density, configuration, and levels of affluence) aids comparison across a broad spectrum. The observations and conclusions reached in this book are based on broad patterns or trends, not finely tuned statistical data.

3 Wienke G. W. Boerma, "Coordination and Integration in European Primary Care," in *Primary Care in the Driver's Seat? Organizational Reform in European Primary Care*, ed. Richard B. Saltman, Ana Rico, and Wienke G. W. Boerma (Maidenhead, UK: Open University Press, 2006), 7.

4 Ibid., 7.

5 Barbara Starfield, Leiyu Shi, and James Macinko, "Contribution of Primary Care to Health Systems and Health," *The Milbank Quarterly* 83(2005); GAO, "Primary Care Physicians"; Rosemary Stevens, *American Medicine and the Public Interest: A History of Specialization* (Berkeley: University of California Press, 1998), 293 ("The role of the generalist in medicine has been, and remains, the most important single issue in modern medicine, for the structure of the medical profession hinges on whether – and how – general practice is recognized").

6 Thomas Bodenheimer, Ellen Chen, and Heather D. Bennett, "Confronting the Growing Burden of Chronic Disease: Can the U.S. Health Care Workforce Do the Job?," *Health Affairs* 28 (2009): 64.

7 US Census Bureau, National Population Projections, 2014.

8 K. A. Paez, L. Zhao, and W. Hwang, "Rising Out-of-Pocket Spending for Chronic Conditions: A Ten-Year Trend," *Health Affairs* 28 (2009): 15–25; Marshall Protocol Knowledge Base, Autoimmunity Research Foundation. Available at http://mpkb.org (accessed Dec. 15, 2009).

9 Council on Graduate Medical Education (COGME), *Twentieth Report: Advancing Primary Care*, US Department of Health and Human Services, Health Resources and Services Administration, September, 2007, 4 ("There is compelling evidence that health care outcomes and costs in the United States are strongly linked to the availability of primary care physicians"); Thomas Bodenheimer, Kevin Grumbach, and Robert A. Berenson, "A Lifeline for Primary Care," *New England Journal of Medicine* (hereafter *NEJM*) 360 (2009): 2693; Cathy Schoen, Robin Osborn, Michelle M. Doty, David Squires, Jordon Peugh, and Sandra Applebaum, "A Survey of Primary Care Physicians in Eleven Countries, 2009: Perspectives on Care, Costs, and Experiences," *Health Affairs/Web Exclusive* (2009): w1171; David C. Goodman, "Twenty-Year Trends in Regional Variation in the U.S. Physician Workforce," *Health Affairs/Web Exclusive* (2004): VAR-95; Starfield et al., "Contribution of Primary Care," 466–485; Wienke G. W. Boerma, J. Van Der Zee, and D. M. Fleming, "Service Profiles of General Practitioners in Europe," *British Journal of General Practice* 47 (1997): 481; Molla S. Donaldson, Karl D. Yordy, Kathleen N. Lohr, and Neal A. Vanselow, eds., *Primary Care: America's Health in a New Era*, Institute of Medicine, Committee on the Future of Primary Care (Washington, DC: National Academy Press, 1996), 62–72; Colleen M. Grogan, "Who Gets What? Levels of Care in Canada, Britain, Germany, and the United States," in *The Politics of Health Care Reform: Lessons from the Past, Prospects for the Future*, ed. James A. Morone and Gary Stuart Belkin (Durham, NC: Duke University Press, 1994), 448.

10 Daniel M. Fox, *The Convergence of Science and Governance: Research, Health Policy, and American States* (Berkeley: University of California Press,

2010); Daniel M. Fox, *Health Policies, Health Politics: The British and American Experience, 1911–1965* (Princeton, NJ: Princeton University Press, 1986).

11 Fox, *Health Policies*, 15–16.

12 Report of the Medical Consultative Council for England, "Future Provision of Medical Services," *The British Medical Journal* (hereafter *BMJ*) 1 (1920): 739–743.

13 Ibid., 739.

14 Ibid., 740.

15 Ibid., 741.

16 Boerma, "Coordination and Integration," 8; Michael Calnan, Jack Hutten, and Hrvoje Tiljak, "The Challenge of Coordination: The Role of Primary Care Professionals in Promoting Integration Across the Interface," in Saltman et al., eds., *Primary Care in the Driver's Seat?*, 87–90. See generally Grace Budrys, *Our Unsystematic Health Care System* (Lanham, MD: Rowman & Littlefield, 2012), 121–139.

17 Carl F. Ameringer, *The Health Care Revolution: From Medical Monopoly to Market Competition* (Berkeley: University of California Press, 2008), 173–195.

18 Perhaps the most important restriction is that the physician must be "in-network" for the insured patient to receive full coverage. Patients can see a doctor "out of network" but likely will pay a portion of the costs out-of-pocket. The portion or share that patients must pay will depend on the terms of their health plans. Most provider networks are quite large today, particularly those attached to a Preferred Provider Organization (PPO). Thus, the restrictions on individuals in PPOs, which grew to exceed all other plan types among US employees between 1998 and 2002, are few. Robert E. Hurley, Bradley C. Strunk, and Justin S. White, "The Puzzling Popularity of the PPO," *Health Affairs* 23 (2004): 56–68.

19 The 1946 Hospital Survey and Construction Act, known as Hill-Burton, represented the US government's initial foray into system-wide planning. In sponsoring the legislation, Senator Lester Hill indicated that the law's main purposes were (1) "to make a careful state-wide survey of the hospitals and health facilities," in order to determine "where additional facilities [and federal funding for construction] are needed" and (2) "to encourage the States to correlate and integrate their hospital and public-health services and plan additions so that all parts of the country would be adequately served." Paul Brinker and Burley Walker, "The Hill-Burton Act: 1948–1954," *The Review of Economics and Statistics* 44 (1962): 209.

20 While pyramidal shapes or hub-and-spoke patterns as depicted in Figure 1.1 have been evolving in the United States for over one hundred years – examples include the Mayo Clinic and Kaiser Permanente – these are the exceptions and do not reflect more recent trends. Patrick Shay's 2014 study of multihospital systems in the United States found that only 14%, or 16 out of 114, hospital systems exhibited moderate to high levels of hierarchical integration and "geographic reach." Patrick Shay, "More Than Just Hospitals: An Examination of Cluster Components and Configurations," doctoral dissertation, Virginia

Commonwealth University, 2014. Available at http://scholarscompass.vcu
.edu/cgi/viewcontent.cgi?article=4330&context=etd. See also Roice D. Luke,
"System Transformation: USA and International Strategies in Healthcare
Organization and Policy," *International Journal of Public Policy*, 5 (2010).

21 See Lawton Robert Burns and Ralph W. Muller, "Hospital-Physician Collab-
oration: Landscape of Economic Integration and Impact on Clinical Integration," *The Millbank Quarterly* 86 (2008): 375–434; Sarah L. Krein, "The
Adoption of Provider-Based Rural Health Clinics by Rural Hospitals: A Study
of Market and Institutional Forces," *Health Services Research* 34 (1999): 33–60;
Michael E. Samuels, Sudha Xirasagar, Keith T. Elder, and Janice C. Probst,
"Enhancing the Care Continuum in Rural Areas: Survey of Community Health
Center–Rural Hospital Collaborations," *The Journal of Rural Health* 24 (2008):
24–31.

22 OECD is arguably the most comprehensive and reliable source of comparative
data for its member countries. See *OECD Health Statistics 2016*. Available at
www.oecd.org/els/health-systems/health-data.htm.

23 OECD defines "generalist medical practitioner" to include physicians who
"do not limit their practice to certain disease categories or methods of treatment." "Specialist medical practitioners" are doctors who "specialize in certain disease categories, types of patient or methods of treatment."

24 See US Bureau of Health Professions (BHP), "The Physician Workforce:
Projections and Research into Current Issues Affecting Supply and
Demand," US Department of Health and Human Services, Health
Resources and Services Administration (2008); COGME, *Sixteenth Report:
Physician Supply, Demand, and Need, 2000–2020: Specialty Mix Issues*,
US Department of Health and Human Services, Health Resources and
Services Administration, 2005; Richard A. Cooper, "Seeking a Balanced
Physician Workforce for the 21st Century," *JAMA* 272 (1994): 680; GAO,
"Primary Care Physicians."

25 See Ono et al., "Geographic Imbalances in Doctor Supply"; OECD, *Health at
a Glance 2011*; Paris et al., "Health Systems Institutional Characteristics";
Thomas Bodenheimer, Ellen Chen, and Heather D. Bennett, "Confronting the
Growing Burden of Chronic Disease: Can the U.S. Health Care Workforce Do
the Job?," *Health Affairs* 28 (2009): 69; Starfield et al., "Contribution of
Primary Care"; GAO, "Primary Care Physicians."

26 GAO, "Primary Care Physicians," 2.

27 Jan Heyrman, Margus Lember, Valentin Rusovich, and Anna Dixon,
"Changing Professional Roles in Primary Care Education," in Saltman et al.,
eds., *Primary Care in the Driver's Seat?*, 165–183; Uwe E. Reinhardt, "The
Debt of Medical Students," *New York Times*, Sept. 14, 2012.

28 Steven Simoens and Jeremy Hurst, "The Supply of Physician Services in
OECD Countries," OECD Health Working Papers, 29.

29 See National Health Service (NHS) Careers, "Registration for Doctors."
Available at www.nhscareers.nhs.uk/explore-by-career/doctors/registration-
for-doctors/ (accessed Oct. 8, 2013); Royal College of Physicians. Available
at www.rcplondon.ac.uk/ (accessed Feb. 5, 2015); Graduate Medical Council.
Available at www.gmc-uk.org/ (accessed Feb. 5, 2014).

30 Approximately 8,600 students were admitted to medical schools in France in 1971, but a perceived oversupply reduced that number to 3,500 in 1993. Martine M. Bellanger and Philippe R. Mosse, "The Search for the Holy Grail: Combining Decentralised Planning and Contracting Mechanisms in the French Health Care System," *Health Economics* 14 (2005): S/27.

31 Between 2005 and 2012, 43% of new training places were allocated to general medicine. Ono et al., "Geographic Imbalances," 31.

32 Simoens and Hurst, "Supply of Physician Services in OECD Countries," 29; Jane Hall, "Incremental Change in the Australian Health Care System," *Health Affairs* 18 (1999): 107.

33 Ono et al., "Geographic Imbalances," 27.

34 Ibid., 39; Simoens and Hurst, "Supply of Physician Services in OECD Countries," 41.

35 Ono et al., "Geographic Imbalances," 39.

36 GAO, "Primary Care Physicians," 3, 11.

37 Ibid., 11; COGME, *Twentieth Report*, 32 ("In 1998, the Canadian Residency Matching Service (CaRMS) reported that 32 percent of Canadian medical students had chosen family medicine as their career choice. By 2004, this percentage fell to 24.5 percent. Public officials and primary care physicians considered this a national emergency and plans were implemented to reverse the trend. The plans were successful and the CaRMS reports that 32.5 percent of Canadian medical school students chose family medicine residences in 2009").

38 Paris et al., "Health Systems Institutional Characteristics," 50.

39 COGME, *Third Report: Improving Access to Health Care through Physician Workforce Reform: Directions for the 21st Century*, US Department of Health and Human Services, Public Health Service, 1992, 8.

40 Ibid., Ch. II, 10 ("In most Western nations, the percentage of generalist physicians far exceeds that of the United States. Fifty percent of Canadian physicians and 70 percent of British physicians are general practitioners or family physicians"); Ch. I, 3 ("Studies suggest that the cost of physician services is much greater in the United States and that patients undergo more intense medical services per visit because of the exceptionally high proportion of nonprimary care specialists in this country").

41 Ibid., "Executive Summary," 8.

42 Ibid., Ch. I, 3.

43 Ibid., Ch. I, 3.

44 Ibid., Ch. 1, 3 ("[T]he United States has a rather dismal health status scorecard due to its failure to provide routine, ongoing primary care to surprisingly large segments of its population").

45 COGME, Cover Memo to *Twentieth Report*, May 5, 2009 ("Between 2002 and 2006, despite a Medicare GME payment cap, teaching hospitals increased subspecialty training positions by nearly 25% but reduced family medicine training by almost 3%. Since the GME cap was put in place in 1996, primary care internal medicine positions in the annual student Match have fallen by 57%, primary care pediatric positions by 34%, and family medicine by 18%").

46 An influx of international medical graduates, the creation of new subspecialties, and the late 1990s backlash against managed care were among the explanations that several analysts gave. Edward Salsberg, Paul H. Rockey, and Kerri L. Rivers, "US Residency Training before and after the 1997 Balanced Budget Act," *JAMA* 300 (2008): 1174–1180; BHP, "Physician Supply and Demand: Projections to 2020," Department of Health and Human Services, Health Resources and Services Administration (2006), 23; David Blumenthal, "New Steam from an Old Cauldron – The Physician-Supply Debate," *NEJM* 350 (2004): 1780–1787; COGME, *2002 Summary Report,* US Department of Health and Human Services, Health Resources and Services Administration, June 2002, 3–6, 12–14.

47 Edward S. Salsberg and Gaetano J. Forte, "Trends in the Physician Workforce, 1980–2000," *Health Affairs* 21 (2002): 168. See also Robert C. Bowman, "The 25th Anniversary of the COGME Third Report and No Change by Design," Basic Health Access Blog, 2016 ("Hardly a month goes by without some new proposal for more study regarding physician workforce. New studies funded and implemented and reported will not do anything but cost much more and even do less. There are reports from the 1990s that outline concisely what is needed. There has been little progress as the nation has not acted on the recommendations. New reports only allow those with their own agenda to add their own spin. At one point in time the experts were more in tune with workforce needs in the nation. The COGME Reports such as the Third Report have been on target – and they have been ignored"). Available at http://basichealthaccess.blogspot.com/2016/11/the-25th-anniversary-of-cogme-third.html.

48 Salsberg and Forte, "Trends," 168.

49 Wienke G. W. Boerma and Ana Rico, "Changing Conditions for Structural Reform in Primary Care," in Saltman et al., eds., *Primary Care in the Driver's Seat?,* 62.

50 Ibid., 62.

51 Wienke G. W. Boerma and Carl-Ardy Dubois, "Mapping Primary Care across Europe," in Saltman et al., eds., *Primary Care in the Driver's Seat?,* 25–27; Laurene A. Graig, *Health of Nations,* 3rd ed. (Washington, DC: Congressional Quarterly, 1999), 2–3.

52 The Commonwealth Fund, *International Profiles of Health Care Systems,* June 2010, 10.

53 Ibid., 9.

54 Paris et al., "Health Systems Institutional Characteristics," 36; Robert Evans, "Canada: The Real Issues," in Morone and Belkin, eds., *The Politics of Health Care Reform,* 470–471.

55 Commonwealth Fund, *International Profiles,* 1; Paris et al., "Health Systems Institutional Characteristics," 41–43.

56 Victor G. Rodwin and Simone Sandier, "Health Care under French National Health Insurance," *Health Affairs* 12 (1993): 111–131.

57 Paris et al., "Health Systems Institutional Characteristics," 32.

58 Victor G. Rodwin, "The Health Care System under French National Health Insurance: Lessons for Health Reform in the United States," *American Journal of Public Health* 93 (2003): 36.

59 Rie Fujisawa and Gaetan Lafortune, "The Remuneration of General Practitioners and Specialists in 14 OECD Countries," OECD Health Working Papers No. 41 (2008), 49.

60 Fujisawa, "Remuneration of General Practitioners and Specialists," 49.

61 Paris et al., "Health Systems Institutional Characteristics," 42.

62 Commonwealth Fund, *International Profiles*, 2.

63 Michael J. Roy, "The German Health Care System: Model or Mirage?," *Southern Medical Journal* 86 (1993): 1390. While about a quarter of German hospitals are government owned, these hospitals command a disproportionate share of the country's acute care beds (49% of all acute care beds in 2009). Paris et al., "Health Systems Institutional Characteristics," 32; Markus Worz and Reinhard Busse, "Analyzing the Impact of Health-Care System Change in the EU Member States – Germany," *Health Economics* 14 (2005): S134–S135.

64 Grogan, "Who Gets What?," 451 ("Germany makes a rigid distinction between office-based and hospital-based physicians. A patient is required to have an admission prescription written by an office-based physician to receive hospital care"); John K. Iglehart, "Germany's Health Care System," *NEJM* 324 (1991): 507 (There are two regional associations that represent doctors in Germany, one for ambulatory care physicians and the other for hospital-based physician. "These different organizations are a reflection of one of the key features that distinguish German medical care – the sharp distinction that separates ambulatory care physicians and hospital-based physicians").

65 Commonwealth Fund, *International Profiles*, 2.

66 See, generally, Martin Gorsky, "The British National Health Service 1948–2008: A Review of the Historiography," *Social History of Medicine* 21 (2008): 437–460; Rudolf Klein, "The Troubled Transformation of Britain's National Health Service," *NEJM* 355 (2006): 409–415; Graig, *Health of Nations*, 151–175.

67 Paris et al., "Health Systems Institutional Characteristics," 29–56; Graig, *Health of Nations*, 160–161.

68 "Closed staffing" means that hospital privileges are restricted to hospital-based physicians, most of whom are salaried specialists. William A. Glaser, "How Other Countries Do It," HealthPac Online. Available at www.health paconline.net/rekindling/Articles/Glasser.htm (accessed Dec. 17, 2013); Milton I. Roemer, *Health Care Systems in World Perspective* (Ann Arbor, MI: Health Administration Press, 1976), 104–115.

69 In connection with the last of these categories, the American Medical Association formulates and maintains the Current Procedural Terminology (CPT) codes, which private and public insurers assign to outpatient and office-based procedures. As of 1992, the AMA in conjunction with the specialty societies then calculates the corresponding "relative value" for each coded procedure, and then "recommends" the "relative value" to the Medicare and Medicaid programs for use in determining the payment amount. See AMA, "RBRVS: Resource-Bases Relative Value Scale." Available at www.ama-assn.org/rbrvs-overview.

70 See, generally, Andrew Abbott, *The System of Professions: An Essay on the Division of Expert Labor* (Chicago: University of Chicago Press, 1988); Eliot

Freidson, *Professionalism: The Third Logic* (Chicago: University of Chicago Press, 2001).

71 See, generally, James C. Robinson, *The Corporate Practice of Medicine: Competition and Innovation in Health Care* (Berkeley: University of California Press, 1999); D. Pulane Lucas, "Disruptive Transformations in Health Care: Technological Innovation and the Acute Care General Hospital," doctoral dissertation, Virginia Commonwealth University, 2013.

72 See, generally, Carol S. Weissert and William G. Weissert, *Governing Health: The Politics of Health Policy* (Baltimore, MD: Johns Hopkins University Press, 1996).

73 See, for example, Alan Derickson, *Health Security for All: Dreams of Universal Health Care in America* (Baltimore, MD: Johns Hopkins University Press, 2005); Jill Quadagno, *One Nation Uninsured: Why the U.S. Has No National Health Insurance* (New York: Oxford University Press, 2005); Rick Mayes, *Universal Coverage: The Elusive Quest for National Health Insurance* (Ann Arbor: University of Michigan Press, 2004); Jennie Jacobs Kronenfeld, *The Changing Federal Role in U.S. Health Care Policy* (Westport, CT: Praeger, 1997); Kant Patel and Mark E. Rushefsky, *Health Care Politics and Policy in America* (Armonk, NY: M. E. Sharpe, 1999). Some notable exceptions include Paul Starr, *The Social Transformation of American Medicine* (New York: Basic Books, 1982); Lawrence Brown, *Politics and Health Care Organizations: HMOs as Federal Policy* (Washington, DC: Brookings Institution, 1983); Budrys, *Our Unsystematic Health Care System.* Except for Budrys, these are not recent attempts. Starr's book, for instance, was published in 1982, before the formation of the type of corporate health systems that exist today. Starr's book, moreover, did not cover the influence of federal antitrust policy and Medicare prospective payment on the trajectory of health care delivery after 1983. There are also several textbooks on the US health care system that instructors use in teaching courses on health care organizations and administration. These are not historical accounts. They include Leiye Shi and Douglas A. Singh, *Essentials of the U.S. Health System*, 4th ed. (Burlington, MA: Jones & Bartlett Learning, 2017); Harry A. Sultz and Kristina M. Young, *Health Care USA: Understanding Its Organization and Delivery*, 2nd ed. (Gaithersburg, MD: Aspen, 1999); Beaufort B. Longest, Jr., Jonathon S. Rakich, and Kurt Darr, *Managing Health Services Organizations and Systems*, 4th ed. (Baltimore, MD: Health Professions Press, 2000).

74 Grogan, "Who Gets What?," 448 ("It is not an explicit benefit structure that has enabled [Canada, Britain, and Germany] to control their health care costs but the structure of the health care system itself"); Stevens, *American Medicine and the Public Interest*, 293.

75 Carl F. Ameringer, *State Medical Boards and the Politics of Public Protection* (Baltimore, MD: Johns Hopkins University Press, 1999), 117–118.

76 See Jeffrey Chase-Lubitz, "The Corporate Practice of Medicine Doctrine: An Anachronism in the Modern Health Care Industry," *Vanderbilt Law Review* 40 (1987): 445–488.

77 See Ameringer, *Health Care Revolution*, 106–110.

Chapter 2

1 Stevens, *American Medicine and the Public Interest*, 528.
2 Ibid., 528.
3 See Eliot Freidson, *Professional Powers: A Study of the Institutionalization of Formal Knowledge* (Chicago, IL: University of Chicago Press, 1986); Magali Sarfatti Larson, *The Rise of Professionalism: A Sociological Analysis* (Berkeley: University of California Press, 1977).
4 James C. Mohr, *Licensed to Practice: The Supreme Court Defines the American Medical Profession* (Baltimore, MD: Johns Hopkins University Press, 2013), 18; Starr, *Social Transformation*, 102–107.
5 Eliot Freidson, *Profession of Medicine: A Study in the Sociology of Applied Knowledge* (Chicago, IL: University of Chicago Press, 1970), 23.
6 Charles De Paolo, "Pasteur and Lister: A Chronicle of Scientific Influence," *The Victorian Web*, available at www.victorianweb.org/science/health/depaolo.html (accessed May 26, 2015).
7 Mohr, *Licensed to Practice*, 16, 157–161.
8 Ibid., 16, 66, 104, 120, 157–161.
9 *Dent v. State of West Virginia*, 129 U.S. 114 (1889).
10 Ibid. at 124.
11 Ibid. at 122.
12 Mohr, *Licensed to Practice*, 28, 80.
13 Ameringer, *State Medical Boards*, 49–50; Frank P. Grad and Noelia Marti, *Physician's Licensure and Discipline* (Dobbs Ferry, NY: Oceana Publications, 1979); Robert C. Derbyshire, *Medical Licensure and Discipline in the United States* (Baltimore, MD: Johns Hopkins University Press, 1969).
14 Mohr, *Licensed to Practice*, 69.
15 Georgia Medical Practice Act (1907).
16 Maryland Medical Practice Act (1908).
17 *Long v. Metzger*, 152 A. 572, 573 (Pa. 1930).
18 Thomas Neville Bonner, *Becoming a Physician: Medical Education in Britain, France, Germany, and the United States, 1750–1945* (Baltimore, MD: Johns Hopkins University Press, 1995), 28–30.
19 Bonner, *Becoming a Physician*, 14–32.
20 Ibid., 167.
21 Ibid., 194.
22 Larson, *Rise of Professionalism*, 15–17.
23 Ibid., 17 (emphasis in original).
24 Ibid., 17 ("the emergence of modern systems of education … appears as the central hinge of the professional project").
25 Mohr, *Licensed to Practice*, 158–159.
26 Larson, *Rise of Professionalism*, 110; Stevens, *American Medicine and the Public Interest*, 38–39; Bonner, *Becoming a Physician*, 136–141, 159–181, 187, 190–195.
27 Bonner, *Becoming a Physician*, 291.
28 Ibid., 42–43, 136, 187–190.

29 Gerald Imber, *Genius on the Edge: The Bizarre Double Life of Dr. William Stewart Halsted* (New York: Kaplan Publishing, 2011); Johns Hopkins Medicine, "The Four Founding Physicians," available at www.hopkinsmedicine .org/about/history/history5.html (accessed June 18, 2015).
30 Bonner, *Becoming a Physician*, 228.
31 Ibid., 298.
32 Ibid., 294.
33 Rosemary A. Stevens, "The Challenge of Specialism in the 1900s," in *The American Medical Ethics Revolution: How the AMA's Code of Ethics Has Transformed Physicians' Relationships to Patients, Professionals, and Society*, ed. Robert B. Baker, Arthur L. Caplan, Linda L. Emanuel, and Stephen R. Latham (Baltimore, MD: Johns Hopkins University Press, 1999), 71.
34 Abraham Flexner, *Medical Education in the United States and Canada*, "A Report to the Carnegie Foundation for the Advancement of Teaching" (1910), 59.
35 George Rosen, *The Structure of American Medical Practice 1875–1941*, ed. Charles E. Rosenberg (Philadelphia: University of Pennsylvania Press, 1983), 63.
36 Bonner, *Becoming a Physician*, 169, 309.
37 Flexner, *Medical Education in the United States and Canada*, 59.
38 Ibid., 59.
39 Ibid., 59.
40 Ibid., 57. The CME had deemed 32 schools unsatisfactory in its earlier survey for failure to meet certain standards, including preadmission instruction in the basic sciences, a four-year course of study, and access to a hospital for clinical training.
41 Rosen, *Structure of American Medical Practice*, 65.
42 Editorial, "Medical Education in the United States," *JAMA* 47 (1906): 589.
43 Bonner, *Becoming a Physician*, 293; Starr, *Social Transformation*, 124; Editorial, "Medical Education in the United States," 589. It was not as if the pecuniary rewards of medical practice were particularly favorable. Most physicians outside the big cities made very little money. See Rosen, *Structure of American Medical Practice*, 35.
44 Quoted in Editorial, "Medical Legislation in Virginia," *JAMA* 2 (1884): 240 ("If free instruction is to be given to young doctors, why not to young aspirants to the bar? – why not to clergymen? – to civil and mining engineers? If *professional* men of any class are to be furnished for their special business – equipped for their life work at State expense, why not have commercial and business colleges for clerks, and so on without end?").
45 Editorial, "Medical Legislation in Virginia," 239.
46 Bonner, *Becoming a Physician*, 67, 120.
47 Ibid., 240, 258.
48 Larson, *Rise of Professionalism*, 84.
49 Stevens, *American Medicine and the Public Interest*, 10.
50 Editorial, "Our Medical Colleges," *JAMA* 12 (1889): 740–741.
51 Bonner, *Becoming a Physician*, 309–310.
52 Starr, *Social Transformation*, 124.

53 Ibid., 124 ("[D]eliberate policies of discrimination against Jews, women, and blacks promoted still greater social homogeneity. The opening of medicine to immigrants and women, which the competitive system of medical education allowed in the 1890s, was now reversed").

54 Bonner, *Becoming a Physician,* 309.

55 Rosen, *Structure of American Medical Practice,* 38.

56 Quoted in "Specialism in Medicine," *NEJM* 143 (1900): 379.

57 Quoted in ibid., 379. Over a century later, COGME would attribute the decline of family medicine in part to the educational emphasis on specialization: "One reason for this decline in interest levels has been termed the 'hidden curriculum.' During clinical training, impressionable medical students work shoulder-to-shoulder with residents, interns, and their supervising faculty. This is their first glimpse of the 'real world' of medical practice and they are fed a steady diet of subspecialization. This is because most medical schools have, in one form or another, a faculty practice plan anchored to a large hospital that attracts acutely ill patients." COGME, Twentieth Report (2010), 13.

58 H. G. Bonney, "Internal Medicine, to What Extent Required or Elective in the Medical Course?," *NEJM* 149 (1903): 508. Bonney also claimed, rather presumptively, that "[t]he day of the general practitioner … is nearly at an end … [I]n his place are to be found men, who, if they are less courageous, less self-reliant than the time-honored country doctor, are, nevertheless, more cognizant of their limitations. The sociologic and economic conditions of the country do not at present, as formerly, require a large number of physicians to supply from time to time the needs of the smaller communities. There is on the contrary an appeal for relief from the incubus of the insufficiently prepared practitioner, in order that more encouraging inducements may be offered to … the educated physician."

59 See E. T. Nelson, "The Relation of the Literary to the Medical Colleges," *JAMA* (1885): 253–256; C. M. Jackson, "Skill and Scholarship as Ideals in Medical Graduate Education," *JAMA* 73 (1919): 307–311; Bonney, "Internal Medicine," 507–508.

60 David W. Cheever, "The Changed Position of the Profession of Medicine," *NEJM* 172 (1915): 475.

61 W. M. Leonard, "Reading for Physicians," *NEJM* 163 (1910): 959.

62 Ibid., 959.

63 Medical News, "The Question of Specialization by Undergraduates," *JAMA* (1901): 983.

64 Rosen, *Structure of American Medical Practice,* 38.

65 Edward Jackson, "The Optometry Question and the Larger Issue Behind It," *JAMA* 57 (1911): 269.

66 Jackson, "The Optometry Question," 270.

67 Andrew F. Downing, "The General Practitioner's *Apologia Pro Vita Sua,*" *NEJM* 175 (1916): 18.

68 Ibid., 18.

69 Beverly Robinson, "Loss of Faith as a Woeful Outcome of Today's Specialism," *NEJM* 179 (1918): 800.

70 Ibid., 80.
71 Elliott P. Joslin, "The Diabetic Situation in Massachusetts," *NEJM* 219 (1938): 551, 555.
72 Stevens, *American Medicine and the Public Interest*, 46.
73 Ibid., 54.
74 Ibid., 124–131.
75 Ibid., 124–131.
76 Ibid., 213.
77 The compromise involved the creation of the Advisory Board for Medical Specialties (ABMS) to oversee and approve the formation of future specialty boards. The formulation of standards for specialty board certification would occur under the auspices of the AMA Council on Medical Education and the respective specialty board. The AMA would continue to approve hospitals for residency training, something it had done since 1924. Rosen, *Structure of American Medical Practice*, 78–87; Stevens, *American Medicine and the Public Interest*, 212–217.
78 Rosen, *Structure of American Medical Practice*, 85.
79 Charles Gordon Heyd, "Relation of American Medical Association to Certification of Specialists," *JAMA* 108 (1937): 1017.
80 Stevens, *American Medicine and the Public Interest*, 77–78. Notwithstanding the progress of scientific medicine in universities and medical schools, medical practitioners still had much to prove. "Indeed, medical science made only modest therapeutic advances, especially in internal medicine, prior to the early sulfa drugs in the 1930s and the mass production of penicillin, which was not available to the general public, until the 1940s," historian James Mohr has pointed out. Mohr, *Licensed to Practice*, 158–159. Unity therefore was important to a profession that had yet to fully earn the public's trust. Though state societies controlled medical licensing at this time, specialty licensing would have been professional suicide. As law professor Lawrence Friedman has keenly observed: "Occupational associations take as their goal the task of defining an area of exclusive economic jurisdiction and protecting that area against competition … Each occupational association thus sought to claim territory and hold that territory against competitors, choosing methods of economic warfare appropriate to the occupation and the type of association. Doctors could hardly have formed a labor union; they had to preserve their professional status, and if possible, enhance it, which required rejection of the associational forms of workmen. Besides, doctors had no employers to strike against. The doctors had to insist that they were a learned, technical, elite occupation, a profession. And by the same token they had the right to exclude those who did not measure up to their standard. Strong medical societies and mandatory licensing laws proved to be appropriate and effective tools of economic warfare." Friedman, "Freedom of Contract and Occupational Licensing," 504–505.
81 Heyd, "Relation of AMA to Certification of Specialists," 1017.
82 Ibid., 1018.
83 See Stevens, *American Medicine and the Public Interest*, 124.
84 Rosen, *Structure of American Medical Practice*, 86–90.

85 See Stevens, *American Medicine and the Public Interest*, 147, 185, 295.

86 Rosemary Stevens, *In Sickness and in Wealth: American Hospitals in the Twentieth Century* (Baltimore, MD: Johns Hopkins University Press, 1999), 53.

87 James C. Robinson, *The Corporate Practice of Medicine: Competition and Innovation in Health Care* (Berkeley: University of California Press, 1999), 196–197; Rosen, *Structure of American Medical Practice*, 49.

88 Stevens, *American Medicine and the Public Interest*, 185; Starr, *Social Transformation*, 224.

89 Rosen, *Structure of American Medical Practice*, 19.

90 Ibid., 24 ("Fee bills were adopted to standardize and regulate service charges and to discourage underbidding by rival physicians").

91 See Baker et al., eds., *American Medical Ethics Revolution*, xxix–xxxi. The introduction to the 1847 Code was lengthy, but its key provisions, contained in eleven articles, were not. Though subsequent Code revisions reconfigured and reframed parts of the Code, many of the original provisions remained largely intact until federal agencies and federal courts intervened in the 1970s and 1980s. Over the course of the twentieth century, the Code was divided into multiple parts, the most important parts being the "Principles of Medical Ethics" and the "Opinions of the AMA's Judicial Council," later renamed the Council on Ethical and Judicial Affairs.

92 According to Frank Campion, the Judicial Council has had two important functions – recommending Code revisions to the House of Delegates and interpreting the Principles. In its latter role, "the Judicial Council is more of a court than a council, acting independently of the house and board on matters of ethics, discipline, and constitutional interpretation." Frank D. Campion, *The AMA and U.S. Health Policy since 1940* (Chicago, IL: American Medical Association, 1984), 101.

93 AMA Bureau of Medical Economics, *Economics and the Ethics of Medicine* (Chicago, IL: American Medical Association, 1936), 54, 67.

94 Comment, "British Control of Misconduct," *JAMA* 46 (1906): 438.

95 Joslin, "The Diabetic Situation," 551, 555.

96 "Reports of Societies," *NEJM* 119 (1888): 81–86.

97 John Harley Warner, "The 1880s Rebellion against the AMA Code of Ethics," in Baker et al., eds., *The American Medical Ethics Revolution*, 59.

98 Warner, "The 1880s Rebellion," 57.

99 AMA Code 1847.

100 Warner, "The 1880s Rebellion," 59–60.

101 Ibid., 63. The rhetoric on occasion became intense. In 1893, a speaker at an AMA meeting in Milwaukee warned that "[c]onsultation with a homeopath ... is worse than a sham, worse than an imposture. It is a crime. The arguments that are sometimes used to indicate that the refusal of a practitioner of good standing to consult professionally with a homeopathic practitioner is contrary to the public good and a mark of illiberality and intolerance amongst regular practitioners, are a false, fabricated, specious, and worthless plea." Quoted in "The American Medical Association and the Code," *NEJM* 128 (1893): 632–633.

102 Warner, "The 1880s Rebellion," 59.

103 Ibid., 55.

104 Ibid., 65.
105 A. E. P. Rockwell, "The Testimony of the Fathers," *NEJM* 154 (1906): 654.
106 Warner, "The 1880s Rebellion," 65.
107 433 U.S. 350, 368 (1977).
108 Editorial, "Specialties and Their Ethical Relations," *JAMA* (1883): 511; Editorial, "Medical Advertising," *JAMA* 42 (1904): 1025–1026.
109 AMA Code 1847.
110 Editorial, "Specialties and Their Ethical Relations," 511.
111 Ibid., 511.
112 Editorial, "Ethical Advertising," *JAMA* (1883): 540, 541 (emphasis in original). Despite the AMA's disapproval, specialists often violated the rule, with little consequence. A letter from a doctor in 1883 to Nathan Smith Davis complained about "a number of prominent men who are daily advertising in the various medical journals as *specialists* and calling attention ... to their facilities for treating special claims of disease." A 1904 editorial in *JAMA* declared that "specialists" who advertise in newspapers and journals were no better than "the proprietary medicine house, or ... the advertising quacks." Editorial, "Medical Advertising," 1025. And a 1902 commentary in *JAMA* noted the AMA's receipt of several "newspaper clippings" calling attention to surgeons' exploits. Admonishing the surgeons, the writer of the commentary warned: "If it is wrong for one physician to allow himself to be written up in the newspapers, it is wrong for another. The great city surgeon or physician whose conduct is dishonorable is a sad example to the country practitioner." Comment, "The Self-Advertising Practitioner," *JAMA* (1902): 1261.
113 AMA Code 1912.
114 Rosen, *Structure of American Medical Practice*, 38.
115 Joseph Grindon, "Advertising by Physicians," *JAMA* 52 (1909): 1756.
116 Marc A. Rodwin, *Medicine, Money, and Morals: Physicians' Conflicts of Interest* (New York: Oxford University Press, 1993), 22–26.
117 AMA Code 1903.
118 Robert M. Cunningham, Jr., "Fee Splitting: Why Is It Unethical?," *Medical Economics* 29 (1952): 67.
119 Jason T. Miller, Scott Y. Rahimi, and Mark Lee, "History of Infection Control and Its Contributions to the Development and Success of Brain Tumor Operations," *Neurosurgical Focus* 18 (2005): 1.
120 Imber, *Genius on the Edge*, 98.
121 Imber, *Genius on the Edge*, 99.
122 Atul Gawande, "Two Hundred Years of Surgery," *NEJM* 366 (2012): 1720.
123 Ibid., 1720; Imber, *Genius on the Edge*, 98.
124 Rosen, *Structure of American Medical Practice*, 48.
125 Stevens, *In Sickness*, 30, 36.
126 Rodwin, *Medicine, Money, and Morals*, 29; Stevens, "The Challenge of Specialism," 86–87.
127 Rodwin, *Medicine, Money, and Morals*, 29. The requirement was in effect from 1918 to 1952.
128 Editorial, "Fee Splitting – An Old Ethical Problem," *JAMA* 97 (1931): 1710.

129 The full quote is as follows: "It has become a Privilege for the lowly General Practitioner to be allowed to refer his surgical patient to Doctor Scalpel. They used to allow the family physician to administer the anesthetic and in due course perhaps humbly demand the large sum of ten dollars therefor; but those good old days have about went . . . If he bills for $10.00 – attendance at operation – he may get it with scowl. Suppose he had devoted half a practice day to hanging around that hospital, and bills $25.00. Does he get it? He does, but not $25.00. He gets the door, and he gets it promptly. Why the very idea of sending us a bill! What for? What did you do? We paid Dr. So-and-So $300.00 for that operation. We paid Dr. Morpheus, the Anesthetist, $15.00 or $25.00 for his anesthetic. We paid our hospital bill. That covers everything." J. B. H. Waring, "A Specialist Looks at Fee-Splitting with the G.P.'s Eyes," *Medical Economics* 9 (1932): 43.

130 AMA Code 1912 (emphasis added).

131 Editorial, "Can Fee-Splitting Be Made Ethical?," *NEJM* 18 (1937): 801.

132 Editorial, "The Stand of an Organized Profession in Germany," *JAMA* 42 (1904): 596.

133 AMA Bureau of Medical Economics, *Economics and the Ethics of Medicine*, 15; Alexander Lambert, "Health Insurance and the Medical Profession," *JAMA* 68 (1917): 259; Faith Lagay, "Right to Choose Patients and Duty Not to Neglect," *Virtual Mentor* 2001, vol. 3, available at http://virtualmentor.ama-assn.org/2001/09/code1-0109.html (accessed 10/7/2013).

134 According to Daniel Fox, "the purpose of compulsory health insurance was subtly but decisively redefined" in the second decade of the twentieth century. "A policy to avoid destitution was transformed into a policy to expand access to desirable services in order to alleviate disease." Fox, *Health Policies Health Politics*, 4–5. See also Frank D. Boudreau, "Relation of Private Medical Practice to Public Health in Europe," *JAMA* 99 (1932): 721.

135 Rosen, *Structure of American Medical Practice*, 109.

136 Morris Fishbein, "History of the American Medical Association: The War," *JAMA* 133 (1947): 836–847; Lambert, "Health Insurance and the Medical Profession," 257–262.

137 AMA Committee on Social Insurance, "Invalidity, Old Age and Unemployment Insurance, and a General Summary of Social Insurance," *AMA Bulletin* 12 (1917): 418.

138 Fox, *Health Policies Health Politics*, 34–36.

139 See Nathaniel W. Faxon, "The Country Doctor and the Hospital," *NEJM* 177 (1917): 167–171; Philemon E. Truesdale, "Group Practice," *NEJM* 196 (1927): 973–983; William Mason, "Medical Co-operation in the Management of the Surgical Case," *NEJM* 201 (1929): 503–506.

140 Hugh Cabot, "Medicine – A Profession or a Trade," *NEJM* 173 (1915): 686.

141 Ernest L Hunt, "The Hospital as a Diagnostic Centre," *NEJM* 185 (1921): 354.

142 Cabot, "Medicine – A Profession or a Trade," 686.

143 Mason, "Medical Co-operation," 504.

144 Truesdale, "Group Practice," 975.

145 Ibid., 977.

146 Report of the Medical Consultative Council for England, "Future Provision."

147 Cabot, "Medicine – A Profession or a Trade," 686.

148 Mason, "Medical Co-operation," 504.

149 Faxon, "The Country Doctor and the Hospital," 168 (emphasis in original).

150 Dawson proposed that GPs treat patients at Primary Care Centres, which "vari[ed] in their size and complexity according to local needs, and as to their situation in town or country ... A group of Primary Care Centres should in turn be based on a Secondary Health Centre. Here cases of difficulty, or cases requiring special treatment, would be referred from Primary Centres, whether the latter were situated in the town itself or in the country round. The equipment of the Secondary Centres would be more extensive, and the medical personnel more specialized. Patients entering a Secondary Health Centre would be passed from the hands of their own doctors under the care of the medical staff of that centre. Whereas a Primary Health Centre would be mainly staffed by general practitioners, a Secondary Health Centre would be staffed mainly by consultants and specialists." Report of the Medical Consultative Council for England, "Future Provision."

151 Cabot, "Medicine – A Profession or a Trade," 686.

152 Bonney, "Internal Medicine," 508.

153 Faxon, "The Country Doctor and the Hospital," 168.

154 Ibid., 169. See also Gilbert W. Haigh, "How Medicine Can Best Serve," *NEJM* 192 (1925): 1163.

155 Fox, *Health Policies Health Politics*, 42–51; Rosen, *Structure of American Medical Practice*, 116–117.

156 AMA Bureau of Medical Economics, *Economics and the Ethics of Medicine*, 68.

Chapter 3

1 AMA House of Delegates Proceedings, *Minutes of the Seventieth Annual Session*, Atlantic City, June 9–13, 1919, 2 (from an address by Hubert Work, Speaker of the House of Delegates); Morris Fishbein, "Present-Day Trends of Private Practice in the United States," *JAMA* 98 (1932): 2041.

2 AMA Proceedings, *Seventieth Annual Session*, 2.

3 Fishbein, "Present-Day Trends of Private Practice," 2041; AMA Code 1934.

4 See Wyatt Wells, *Antitrust and the Formation of the Postwar World* (New York: Columbia University Press, 2002), 38. According to Wells, the Roosevelt administration "embraced antitrust out of desperation" in a "radical effort to restore economic competition." Thus, the events described in this chapter were not unique to the health care industry. The Roosevelt administration's antitrust policy was consistent with many of its other activities.

5 Campion, *AMA and U.S. Health Policy*, 103.

6 Alexander Lambert, "The Obliteration of the Craving for Narcotics," *JAMA* 53 (1909); "Dr. Alexander Lambert, Skull & Bones 1884," available at www.smokerhistory.com/Whitney.htm (accessed July 9, 2015); Starr, *Social Transformation*, 247.

7 Starr, *Social Transformation*, 247; Rosen, *Structure of American Medical Practice*, 108–112.
8 Fishbein, "History: The War," 838–839.
9 Lambert, "Health Insurance and the Medical Profession," 257, 258.
10 Fishbein, "History: The War," 846–847.
11 Lambert, "Health Insurance and the Medical Profession," 257.
12 AMA Proceedings, *Seventieth Annual Session*, 47–48.
13 Ibid.,47–48.
14 Ibid., 47.
15 Lambert, "Health Insurance and the Medical Profession," 258.
16 Ibid., 259, 260.
17 Ibid., 259.
18 Fox, *Health Policies Health Politics*, 27.
19 "The President-Elect, Major Alexander Lambert," *JAMA* 70 (1918): 1948–1949.
20 Lambert, "Health Insurance and the Medical Profession," 259.
21 Richard Cabot, as quoted in Nathaniel W. Faxon, "The Country Doctor and the Hospital," *NEJM* 177 (1917): 167.
22 AMA House of Delegates Proceedings, *Minutes of the Seventy-First Annual Session*, New Orleans, April 26–30, 1920, 15.
23 AMA Proceedings, *Seventieth Annual Session*, 19. Morris Fishbein, an ardent opponent of sickness insurance who would soon become *JAMA*'s editor, agreed that the House of Delegates had endorsed much of Lambert's work. The House of Delegates gave its "qualified acceptance" to "compulsory sickness insurance," Fishbein reported. Fishbein, "History: The War," 841.
24 Richard Harris, *A Sacred Trust* (Baltimore, MD: Penguin Books, 1966), 6; Rosen, *Structure of American Medical Practice*, 112; Starr, *Social Transformation*, 253. Morris Fishbein encouraged this interpretation of events, noting that "[i]t is interesting to think what might have happened relating to social insurance if the war had not intervened." Fishbein, "History: The War," 843.
25 AMA Proceedings, *Seventieth Annual Session*, 33.
26 Rosen, *Structure of American Medical Practice*, 97.
27 Ibid., 113.
28 Hugh Cabot, "Medicine – A Profession or a Trade," *NEJM* 173 (1915): 686.
29 Paul W. Goldsbury, "Medical Practice and the Future Field," *NEJM* 185 (1921): 246–247.
30 Rosen, *Structure of American Medical Practice*, 36.
31 Ibid., 36.
32 AMA Bureau of Medical Economics, *Economics and the Ethics of Medicine* (American Medical Association, 1936), 68.
33 See, for ex., *People v. Woodbury Dermatological Inst.*, 85 N.E. 697 (1908); *Parker v. Board of Dental Exam'rs*, 14P.2d 67 (Cal. 1932); *People v. United Medical Services, Inc.*, 200 N.E. 157 (1936); *State v. Boren*, 219 P.2d 566 (1950); Joseph Rosenheck, "The American Medical Association and the Antitrust Laws," *Fordham Law Rev.* 8, no. 1 (1939): 82–102; Chase-Lubitz, "The Corporate Practice of Medicine Doctrine," 445–488; Sara Mars, "The Corporate Practice of Medicine: A Call for Action," *Health Matrix* 7 (1997): 241–279;

E. Haavi Morreim, "Playing Doctor: Corporate Medical Practice and Medical Malpractice," *U. Mich. J.L. Reform* 32 (1999): 939.

34 Chase-Lubitz, "The Corporate Practice of Medicine Doctrine," 445–488; Mars, "Corporate Practice of Medicine: A Call for Action," 241–279; Morreim, "Playing Doctor," 939.

35 "Contract Practice," *JAMA* 46 (1906): 199.

36 "Contract Practice," *JAMA* 47 (1906): 1923.

37 Francis W. Gallagher, Letter to the Editor, *JAMA* 57 (1911): 918.

38 "Contract Practice," *JAMA* 47 (1906): 1923.

39 "Municipal Contract Practice," *JAMA* 43 (1904): 1067.

40 "Contract Practice," *JAMA* 42 (1904): 742.

41 Letter to the Editor, *JAMA* 68 (1917): 1140.

42 Morris Fishbein, "Socialized Medicine," *NEJM* 199 (1928): 472–473.

43 "Contract Practice in Massachusetts," *JAMA* 34 (1900): 883.

44 Ralph S. Cone, "Why I Do Not Favor Compulsory Health Insurance," *JAMA* 68 (1917): 1141.

45 R. G. Leland, "Contract Practice," *JAMA* 98 (1934): 811, 813.

46 Ibid., 808.

47 Ibid., 809.

48 Editorial, "The Bureau of Medical Economics," *JAMA* 102 (1934): 294–295.

49 Morris Fishbein, "History of the American Medical Association: Changing Views of Sickness Insurance, 1920–1924," *JAMA* 133 (1947): 927.

50 Discontented with the activities of *JAMA*'s editor at the time, George Simmons, the AMA Executive Committee's first order of business in 1919 was to restrict *JAMA*'s publication of "abstracts from German medical periodicals." "There had been an extensive correspondence on the subject," it was later reported in *JAMA*. One Cleveland physician, in particular, "was adamant in refusing to countenance any relationships whatever with Germans or any recognition of their science." Fishbein, "History: The War,"848.

51 Fishbein, "History: Changing Views,"925.

52 Ibid., 923.

53 Lambert never once mentioned social insurance in his keynote address at the association's annual meeting in New Orleans, Louisiana, in 1920. AMA Proceedings, *Seventy-First Annual Session*, 4.

54 Campion, *AMA and U.S. Health Policy*, 114.

55 Morris Fishbein, "History of the American Medical Association: By Leaps and Bounds" 133 *JAMA* (1947): 605.

56 "Angry Voice," *Time* (June 16, 1947): 61.

57 Campion, *AMA and U.S. Health Policy*, 83.

58 Lawrence M. Friedman, "Freedom of Contract and Occupational Licensing 1890–1910," *California Law Review* 53 (1965): 504–505.

59 Campion, *AMA and U.S. Health Policy*, 79.

60 Oliver Garceau, *The Political Life of the American Medical Association* (Cambridge, MA: Harvard University Press, 1941), 132.

61 Fishbein, "History: By Leaps and Bounds," 606; Fishbein, "History: The War," 848. At the AMA's annual meeting in 1906, the association's president, Lewis McMurtry, advised that neither the president nor the secretary were any longer

involved in the organization's daily affairs, that "the great power of the Association was concentrated in the Board of Trustees." The board has "sole charge of the extensive property and controls all the financial and business affairs," McMurtry stated. Morris Fishbein, "History of the American Medical Association: Development of the Councils," 133 *JAMA* (1947): 683–684. Still, board members, mostly practicing physicians, met only "twice each year – once in February and once at the annual session." Fishbein, "History: The War," 848.

62 Morris Fishbein, "History of the American Medical Association: The Journal Gains"133 *JAMA* (1947): 310.

63 AMA Proceedings, *Seventieth Annual Session*, 11.

64 Ibid., 7.

65 Fishbein, "History: The Journal Gains," 312. "Writing an editorial to stimulate discussion in the correspondence columns," Fishbein indicated, boosted interest and readership while educating members "in the problems" that the AMA faced.

66 Morris Fishbein, "History of the American Medical Association: The Permanent Secretary Retires and Dr. George H. Simmons Succeeds," 133 *JAMA* (1947): 474.

67 Morris Fishbein, "History of the American Medical Association: The Medical Trust and Oligarchy?," 133 *JAMA* (1947): 764. Not all GPs agreed with this assessment, as the following letter from Colorado physician R. A. Allen indicated: "In reading over your 'Knocks and Boosts,' I am rather surprised that the 'knockers' criticize *The Journal* on the ground that it has too little of value to the general practitioner – that it does not help the country doctor. I have been a subscriber to *The Journal* ever since my senior year in medical school and have been what might be called a 'country practitioner,' but I never have received an issue of *The Journal* that has not contained something of interest or value to me." Correspondence, "The Value of the Journal to the Country Practitioner," *JAMA* 59 (1912): 135.

68 In an editorial announcing *Archives'* publication, William Mayo stated that *Archives* would not compete with "the journals of surgery now in existence," that it would "establish a sphere of its own." The reason for *Archives'* publication, Mayo said, was because "contributions to [*JAMA*'s] surgical section" had become "so numerous as to make it difficult to publish them all," and that "these contributions are too technical to be of interest to the entire profession." In a mild rebuke to *Annals*, Mayo observed that *Archives* "will attempt ... to enlarge the surgical horizon and assist in establishing surgery on a sounder basis." William J. Mayo, "Editorial Announcement," *Archives of Surgery* 1 (1920): 1.

69 Milton Mayer, "The Rise and Fall of Dr. Fishbein," *Harper's Magazine*, Nov. 1, 1949, 77.

70 Morris Fishbein, *Morris Fishbein, M.D., an Autobiography* (Garden City, NY: Doubleday, 1969), 265.

71 Campion, *AMA and U.S. Health Policy*, 114.

72 Mayer, "Rise and Fall," 77.

73 Campion, *AMA and U.S. Health Policy*, 116.

74 As quoted in ibid., 116–117.

75 Garceau, *Political Life*, 86.

76 Ibid., 86.

77 Fishbein, "Present-Day Trends of Private Practice," 2041.

78 Ibid., 2041.

79 Morris Fishbein, "Putting the Doctor in the Budget," *The American Scholar* 5 (1936): 186.

80 AMA Proceedings, *Seventieth Annual Session* (address of House Speaker, Hubert Work), 2.

81 Ibid., 2.

82 Ibid., 2.

83 Dean Lewis, "The Restoration of the General Practitioner," *JAMA* 102 (1934): 979.

84 Hugh Cabot, "Specialization in Medicine: A Subject for Undergraduate Planning," *NEJM* 217 (1937): 25.

85 Joseph J. Cobb, "The General Practitioner of Medicine and His Relation to Surgery," *NEJM* 199 (1928): 468.

86 Cobb, "The General Practitioner," 469 (comments of Homer H. Marks).

87 Ibid., 468 (comments of David W. Parker).

88 Stevens, *American Medicine and the Public Interest*, 205, 207.

89 John P. Peters, "Medicine and the Public," *NEJM* 220 (1939): 507.

90 Ibid., 507.

91 Peer P. Johnson, "The Contribution of the Community Hospital to Better Medical Service," *NEJM* 214 (1936): 295.

92 Fishbein, "Present-Day Trends of Private Practice," 2041.

93 Joseph S. Ross, "The Committee on the Costs of Medical Care and the History of Health Insurance in the United States," *Einstein Quarterly Journal of Biology and Medicine* 19 (2002): 130.

94 Ibid., 130.

95 Ibid., 130.

96 Starr, *Social Transformation*, 261; Fox, *Health Policies Health Politics*, 45.

97 Starr, *Social Transformation*, 261–266.

98 "'Final Report' of the Committee on the Costs of Medical Care," *California and Western Medicine* 37 (1932): 397.

99 CCMC Final Report, 399.

100 Editorial, "The Committee on the Costs of Medical Care," *JAMA* 99 (1932): 1952. Fishbein's comments and speeches before 1932 did not specifically target group practice and group insurance. Based on some of his writings, Daniel Fox has suggested that Fishbein was "a member of a loose coalition of doctors who were willing to contemplate changes in the organization of care, though not if they were financed by mandatory insurance." Fox, *Health Policies Health Politics*, 44. Any doubts concerning Fishbein's opposition to group practice were erased after the CCMC issued its final report.

101 F. J. L. Blasingame, *Digest of Official Actions, 1846–1958* (American Medical Association, 1959), 314.

102 Ibid., 315.

103 The AMA Code included most any type of collective activity within the definition of contract practice (groups, clinics, medical schools, and hospitals). While stating that "contract practice per se is not unethical," the Code made any group activity contingent on state medical society "approval." Blasingame, *Digest*, 123–124, 130, 131, 313, 317, 318.

104 Ibid., 123 (emphasis added).

105 AMA Bureau of Medical Economics, *Economics and the Ethics of Medicine*, 50.

106 Blasingame, *Digest*, 419.

107 Stevens, *American Medicine and the Public Interest*, 129–131.

108 When Dr. Mundt first put the resolution before the House in 1932, the House largely rejected it "as an expression of opinion in favor of a standard to be strived for." In 1933, when the resolution came up again, the House found that "general application at this time is undesirable." Yet when it appeared in 1936, the House approved it. Blasingame, *Digest*, 418–419.

109 *Dent*, 129 U.S. at 122–123.

110 Edward D. Berkowitz and Wendy Wolff, *Group Health Association: A Portrait of a Health Maintenance Organization* (Philadelphia: Temple University Press, 1988), 16–17.

111 AMA Organization Section, "The Story of the Indictment," *JAMA* 112 (1939): 59.

112 Berkowitz and Wolff, *Group Health Association*, 38.

113 Morris Fishbein, "American Medicine and the National Health Program," *NEJM* 220 (1939): 502.

114 "Application of the Antitrust Law to Regulation of Medical Practice," *Arizona Republic* (Aug. 2, 1938).

115 Members of the appropriations committees in both the House and the Senate denounced the $40,000 transfer. According to Berkowitz and Wolff: "It became increasingly clear that the $40,000 contribution could not be defended, because it put the federal government in the position of advancing the cause of prepaid group health without legislative sanction." The defeat, they indicated, likely aided the fledgling cooperative by forcing it to expand beyond federal workers at HOLC, to enroll employees from other federal agencies. Berkowitz and Wolff, *Group Health Association*, 41, 43.

116 *Group Health Ass'n v. Moor*, 24 F. Supp. 445, 446 (D.D.C. 1938).

117 Ibid., at 447.

118 Ibid., at 447. The court found that the DC insurance law in question applied only to indemnity insurers. Group Health was not an indemnity insurer.

119 *Group Health Ass'n v. Moor*, 24 F. Supp. at 446. Though the federal court decision was overshadowed when Thurman Arnold announced only three days later on July 30 that he would seek a criminal indictment against the AMA, the ramifications of the ruling were significant. Yet US attorney Pine did not appeal the ruling, nor did he pursue Group Health any further in the DC courts. Rather, Pine reversed course, joining Arnold's cause against the AMA. Indeed, both he and Arnold signed the forthcoming criminal indictment.

120 The Elk City clinic was the first to be targeted. Michael Shadid, the doctor who started the clinic in 1929, claimed that he faced expulsion from his

county medical society, the revocation of his medical license, the cancellation of his medical malpractice insurance, interference with his efforts to recruit physicians to work at the clinic, and the formation of competing cooperatives by local medical societies to force him out of business. Michael A. Shadid, *A Doctor for the People* (New York: Vanguard Press, 1939), 115, 124, 133–142, 152–157, 161–163.

121 AMA Organization Section, "Indictment of the American Medical Association," *JAMA* 111 (1938): 2499 (hereafter referred to as "Indictment").

122 Comment, "The American Medical Association: Power, Purpose, and Politics in Organized Medicine," *Yale Law Journal* 63 (1954): 953.

123 DOJ Appeal Brief in *United States v. American Medical Ass'n* (filed in the D.C. Cir., Nov. 10, 1939), 20.

124 Indictment, 2499.

125 AMA Organization Section, "Statement of Thurman Arnold, Assistant Attorney General, Department of Justice, Relative to Investigation of the American Medical Association," *JAMA* 111 (1938): 538 (hereafter referred to as "Arnold Statement").

126 Science News, "The Reorganization of Medical Practice," 12–13.

127 Editorial, "Principles and Proposals of the Committee of Physicians," *JAMA* 109 (1937): 1816.

128 The rhetorical barbs traded between Cabot and Fishbein spanned several years. See, for example, the exchange of letters between Cabot and Fishbein in *The American Scholar* 10 (1940–1941): 124–125.

129 "Mayo Physician Hits Fascism in Medical Control: Calls Group Practice People's Need," *Chicago Tribune* (May 5, 1938).

130 Patricia Spain Ward, "United States versus the American Medical Profession, et al.: The Medical Anti-Trust Case of 1938–1943," *American Studies* 30 (1989): 139.

131 Starr, *Social Transformation*, 276–279.

132 Ward, "Medical Anti-Trust Case," 139.

133 Beginning in May 1938, the Department of Justice released several statements concerning the forthcoming criminal indictment of the AMA. Arnold's July 30 statement is the most detailed and important of the pre-indictment announcements. See AMA Organization Section, "Story of the Indictment," 61; Arnold Statement, 537–539.

134 Arnold Statement, 537, 538.

135 Ibid., 539.

136 "Prosecuting the Doctors," *Chicago Tribune* (Aug. 2, 1938).

137 "A Preposterous Indictment," *Daily Globe-Democrat* (Dec. 21, 1938).

138 "A New Use for Antitrust Laws," *Philadelphia Inquirer* (Aug. 2, 1938).

139 "Socialized Medicine?," *Chicago Daily News* (Aug. 2, 1938).

140 Edward N. Kearny, *Thurman Arnold, Social Critic: The Satirical Challenge to Orthodoxy* (University of New Mexico Press, 1970), 92.

141 Spencer Weber Waller, "The Antitrust Legacy of Thurman Arnold," *St. John's Law Review* 78 (2004): 581.

142 Waller, "Antitrust Legacy," 592.

143 Henry N. Dorris, "Arnold Tries New Plan to Smash Monopolies," *New York Times* (Dec. 10, 1939). See also Arnold Statement, 539.

144 Frederick R. Barkley, "Big Drive on Monopoly Pressed by New Deal," *New York Times* (Nov. 13, 1938).
145 Arnold Statement, 537.
146 Ibid., 538.
147 Ibid., 537.
148 "The Soft Impeachment," *New York Herald Tribune* (Aug. 2, 1938).
149 "New Deal Medical Bluff," *Indianapolis Star* (Aug. 2, 1938).
150 "Group Medical Practice," *New York Times* (Aug. 2, 1938).
151 "Club for Medical 'Trade,'" *Philadelphia Evening Bulletin* (Aug. 2, 1938).
152 Fishbein, "American Medicine and the National Health Program," 503. See also "Battle to Clear AMA Promised," *New York Times* (June 10, 1940).
153 Indictment, 2497.
154 "The Medical 'Trust,'" *Constitution* (Dec. 25, 1938).
155 "Indicting the Doctors," Springfield, Massachusetts *Union* (1938).
156 "'Doc' Indicted," *World Telegram* (Dec. 21, 1938).
157 AMA Organization Section, "Press Comment on the Indictment," *JAMA* 112 (1939): 64.
158 "About Doctors," *Daily Mirror* (Dec. 22, 1938).
159 15 U.S. Code §1 (July 2, 1890, ch. 647, §1, 26 Stat. 209).
160 *United States v. American Medical Ass'n*, 28 F. Supp. 752, 755 (D.D.C. 1939).
161 *The NYMPH*, 18 F. Cas. 506 (Cir. Ct., D. Maine 1834).
162 *Federal Trade Commission v. Raladam Co.*, 283 U.S. 643 (1931); *Atlantic Cleaners & Dyers v. United States*, 286 U.S. 427 (1932).
163 *United States v. American Medical Ass'n*, 110 F.2d. 703 (D.C. Cir. 1940).
164 Berkowitz and Wolff, *Group Health Association*, 53.
165 "Medical Societies Convicted as Trust," *New York Times* (April 5, 1941).
166 Ward, "Medical Anti-Trust Case," 130.
167 *American Medical Ass'n v. United States*, 130 F.2d 233, 237 (D.C. Cir. 1942).
168 *American Medical Assn. v. U.S.*, 317 U.S. 519, 528 (1943).
169 See Derickson, *Health Security*, 122, 132.
170 Waldemar Kaempffert, "Group-Medicine Fight Growing More Bitter," *New York Times* (Aug. 7, 1938).
171 This statement requires qualification. In the late 1940s and early 1950s, Cold War rhetoric conflated the two again for a brief interval. See, for example, the federal district judge's opinion in *United States v. Oregon State Medical Society*, 95 F. Supp. 103, 109, 113 (D. Or. 1950).
172 Campion, *AMA and U.S. Health Policy*, 141.

Chapter 4

1 C. F. Wilinsky, "Preventive Medicine and the General Practitioner," *American Journal of Public Health* 15 (1925): 610.
2 Ibid., 612.
3 C. F. Wilinsky, "The Health Center," *American Journal of Public Health* 17 (1927): 677.
4 Ibid., 677.

5 Ibid., 678.
6 Starr, *Social Transformation of American Medicine*, 194–197.
7 Wilinsky, "Health Center," 679.
8 Miguel Faria, "Medical History – Hygiene and Sanitation," available at www .haciendapub.com/medicalsentinel/medical-history-hygiene-and-sanitation (accessed Dec. 4, 2015).
9 Centers for Disease Control and Prevention (CDC), National Center for Health Statistics, *Trend Tables*, 2010. Available at www.cdc.gov/nchs/data/ hus/2010/022.pdf.
10 C. F. Wilinsky, "The Public Health of Tomorrow," *American Journal of Public Health* 39 (1949): 1399.
11 C. F. Wilinsky, "The Relation of Hospitals and Health Departments in Tomorrow's World," *NEJM* 251 (1954): 325.
12 Edwin Crosby, "The Hospital as a Community Health Center," *Public Health Reports* 73 (1958): 765–772.
13 Nitin Puri, Vinod Puri, and R. P. Dellinger, "History of Technology in the Intensive Care Unit," *Critical Care Clinics* 25 (2009): 185–200; "The History of Dialysis," available at www.davita.com/kidney-disease/dialysis/the-basics/ the-history-of-dialysis/e/10431 (accessed on March 30, 2016).
14 Milton I. Roemer, "World Trends in Medical-Care Organization," *Social Research* 26 (1959): 303–306; Charles F. Neergaard, "How Many Hospital Beds Are Enough?," *JAMA* 108 (1937): 1029–1033. The 1951 edition of a leading US textbook on health administration noted, for instance, that "until recent years," only "the largest hospitals" had the money to purchase and "the highly skilled technicians" needed to operate "the electrocardiograph ... [B]ut there is in general use [today] a portable machine which can be taken to the bedside, is not so easily damaged, and is reasonably priced in both original cost and maintenance." Malcolm MacEachern, *Hospital Organization and Management* (Chicago, IL: Physicians' Record Co., 1951), 271.
15 Joint Statement of Recommendations by the American Hospital Association and the American Public Health Association, "Coordination of Hospitals and Health Departments," *American Journal of Public Health* 38 (1948): 700.
16 Ibid., 700–703.
17 Evan M. Melhado, "Health Planning in the United States and the Decline of Public-interest Policymaking," *The Milbank Quarterly* 84 (2006): 364–367.
18 Paul Brinker and Burley Walker, "The Hill-Burton Act: 1948–1954," *The Review of Economics and Statistics* 44 (1962): 209.
19 Judith Lave and Lester Lave, *The Hospital Construction Act: An Evaluation of the Hill-Burton Program, 1948–1973* (Washington, DC: American Enterprise Institute for Public Policy Research, 1974), 8, 13–15; Brinker and Walker, "The Hill-Burton Act," 744–745.
20 John Cronin, Louis Reed, and Helen Hollingsworth, "Hospital Construction under the Hill-Burton Program: Analysis of the Type, Size, and Location of Projects Being Built with Federal Aid," *Public Health Reports* 65 (1950): 744.
21 Ibid., 744–753.
22 Ibid., 752–753.
23 Ibid., 753.

24 Ibid., 749.

25 By regulation, intermediate areas had 25,000 or more inhabitants and one general hospital of 100 beds or more, while base areas contained a teaching hospital or comprised over 100,000 persons and a 200-bed hospital. Brinker and Walker, "The Hill-Burton Act," 212.

26 Cronin et al., "Hospital Construction under Hill-Burton," 750; Brinker and Walker, "The Hill-Burton Act," 212.

27 Lave and Lave, *The Hospital Construction Act*, 5.

28 Melhado, "Health Planning," 367.

29 Testifying before Congress in 1945, US Surgeon General Thomas Parran remarked that "hospital and diagnostic facilities, possibly more than any other factor, determines [*sic*] the distribution and professional skill of physicians." Quotation in Lave and Lave, *The Hospital Construction Act*, 41. But the connection between hospitals and physicians that Parran mentioned was not an important piece of evaluators' reports. Though the 1974 evaluation "conclude[d] that the Hill-Burton program probably has affected the distribution of physicians," it did not go much beyond that. Ibid., 43.

30 Beatrix Hoffman, "Emergency Rooms: The Reluctant Safety Net," in *History and Health Policy in the United States*, ed. Rosemary Stevens, Charles Rosenberg, and Lawton Burns (New Brunswick, NJ: Rutgers University Press, 2006), 252; Jean-Louis Vincent, "Critical Care – Where Have We Been and Where Are We Going?," *Critical Care* 17(Suppl. 1, 2013), available at www.ncbi.nlm.nih.gov/pmc/articles/PMC3603479/ (accessed March 2, 2016).

31 Ernest Shortliffe, T. Stewart Hamilton, and Edward Noroian, "The Emergency Room and the Changing Pattern of Medical Care," *NEJM* 258 (1958): 20–22.

32 Ibid., 25.

33 Hoffman, "Emergency Rooms," 254–255.

34 Ibid., 254–255.

35 Allen Daley, "The Place of the Hospital in the National Health Service," *BMJ* 2 (1953): 246; Peter MacDonald, "Hospital Policy of the British Medical Association," *BMJ* 2 (1939): 16–17.

36 Melissa Thomasson, "Health Insurance in the United States," Eh.net (Economic History Services), available at https://eh.net/encyclopedia/health-insurance-in-the-united-states/ (accessed on Jan. 19, 2016).

37 Raymond Munts, *Bargaining for Health: Labor Unions, Health Insurance, and Medical Care* (Madison: University of Wisconsin Press, 1967), 9; Jennifer Klein, *For All These Rights: Business, Labor, and the Shaping of America's Public-Private Welfare State* (Princeton, NJ: Princeton University Press, 2003), 210; Thomas Buchmueller and Alan Monheit, "Employer-Sponsored Health Insurance and the Promise of Health Insurance Reform," National Bureau of Economic Research, Working Paper No. 14839, April 2009.

38 Flush with excess cash reserves from sales of life insurance policies, commercial insurers found a ready source of fund investment in large manufacturing firms that were seeking loans for capital expansion in the early 1940s. Klein, *For All These Rights*, 227.

39 Ibid., 223. See also Starr, *Social Transformation*, 310–315; Munts, *Bargaining for Health*, 7–12, 48–52.

40 Klein indicates that the percentage of individual hospital costs that carriers paid typically ranged from 45 percent to 55 percent. Klein, *For All These Rights*, 217.

41 Ibid., 214; Munts, *Bargaining for Health*, 131.

42 Lewis Weeks, "C. Rufus Rorem: A First-Person Profile," *Health Services Research* 18 (1983, Part II): 331.

43 AMA Council on Medical Service, "Physician-Hospital Relations," *JAMA* 190 (1964): 186.

44 Weeks, "C. Rufus Rorem," 335–337; Stevens, *In Sickness*, 187–193.

45 Starr, *Social Transformation*, 298.

46 Thomasson, "Health Insurance in the United States."

47 Milton I. Roemer, "Hospital Utilization and the Supply of Physicians," *JAMA* 178 (1961): 126 (emphasis in original).

48 Arestad, "Hospital Service," 260. Rosemary Stevens confirmed these trends using AHA data. According to Stevens, "the rate of hospital admissions in 1960 was double that of 1935: 129 compared with 54 admissions per 1,000 population." Stevens, *In Sickness*, 229.

49 Ibid.,126.

50 William Hunt, "Role of Insurance Abuse in Hospital-Bed Utilization," *JAMA* 187 (1964): 934.

51 Ibid., 934.

52 The ten hospitals were Mount Sinai Hospital, Montefiore Hospital, Beth Israel Hospital, Lebanon Hospital, Jewish Hospital of Brooklyn, Hospital for Joint Diseases, Bronx Hospital, Maimonides Hospital, Hillside Hospital, and Long Island Jewish Hospital. Combined, these hospitals were responsible for about 22 percent of the patient load in New York City in 1958. Eli Ginzberg and Peter Rogatz, *Planning for Better Hospital Care: Report on the Hospitals and Health Agencies of the Federation of Jewish Philanthropies of New York* (New York: King's Crown Press, 1961), 29.

53 Ibid., 66.

54 Ibid., 66.

55 Lawrence D. Brown, "Capture and Culture: Organizational Identity in New York Blue Cross," *Journal of Health Politics, Policy and Law* 16 (1991): 664.

56 Milton Irwin Roemer, *Doctors in Hospitals: Medical Staff Organization and Hospital Performance* (Baltimore, MD: Johns Hopkins University Press, 1971), 37.

57 Ibid., 36–37.

58 Milton Roemer, "Health Service Organization in Western Europe," *The Milbank Memorial Fund Quarterly* 29 (1951): 146.

59 Veronica Strong-Boag and Kathryn McPherson, "The Confinement of Women: Childbirth and Hospitalization in Vancouver, 1919–1939," in *Vancouver Past: Essays in Social History*, ed. Ronald A. J. MacDonald and Jean Barman (Vancouver: University of British Columbia Press, 1986), 162.

60 Roemer, *Doctors in Hospitals*, 37.

61 MacEachern, *Hospital Organization*.

62 Strong-Boag and McPherson, "Confinement of Women," 162.

63 MacEachern, *Hospital Organization*, 155.

64 Ibid., 154.
65 Ibid., 187.
66 Ibid., 158.
67 MacEachern's organizing principles included six hospital "divisions" by function and status: "(1) an honorary staff, (2) a consulting staff, (3) an active
   staff, (4) an associate staff, (5) a courtesy staff, and (6) a resident staff."
   "Honorary medical staff" comprised retired physicians from the active staff;
   "consulting medical staff" consisted of physicians available to assist or consult
   with the active staff; "active staff" were in charge of the hospital's clinical
   affairs; "associate staff" involved mostly junior physicians who were seeking
   to become members of the active staff; "courtesy medical staff" could
   "attend" private patients in the hospital but were ineligible for membership
   on the active staff; and "resident medical staff" included recent medical
   graduates in training. MacEachern, *Hospital Organization*, 157–159.
68 Editorials, "Hospitals and the General Practitioner," *JAMA* 134 (1947):
   1484; Supplementary Report of [AMA] Council on Medical Education and
   Hospitals 134 (1947): 711.
69 AMA Supplementary Report, 711.
70 Editorials, "Hospitals and the General Practitioner," 1484.
71 Lewis E. Weeks, "George Bugbee: A First-Person Profile (Part 2)," *Health
   Services Research* 16 (1981): 460.
72 "The AHA's First Nonphysician Leader, George Bugbee," *AHA News* (March
   30, 1998): 2; Stevens, *In Sickness*, 156–157; Lewis Weeks, "George Bugbee:
   A First Person Profile (Part 1)," *Health Services Research* 16 (1981): 343–349.
73 Weeks, "Bugbee (Part 1)," 345.
74 Editorials and Comments, "Inspection of Hospitals by Hospitals," *JAMA* 144
   (1950): 394.
75 Editorials, "Inspection of Hospitals," 395. According to the editorial, "The
   [AMA] was not invited to participate in the early discussions, although the
   Association for many years has been in inspection and approval programs. In
   fact, it was quite by accident that an official of the [AMA] learned what was
   contemplated. Immediately he requested further consideration, but little progress was made in developing a satisfactory program." A 1987 article recount-
   ing the Joint Commission's history, on the other hand, states that the ACS
   "solicited the support and participation of other national professional organizations in the creation of an independent organization." See James Roberts,
   Jack Coale, and Robert Redman, "A History of the Joint Commission on
   Accreditation of Hospitals," *JAMA* 258 (1987): 938. This rendering suggests
   that the AMA had been contacted.
76 Weeks, "Bugbee (Part 2)," 460.
77 Editorials and Comments, "Joint Commission for the Accreditation of Hospitals," *JAMA* 147 (1951): 761. According to Bugbee, the main obstacle to
   reaching an agreement was the GPs. The "general practitioners ... have
   always been threatened by the standardization program ... The AHA by that
   time, with people like Wilinsky [Charles Wilinsky was AHA President in
   1951], were not worried about doctors, they were worried about the AMA
   and the attitude of the general practitioner either emasculating the program or

killing it. They thought it was a program primarily approved by specialists, rather than generalists." Weeks, "Bugbee (Part 2)," 461.

78 Weeks, "Bugbee (Part 2)," 461.

79 Differences soon arose over the extent of the Joint Commission's ability to determine the organization of hospital governance. The AMA's 1956 Stover Report called for "local" forms of hospital governance to prevail. In essence, doctors were concerned that the Joint Commission would standardize hospital governance in ways that diminished the power of medical staff. The Stover Report sought greater flexibility. "Very close liaison between the medical staff and the governing board of a hospital must be maintained," the Report said. "The method used to accomplish this should be determined locally." AMA Organization Section, "Report of Joint Commission on Accreditation of Hospitals," *JAMA* 162 (1956): 978.

80 Editorials, "Joint Commission," 761.

81 George Bugbee, "The Physician in the Hospital Organization," *NEJM* 261 (1959): 901.

82 Ibid., 901.

83 Cf., Roemer, "World Trends," 305; Roemer, "Health Service Organization," 145–147, 159–161.

84 Rosemary A. Stevens, "History and Health Policy in the United States: The Making of a Health Care Industry, 1948–2008," *Social History of Medicine* 21 (2008): 471; W. Richard Scott, Martin Ruef, Peter J. Mendel, and Carol A. Caronna, *Institutional Change and Healthcare Organizations: From Professional Dominance to Managed Care* (Chicago, IL: University of Chicago Press, 2000), 206; Starr, *Social Transformation*, 377.

85 US Department of Health and Human Services, Centers for Disease Control and Prevention, National Center for Health Statistics, *Health, United States, 2004 with Chartbook on Trends in the Health of Americans* (Hyattsville, MD, 2004), 311. Available at www.cdc.gov/nchs/data/hus/hus04.pdf.

86 Glen Garrison, "Primary Medical Care – Its Attractiveness to Physicians Should Be Improved," *NEJM* 282 (1970): 1268.

87 Editorials, "Hospitals and the General Practitioner," 1484.

88 According to Ann Somers, the AMA did not take steps to address the imbalance until the 1950s when "the proportion of general practitioners and family practitioners ... dropped to less than 25%." Ann Somers, "And Who Shall Be the Gatekeeper? The Role of the Primary Physician in the Health Care Delivery System," *Inquiry* 20 (1983): 304. Cf. Phillip R. Canfield, "Family Medicine: An Historical Perspective," *Journal of Medical Education* 51 (1976): 905–906.

89 Stevens, *American Medicine and the Public Interest*, 310–314.

90 Canfield, "Family Medicine: An Historical Perspective," 907–911; James Dennis, "The Shifting Social Scene and Family Medicine," *JAMA* 206 (1968): 1069.

91 The composition of the AMA's Citizens Commission on Graduate Medical Education was uncommon in that Millis was not an M.D., and eight of the eleven commission members were nonphysicians. The final report, known as the Millis Report, came three years after the AMA Board of Trustees established the commission. The section concerning "comprehensive health

care – graduate education for primary physicians" comprised only one portion of the report (there were nine chapters altogether), and represented a small handful of the total number of recommendations (there were twenty-three). Medical News, "Abandon Internship; Establish New 'Primary Physicians,' Commission Urges," *JAMA* 197 (1966): 37.

92 The origin and use of the term "primary care physician" is difficult to pinpoint. A prominent professor of internal medicine, Jeremiah Barondess, claims that Kerr White "introduced" the term "primary care" in a 1961 article. Jeremiah A. Barondess, "The Future of Generalism," *Annals of Internal Medicine* 119 (1993): 154. White sought to determine how patients "decide to seek help" when confronting serious illness. White and colleagues wanted to know how "patients move from level to level up and down the hierarchy of medical-care resources." The study revealed and confirmed a significant discontinuity in America's health care delivery system – the lack of any discernible pattern of physician selection and referral. "Many patients in the United States receive primary, continuing medical care from a specialist; some may visit several specialists concurrently. Frequently, patients 'refer' themselves, and in general, patients appear to control the referral process about half the time," White and colleagues reported. Kerr White, Franklin Williams, and Bernard Greenberg, "The Ecology of Medical Care," *NEJM* 265 (1961): 885, 886, 889. White, of course, was not the first to broach the subject; labor leaders and reformers frequently had raised concerns about the lack of access to good primary care and the need to integrate generalists and specialists in a group or clinic setting.

93 Quotation in Medical News, "Abandon Internship," 38.

94 Quotation in Somers, "And Who Shall Be the Gatekeeper?," 304.

95 Medical News, "Abandon Internship," 38.

96 Quotation in Medical News, "Abandon Internship," 38.

97 Ibid., 37.

98 Much of the subsequent controversy surrounding the report centered on the report's recommendation to end the one year of internship training. James Haviland, "Implementing the Report of the Citizens Commission on Graduate Medical Education," *JAMA* 210 (1969): 1902–1905. Still, it was clear that the part of the report on primary physicians was significant. The press announcement accompanying the issuance of the report stated: "Abandonment of the traditional year of internship and the *creation of a new specialty composed of 'primary physicians'* are among the major recommendations of the Citizens Commission on Graduate Medical Education." Medical News, "Abandon Internship," 37 (emphasis added).

99 Eric Larson, "Health Care System Chaos Should Spur Innovation: Summary of a Report of the Society of General Internal Medicine Task Force on the Domain of General Internal Medicine," *Annals of Internal Medicine* 140 (2004): 639–640; John Geyman, "Training Primary Care Physicians for the 21st Century: Alternative Scenarios for Competitive vs Generic Approaches," *JAMA* 255 (1986): 2631; Jane Spiegel, Lisa Rubenstein, Bonnie Scott, and Robert Brook, "Who Is the Primary Care Physician?," *NEJM* 308 (1983): 1208.

100 Somers, "And Who Shall Be the Gatekeeper?," 303.

101 Klein, *For All These Rights*, 240; Brown, *Politics and Health Care Organization*, 120–124; Somers, "And Who Shall Be the Gatekeeper?," 306.

102 The approach was deeply embedded in Europe; it was not just something that governments required or reimbursement schemes generated. "There was a widespread feeling that 'family doctoring' was simply what most people wanted as well as needed," Ann Somers indicated. Somers, "And Who Shall Be the Gatekeeper?," 303.

103 Geyman, "Training Primary Care Physicians," 2631.

104 Kerr White, "General Practice in the United States," *Journal of Medical Education* 39 (1964): 340.

105 Phillip Kletke, Mary Kay Schleiter, and Alvin Tarlov, "Changes in the Supply of Internists: The Internal Medicine Population from 1978 to 1998," *Annals of Internal Medicine* 107 (1987): 96.

106 Ibid., 96.

107 Klein, *For All These Rights*, 213–214.

108 Ibid., 240.

109 Richard Mulcahy, "A New Deal for Coal Miners: The UMWA Welfare and Retirement Fund and the Reorganization of Health Care in Appalachia," *Journal of Appalachian Studies* 2 (1996): 29–52.

110 *Parker v. Brown*, 317 U.S. 341 (1943).

111 *Group Health Cooperative of Puget Sound v. King County Medical Soc.*, 237 P.2d 737 (Wash. 1952); Munts, *Bargaining for Health*, 144–172.

112 *Group Health Cooperative of Puget Sound*, 237 P.2d 737.

113 Lawrence G. Goldberg and Warren Greenberg, "The Effect of Physician-Controlled Health Insurance: *United States v. Oregon State Medical Society*," *Journal of Health Politics, Policy and Law* 2 (1997): 58–62.

114 *United States v. Oregon State Medical Society*, 343 U.S. 326, 336 (1952).

115 Starr, *Social Transformation*, 306.

116 *Parker v. Brown*, 317 U.S. 341 (1943).

117 *Dent v. State of West Virginia*, 129 U.S. 114 (1889).

118 Starr, *Social Transformation*, 306.

119 Munts, *Bargaining for Health*, 170.

120 Doctors who treated UMW workers "ignored the [AMA's] condemnation and continued working" for the plan. Mulcahy, "A New Deal for Coal Miners," 43, 44.

121 Somers, "And Who Shall Be the Gatekeeper?," 301–306.

122 Cecil G. Sheps and Daniel J. Drosness, "Prepayment for Medical Care," *NEJM* 264 (1961): 498.

123 After he finished his work on the commission, Larson served as the association's president from 1961 to 1962. Campion, *AMA and U.S. Health Policy*, 190–191; Stevens, *American Medicine and the Public Interest*, 424; Dr. Leonard W. Larson papers, 1948–1968, available at http://apps.library.und.edu/archon/index.php?p=collections/controlcard&id=620 (accessed on Feb. 5, 2016).

124 Comment, "The American Medical Association: Power, Purpose, and Politics in Organized Medicine," *Yale Law Journal* 63 (1954): 944–947; Garceau, *Political Life*, 55–58.

125 See Larson papers, Administrative/Biographical History.
126 Organization Section, "Progress Report of Commission on Medical Care Plans," *JAMA* 159 (1955): 1371.
127 Ibid., 1371.
128 Leonard Larson, *Report of the Commission on Medical Care Plans, JAMA* (Special Issue, Jan. 17, 1959): 4–96; Sheps and Drosness, "Prepayment for Medical Care," 499.
129 Louis Orr, "President's Page," *JAMA* 170 (1959): 1554.
130 Ibid., 1554.
131 Stevens, *American Medicine and the Public Interest*, 424–425. See also Roemer, *Doctors in Hospitals*, 60–61.
132 Rosemary Stevens reported that specialty groups increased in number from 404 in 1946 to 6,371 in 1969, the greatest increase occurring after 1959, the year the Larson commission issued its report and the AMA changed its policy on physician group practice. From 1959 to 1969, the number of single specialty groups increased from 392 to 3,953, while the number of multispecialty groups increased from 1,154 to 2,418. Of the 3,953 single specialty groups in 1969, about 1 in 5 were general practice groups. Stevens, *American Medicine and the Public Interest*, 425. See also Roemer, *Doctors in Hospitals*, 12.
133 Ray Brown, "Medical Care: Its Social and Organizational Aspects," *NEJM* 269 (1963): 611.
134 Dorsey indicated that "community-based physicians potentially available for primary care" (GPs, pediatricians, obstetrician–gynecologists, and internists) decreased from 166.9 (per 100,000 population) in 1940 to 117.8 in 1961, just as "hospital-based physicians" increased from 119.4 to 289.4. Joseph Dorsey, "Physician Distribution in Boston and Brookline, 1940 and 1961," *Medical Care* 7 (1969): 432, 436.
135 Ibid., 436.
136 Ibid., 435.
137 Joint Statement of the American Hospital Association, American Public Welfare Association, American Public Health Association, American Medical Association, "Planning for the Chronically Ill," *American Journal of Public Health* 37 (1947): 1257, 1259, 1260. See also Editorials, "Aid for Chronic Illness," *JAMA* 139 (1949): 649–650; Editorials and Comments, "Commission on Chronic Illness," *JAMA* 160 (1956): 292; Commission on Chronic Illness, *Chronic Illness in the United States*, vol. I: *Prevention of Chronic Illness* (Cambridge: Harvard University Press, 1957).
138 Melhado, "Health Planning in the United States," 402, 403.
139 Ibid., 374.
140 Ibid., 374.
141 Ibid., 378.
142 Ibid., 376.
143 Fox, *Health Policies, Health Politics*, 207–208.
144 In addition to federal Hill-Burton dollars for teaching hospitals, state governments also increased funding for university medical centers in the 1950s. Ibid., 191.
145 Starr, *Social Transformation*, 372.

16 Clark C. Havighurst, ed., "Speculations on the Market's Future in Health Care," in *Regulating Health Facilities Construction: Proceedings of a Conference on Health Planning, Certificates of Need, and Market Entry* (Washington, DC: American Enterprise Institute, 1974), 263.

17 Congress, Statement of Clark Havighurst, 1046.

18 *Goldfarb v. Virginia State Bar*, 421 U.S. 773, 787 (1975).

19 The FTC's initial complaint did not include contract practice. Contract practice was a later addition. *In the Matter of the American Medical Association*, 94 F.T.C. 701, 702–703 (1979). The FTC's ruling was affirmed on appeal. *American Medical Association v. F.T.C.*, 638 F.2d 443 (2nd Cir. 1980); *American Medical Association v. F.T.C.*, 455 U.S. 676 (1982).

20 *Arizona v. Maricopa County Medical Society*, 457 U.S. 332 (1982).

21 Ibid. at 356–357 (1982).

22 Lawrence D. Brown, *Politics and Health Care Organization: HMOs as Federal Policy* (Washington, DC: The Brookings Institution, 1983), 34.

23 See Thomas Bodenheimer, "Physicians and the Changing Medical Marketplace," *NEJM* 340 (1999): 584–586.

24 Brown, *Politics and Health Care Organization*, 274.

25 Ibid., 47, 267, 427, 436–437.

26 Ibid., 276.

27 Mayes and Berenson, *Medicare Prospective Payment*, 77.

28 Ibid., 37.

29 Ibid., 47–48.

30 Ibid.,, 47–63, 70–71.

31 Ibid., 74.

32 Thomas Bodenheimer and Kip Sullivan, "How Large Employers Are Shaping the Health Care Marketplace," *NEJM* 338 (1998): 1004.

33 John K. Iglehart, "The American Health Care System: Managed Care," *NEJM* 327 (1992): 744; Bodenheimer and Sullivan, "How Large Employers Are Shaping the Health Care Marketplace," 1003.

34 Cigna's website claims that "[t]he plan [was] so successful that within three years enrollment climb[ed] to 110,000 employees and dependents. Available at www.cigna.com/about-us/company-profile/cigna-company-history?WT.z_nav=about-cigna%3BHeader%3BCompany%20Profile%3BCigna%20History.

35 These trends would continue. In 1998, only 14 percent of employees had conventional insurance; by 2003, conventional insurance was an artifact. Leiyu Shi and Douglas A. Singh, *Essentials of the U.S. Health Care System*, 4th ed. (Burlington, MA: Jones & Bartlett Learning, 2017), 224.

36 Gail A. Jensen, Michael A. Morrisey, Shannon Gaffney, and Derek K Liston, "The New Dominance of Managed Care: Insurance Trends in the 1990s," *Health Affairs* 16 (1997): 126–127. An increasing portion of the Medicare population also moved to managed care during these years, the most dramatic growth occurring after 1994. Between 1994 and 1996, annual enrollment in Medicare managed care exceeded 40 percent. Unlike employer-based insurance, however, a large majority of those 65 and older subscribed to traditional Medicare plans. Jo Ann Lamphere, Patricia Neuman, Kathryn Langwell, and

Daniel Sherman, "The Surge in Medicare Managed Care: An Update," *Health Affairs* 16 (1997): 127.

37 Marsha R. Gold, "HMOs and Managed Care," *Health Affairs* 10 (1991): 192–196.

38 Joyce E. Santora, "Allied Signal's Network Cuts Health Care Costs," *Personnel Journal* 70 (1991). Metropolitan and Prudential, along with Cigna, spent over $200 million combined during this time frame on network formation. Robert H. Miller and Harold S. Luft, "Diversity and Transition in Health Insurance Plans," *Health Affairs* 10 (1991): 40.

39 Elizabeth W. Hoy, Richard E. Curtis, and Thomas Rice, "Change and Growth in Managed Care," *Health Affairs* 10 (1991): 33.

40 Gold, "HMOs and Managed Care," 193; Hoy et al., "Change and Growth," 25.

41 There were "hybrid" plans as well – network HMOs that included both independent physicians and group practices, and Point-of-Service (POS) plans that used primary care physicians as gatekeepers, but allowed patients to go outside the network for specialty care. Iglehart, "The American Health Care System: Managed Care," 744–745; Gabel, "Ten Ways HMOs Have Changed,"134–138; Douglas R. Wholey, Jon B. Christianson, John Engberg, and Cindy Bryce, "HMO Market Structure and Performance," *Health Affairs* 16 (1997): 76–82; Jensen et al., "The New Dominance," 125–136.

42 Hoy et al., "Change and Growth," 23.

43 Wholey et al., "HMO Market Structure," 77. There were significant differences across the country, however, in physician network formation, size, and composition. Thomas Bodenheimer, "The American Health Care System," *NEJM* 340 (1999): 584–588; Kevin Grumbach, Janet Coffman, Karen Vranizan, Noelle Blick, and Edward H. O'Neil, "Independent Practice Association Physician Groups in California," *Health Affairs* 17 (1998): 227–237; James C. Robinson, "The Dynamics and Limits of Corporate Growth in Health Care," *Health Affairs* 15 (1996): 156–164.

44 Hoy et al., "Change and Growth," 34.

45 Jon B. Christianson, Roger D. Feldman, and Douglas R. Wholey, "HMO Mergers: Estimating Impact on Premiums and Cost," *Health Affairs* 16 (1997): 133.

46 Gabel, "Ten Ways HMOs Have Changed," 138–139.

47 Robinson, "The Future of Managed Care Organization," 16–17.

48 Roger D. Feldman, Douglas R. Wholey, and Jon B. Christianson, "HMO Consolidations: How National Mergers Affect Local Markets," *Health Affairs* 18 (1999): 96.

49 Peter J. Hammer and William M. Sage, "Critical Issues in Hospital Antitrust Law," *Health Affairs* 22 (2003): 96.

50 Feldman et al., "HMO Consolidations," 102.

51 Hammer and Sage, "Critical Issues," 96.

52 Stephen M. Shortell, Robin R. Gillies, and David A. Anderson, "The New World of Managed Care: Creating Organized Delivery Systems," *Health Affairs* 13 (1994): 47; Lawton R. Burns, Gloria J. Bazzoli, Linda Dynan, and Douglas R. Wholey, "Managed Care, Market Stages, and Integrated

Delivery Systems: Is There a Relationship?," *Health Affairs* 16 (1997): 216; Michael A. Morrisey, Jeffrey Alexander, Lawton R. Burns, and Victoria Johnson, "Managed Care and Physician/Hospital Integration," *Health Affairs* 15 (1996): 70–71.

53 Casalino, "Physicians and Corporations," 873.

54 Iglehart, "The American Health Care System: Managed Care," 744–745.

55 US Department of Justice and Federal Trade Commission, *Statements of Enforcement Policy and Analytical Principles Relating to Health Care and Antitrust*, Trade Regulation Reprint (CCH 1994): 4, para. 13,152.

56 *In re American International, Inc.*, 104 F.T.C. 1 (1984); *In re Hospital Corporation of America*, 106 F.T.C. 361 (1995); affirmed, 807 F.2d 1381 (7th Cir. 1986); *United States v. Rockford Memorial*, 898 F.2d 1278 (7th Cir. 1990).

57 Hammer and Sage, "Critical Issues," 90–91. See also Duke, "Hospitals in a Changing Health Care System," 54.

58 Morrisey et al., "Managed Care and Physician/Hospital Integration," 70–71; Shortell et al., "The New World of Managed Care," 59–63.

59 Quote in Medical News & Perspectives, "A Quarter Century of Health Maintenance," *JAMA* 280 (1998): 2060.

60 Ellwood related the following in an interview conducted in 2011: "The non-group structural arrangements remained an issue. Since Medicare staffers were skeptical, Butler [Lew Butler, Assistant Secretary for Planning and Evaluation at HEW] sent me off to meet with the American Medical Association, which historically had objected to group practice, especially the Kaiser Permanente Health Plan, to find out if there were any other ways to organize physicians. I met with Bert Howard, executive vice president of the AMA, who said, 'We've got something going on with the medical society there that might work.' The medical society was trying to keep Kaiser out of town. They had set up their own HMO-like entity, where the medical society fee for service members were at risk, to provide services on a prepaid basis to cannery workers. It was sort of a medical society insurance company. We dubbed it 'IPA' – independent practice association – and brought that idea back to Butler and Veneman [Jack Veneman, Undersecretary of HEW]. They thought that was fine. It was a way to placate the AMA and gave us another model." Kim M. Garber, ed., "Paul M. Ellwood, Jr., M.D. in First Person: An Oral History," *Hospital Administration Oral History Collection*, Health Research & Educational Trust, 2011.

61 Alain C. Enthoven, "The History and Principles of Managed Competition," *Health Affairs* 12 (1993): 29.

62 Ibid., 29–31, 35–37.

63 Ibid., 27, 37–39.

64 Ibid., 37–38.

65 Ibid., 45.

66 Robinson, "The Future of Managed Care Organization," 18–19.

67 Starr, *Social Transformation*, 421.

68 Robinson, *Corporate Practice of Medicine*, 23–25.

69 Starr, *Social Transformation*, 384, 385–386.

70 Fitzhugh Mullan, Marc L. Rivo, and Robert M. Politzer, "Doctors, Dollars, and Determination: Making Physician Work-Force Policy," *Health Affairs* 12 (1993): 140.

71 Iglehart, "The American Health Care System," 745.

72 Shortell et al., "The New World of Managed Care," 58.

73 COGME, 2002 *Summary Report*, June 2002, 4.

74 COGME, *Third Report*, ch. II, 10.

75 Ibid., 10.

76 COGME, *Third Report*, ch. II, 10.

77 Richard A. Cooper, "Seeking a Balanced Physician Workforce for the 21st Century," *JAMA* 272 (1994): 686.

78 COGME, *Third Report*, ch. II, 10.

79 Kevin Grumbach and Thomas Bodenheimer, "The Organization of Health Care," *JAMA* 273 (1995): 164–165; Thomas Bodenheimer, "Physicians and the Changing Medical Marketplace," *NEJM* 340 (1999): 587.

80 Christopher B. Forrest and Robert J. Reid, "Passing the Baton: HMOs' Influence on Referrals to Specialty Care," *Health Affairs* 16 (1997): 159–160; Sandy Gamliel, Robert M. Politzer, Marc L. Rivo, and Fitzhugh Mullan, "Managed Care on the March: Will Physicians Meet the Challenge?," *Health Affairs* 14 (1995): 131–142.

81 Mullan et al., "Doctors, Dollars," 148.

82 Ibid., 148.

83 COGME, *Sixth Report – Managed Health Care: Implications for the Physician Workforce and Medical Education*, September 1995, 12.

84 Gamliel et al., "Managed Care on the March," 133.

85 Ibid., 138.

86 Peter D. Jacobson, "Who Killed Managed Care? A Policy Whodunit," *Saint Louis University Law Journal* 47 (2003): 365–396.

87 COGME's Twentieth Report from 2010 stated as follows: "Primary care physician maldistribution in the U.S. is a chronic public policy challenge. Despite persistent efforts to address the problem through various initiatives, approximately 50 million Americans live in health professional shortage areas (HPSAs). While the overall numbers of physicians per capita has increased, there remain significant shortages in many rural and inner city areas where many minority and/or low-income individuals reside. While 20 percent of the U.S. population lives in a rural area, only 9 percent of the nation's physicians serve that population." COGME, *Twentieth Report – Advancing Primary Care*, December 2010, 13–14.

Chapter 6

1 Jon R. Gabel, Gail A. Jensen, and Samantha Hawkins, "Self-Insurance in Times of Growing and Retreating Managed Care," *Health Affairs* 22 (2003): 203, 205.

2 Jon Gabel, Larry Levitt, Erin Holve, Jeremy Pickreign, Heidi Whitmore, Kelley Dhont, Samantha Hawkins, and Diane Rowland, "Job-Based Health Benefits in 2002: Some Important Trends," *Health Affairs* 21 (2002): 147.

3 Ibid., 144, 145.

4 Robert Kuttner, "Employer-Sponsored Health Coverage," *NEJM* 340 (1999): 248.

5 Gabel et al., "Job-Based Health Benefits," 144.

6 Robert E. Hurley, Bradley C. Strunk, and Justin S. White, "The Puzzling Popularity of the PPO," *Health Affairs* 23 (2004): 56.

7 Robinson, "Future of Managed Care Organization," 13.

8 Lynn Etheredge, Stanley B. Jones, and Lawrence Lewin, "What Is Driving Health System Change?," *Health Affairs* 15 (1996): 93.

9 Ameringer, *Health Care Revolution*, 177–180.

10 AMA, House of Delegates, *Proceedings* (Chicago, IL: American Medical Association, June 1993), 217.

11 AMA, Council on Ethical and Judicial Affairs, *Opinions and Reports* (Chicago, IL: American Medical Association, 1995), 330–335.

12 Thomas Bodenheimer, Bernard Lo, and Lawrence Casalino, "Primary Care Physicians Should Be Coordinators, Not Gatekeepers," *JAMA* 281 (1999): 2045.

13 Kevin Grumbach, Joe V. Selby, and Cheryl Damberg, "Resolving the Gatekeeper Conundrum: What Patients Value in Primary Care and Referrals to Specialists," *JAMA* 282 (1999) 261.

14 John W. Beasley, "Letter to the Editor," *JAMA* 279 (1998): 908.

15 Michael Bradford, "Is the Gatekeeper Necessary?," *New York Times* (Aug. 2, 1998).

16 Ameringer, *Health Care Revolution*, 174–181. Gag clauses restricted the type of information that doctors could disclose to their patients. Any-willing-provider laws required health plans to open their panels to physicians who were willing to accept the price terms of managed care contracts.

17 Hurley et al.,"Puzzling Popularity," 63, 67; Robert Kuttner, "Health Insurance Coverage," *NEJM* 340 (1999): 167; Kuttner, "Employer-Sponsored Health Coverage," 248.

18 Cf. Debra A. Draper, Robert E. Hurley, Cara S. Lesser, and Bradley C. Strunk, "The Changing Face of Managed Care," *Health Affairs* 21 (2003): 20.

19 Cost-shifting, according to Kuttner, was the most common approach. "Cost-shifting takes a variety of forms," Kuttner stated. It includes "capping the employer's total benefit contribution," making employees pay a portion of the premium, "covering employees but not their family members," and "increasing the amounts of deductibles or copayments for indemnity and PPO plans." Kuttner, "Employer-Sponsored Health Coverage," 249.

20 Kuttner, "Employer-Sponsored Health Coverage," 250–251; Gary Burtless and Sveta Milusheva, "Effects of Employer-Sponsored Health Insurance Costs of Social Security Taxable Wages," *Social Security Bulletin* 73 (2013): 84, 90.

21 Kuttner, "Employer-Sponsored Health Coverage," 250.

22 Ibid., 250.

23 Ibid., 250; Robin A. Cohen and Michael E. Martinez, "Early Release of Estimates from the National Health Interview Survey, January–March 2010," National Center for Health Statistics, September 2010, 11. Available at www.cdc.gov/nchs/nhis.htm.

24 Samuel T. Edwards, John N. Mafi, and Bruce E. Landon, "Trends and Quality of Care in Outpatient Visits to Generalist and Specialist Physicians Delivering Primary Care in the United States, 1997–2010," *Journal of General Internal Medicine* 29 (2014): 952–953; Cover Story, "Multispecialty or Single-Specialty? Managed Care Drives Group Formation," *Physician Practice Options*, September 1997, 5.

25 Bodenheimer et al., "Primary Care Physicians Should Be Coordinators," 2045; Thomas R. Taylor, "Pity the Poor Gatekeeper: A Transatlantic Perspective on Cost Containment in Clinical Practice," *BMJ* 299 (1989): 1325.

26 Hoangmai H. Pham and Paul B. Ginsburg, "Unhealthy Trends: The Future of Physician Services," *Health Affairs* 26 (2007): 1591–1592.

27 Lawrence P. Casalino, Hoangmai Pham, and Gloria Bazzoli, "Growth of Single-Specialty Medical Groups," *Health Affairs* 23 (2004): 84; Allison Liebhaber and Joy M. Grossman, "Physicians Moving to Mid-Sized, Single-Specialty Practices," *Tracking Report No. 18*, Center for Studying Health System Change, August 2007. Available at www.hschange.com/CONTENT/941/?PRINT=1.

28 Casalino et al., "Growth of Single-Specialty Medical Groups," 84.

29 Ibid., 84.

30 Liebhaber, "Physicians Moving," *Tracking Report No. 18*; Joanna Anderson, "Physicians Moving to Midsize, Single-Specialty Practices," *Washington Health Policy Week in Review*, Aug. 20, 2007.

31 Thomas Bodenheimer, "California's Beleaguered Physician Groups – Will They Survive?," *NEJM* 342 (2000): 1065.

32 Bodenheimer, "California's Beleaguered Physician Groups," 1066 ("A California IPA must operate as a business with a strict budget, yet its physician members demonstrate little organizational loyalty and tend to be concerned more about their own private practices").

33 Pham and Ginsburg, "Unhealthy Trends," 1591–1592.

34 James C. Robinson and Lawrence P. Casalino, "Vertical Integration and Organizational Networks in Health Care," *Health Affairs* 15 (1996): 8 ("The central role played by organized physicians – whether in integrated groups or in IPAs – distinguishe[d] the California model of managed care from managed care in other states, in which physicians often [were] employed by hospitals or contracted as individuals with HMOs").

35 Bodenheimer, "California's Beleaguered Physician Groups," 1064–1067.

36 Ibid., 1066.

37 Author interview of William Osheroff, M.D., March 16, 2017.

38 See Hoangmai H. Pham, Kelly J. Devers, Jessica H. May, and Robert Berenson, "Financial Pressures Spur Physician Entrepreneurialism," *Health Affairs* 23 (2004): 70–81.

39 Lawrence P. Casalino, Kelly J. Devers, and Linda R. Brewster, "Focused Factories? Physician-Owned Specialty Facilities," *Health Affairs* 22 (2003): 59.

40 Karen A. Cullen, Margaret J. Hall, and Aleksandr Golosinskiy, "Ambulatory Surgery in the United States," *National Health Statistics Reports*, No. 11, Jan. 28, 2009. Available at www.cdc.gov/nchs/data/nhsr/nhsr011.pdf.

41 Liebhaber, "Physicians Moving," *Tracking Report No. 18*; Pham and Ginsburg, "Unhealthy Trends," 1591; Douglas A. McIntyre, "The Eleven Most

Implanted Medical Devices in America," *Wall Street Journal,* July 8, 2011. Available at http://247wallst.com/healthcare-economy/2011/07/18/the-eleven-most-implanted-medical-devices-in-america/.

42 Bruce J. Hillman and Jeff Goldsmith, "Imaging: The Self-Referral Boom and the Ongoing Search for Effective Policies to Contain It," *Health Affairs* 12 (2010): 2231.

43 Nancy Baum, *Physician Ownership in Hospitals and Outpatient Facilities,* Center for Healthcare Research and Transformation, July 2013. 3. Available at www.chrt.org/publication/physician-ownership-hospitals-outpatient-facilities/.

44 Hillman and Goldsmith, "Imaging," 2232.

45 James Reschovsky, Alwyn Cassil, and Hoangmai H. Pham, "Physician Ownership of Medical Equipment," Data Bulletin No. 36, Center for Studying Health System Change, December 2010, 2. Available at www.hschange.com/CONTENT/1172/1172.pdf.

46 Baum, *Physician Ownership,* 3.

47 Casalino et al., "Focused Factories," 57.

48 US General Accounting Office, *Specialty Hospitals: Geographic Location, Services Provided, and Financial Performance,* Pub. no. GAO-04–167 (Washington, DC: GAO, October 2003), 8. Available at www.gao.gov/new.items/d04167.pdf.

49 Casalino et al., "Focused Factories," 56.

50 Eelco Bredenhoff, Wineke A. M. van Lent, and Wim H. van Harten, "Exploring Types of Focused Factories in Hospital Care: A Multiple Case Study," *BMC Health Services Research* 10 (2010): 154; Lucas Martin Kop, "Process-Alignment in Focused Factories: An International Comparison Between Eye Hospitals, Focused on the Cataract Process," University of Twente, the Netherlands, March 2008. Available at www.utwente.nl/bms/htsr/education/completed%20assignments/Openbaar_IE%26M-MSc_Lucas_Kop.pdf.

51 Regina E. Herzlinger, *Market-Driven Health Care: Who Wins Who Loses in the Transformation of America's Largest Service Industry* (New York: Basic Books, 1997).

52 Bredenhoff et al., "Exploring Types of Focused Factories," 154; Joyce Frieden, "'Focused Factories' on Healthcare Horizon," *Medpage Today,* March 30, 2011. Available at www.medpagetoday.com/meetingcoverage/aapm/25627.

53 Herzlinger, *Market-Driven Health Care,* 158.

54 In addition to Herzlinger, see also Michael E. Porter and Elizabeth Olmstead Teisberg, *Redefining Health Care: Creating Value-Based Competition on Results* (Boston: Harvard Business School Press, 2006).

55 Jason Shafrin, "Are 'Focused Factories' a Good Idea?," *Healthcare Economist,* Dec. 29, 2015, available at http://healthcare-economist.com/2015/12/29/are-focused-factories-a-good-idea/; John N. Fink, "Managing for Value through Focused Factories," Health Care Financial Management Association, Dec. 17, 2012, available at www.hfma.org/Content.aspx?id=14235; David Cook, Jeffrey E. Thompson, Elizabeth B. Habermann, Sue L. Visscher, Joseph A. Dearani, Veronique L. Roger, and Bijan J. Borah, "From 'Solution Shop'

Model to 'Focused Factory' in Hospital Surgery: Increasing Value and Predictability," *Health Affairs* 33 (2014): 746.

56 Kathryn Anne Paez, Lan Zhao, and Wenke Hwang, "Rising Out-of-Pocket Spending for Chronic Conditions: A Ten-Year Trend," *Health Affairs* 28(1) (2009): 17.

57 COGME, *Twentieth Report* (2010), 10.

58 Ibid., 13.

59 American College of Physicians, *The Impending Collapse of Primary Care Medicine and Its Implications for the State of the Nation's Health Care*, 2006. Available at www.acponline.org.

60 The combination of complicated government funding formulas, an influx of international medical graduates, hospital discretion in the allocation of resources for residency training, the creation of new subspecialties, and the backlash against managed care made things worse, not better, particularly in family medicine. Edward Salsberg, Paul H. Rockey, and Kerri L. Rivers, "US Residency Training before and after the 1997 Balanced Budget Act," *JAMA* 300 (2008): 1174–1180; US Bureau of Health Professions, "Physician Supply and Demand: Projections to 2020," Department of Health and Human Services, Health Resources and Services Administration (2006): 23; David Blumenthal, "New Steam from an Old Cauldron – The Physician-Supply Debate," *NEJM* 350 (2004): 1780–1787; COGME, *Summary Report*, 3–6, 12–14.

61 Kenneth E. Thorpe, David H. Howard, and Katya Galactionova, "Difference in Disease Prevalence as a Source of the U.S.-European Health Care Spending Gap, *Health Affairs* 26 (2007): w678–w686; Cathy Schoen, Robin Osborn, Sabtrina K. H. How, Michelle M. Doty, and Jordon Peugh, "In Chronic Condition: Experiences of Patients with Complex Health Care Needs, in Eight Countries," *Health Affairs* 28 (2008): w1–w16; Thomas Bodenheimer, Edward H. Wagner, and Kevin Grumbach, "Improving Primary Care for Patients with Chronic Illness," *JAMA* 288 (2002): 1175–1779; Starfield et al., "Contribution of Primary Care," 466–485; Mark W. Friedberg, Peter S. Hussey, and Eric C. Schneider, "Primary Care: A Critical Review of the Evidence on Quality and Cost of Health Care," *Health Affairs* 29 (2010): 766–772.

62 IOM (Institute of Medicine), *The Future of Nursing: Leading Change, Advancing Health* (Washington, DC: National Academies Press, 2010), 3–23.

63 Nurse practitioners are licensed members of the nursing profession who receive their education and training in nursing schools. Because the nursing profession is distinct from the medical profession, state legislatures can give and in many instances have given NPs the authority under state scope-of-practice laws to diagnose and treat patients on their own, independent of doctors' supervision. As such, primary care physicians often view NPs as competitors. Physician assistants, on the other hand, receive their education and training in physician assistant programs that follow the medical model (disease-centered approach) to patient care. Though licensed to practice under state laws, PAs work under doctors' direct supervision and perform work that doctors delegate to them. They are physician extenders, not independent practitioners.

64 AMA, *Scope of Practice Data Series: Nurse Practitioners*, Oct. 2009. The AMA's Scope of Practice Data Series includes an in-depth report on each of ten professions: audiologists, naturopaths, nurse anesthetists, nurse practitioners, optometrists, oral and maxillofacial surgeons, pharmacists, physical therapists, and psychologists. The series was launched in 2005 by resolution of the AMA House of Delegates. See Stephen Isaacs and Paul Jellinek, *Accept No Substitute: A Report on Scope of Practice* (The Physicians Foundation, Nov. 2012): 2. Available at www.physiciansfoundation.org/uploads/default/ A_Report_on_Scope_of_Practice.pdf.

65 AMA, *Scope of Practice Data Series: Nurse Practitioners*, 6.

66 Mary D. Naylor and Ellen T. Kurtzman, "The Role of Nurse Practitioners in Reinventing Primary Care," *Health Affairs* 29 (2010): 893–899; Angelique Dierek-van Daele, Lotte M. G. Steuten, Job F. M. Metsemakers, Emmy W. C. C. Derckx, Cor Spreeuwenberg, and Hubertus J. M. Vrijhoef, "Economic Evaluation of Nurse Practitioners versus GPs in Treating Common Conditions," *British Journal of General Practice* 60 (2010): e28–e35; Christine M. Everett, Jessica R. Schumacher, Alexandra Wright, and Maureen A. Smith, "Physician Assistants and Nurse Practitioners as a Usual Source of Care," *Journal of Rural Health* 25 (2010): 407–414; Elizabeth R. Lenz, Mary O. Mundinger, and Robert L. Kane, "Primary Care Outcomes in Patients Treated by Nurse Practitioners or Physicians: Two-Year Follow-up," *Medical Care Research and Review* 61 (2004): 332–351; Mary O. Mundinger, Robert L. Kane, and Elizabeth R. Lenz, "Primary Care Outcomes in Patients Treated by Nurse Practitioners or Physicians: A Randomized Trial," *JAMA* 283 (2000): 59–68.

67 OTA (Office of Technology Assessment), US Congress, *Nurse Practitioners, Physician Assistants, and Certified Nurse-Midwives: A Policy Analysis* (Washington, DC: US Government Printing Office, 1986), 6.

68 Mundinger et al., "Primary Care Outcomes," 55.

69 IOM, *Future of Nursing*, 3–23.

70 Stephen Isaacs and Paul Jellinek, *Accept No Substitute: Report on Scope of Practice*, The Physicians Foundation, Nov. 2012, 4. Available at www.physiciansfoundation.org/uploads/default/A_Report_on_Scope_of_Practice.pdf.

71 NCQA (National Committee for Quality Assurance), *Recognizing Nurse Led Practices for Patient-Centered Medical Homes*, 2010. Available at www.ncqa .org.

72 Isaacs, *Accept No Substitute*, 4.

73 Charles M. Kilo and John H. Wasson, "Practice Redesign and the Patient-Centered Medical Home: History, Promises, and Challenges," *Health Affairs* 29 (2010): 775; MacColl Center for Health Care Innovation, "The Chronic Care Model." Available at www.improvingchroniccare.org/index.php?p= Model_Elements&s=18.

74 Patient-centered approaches encompass the "chronic care model," which first appeared in the late 1990s, and the "patient-centered medical home," the term in use today. Kilo and Wasson, "Practice Redesign," 775; Thomas T. Bodenheimer and Rachel Berry-Millett, *Care Management of Patients with Complex Health Care Needs*, Research Synthesis Report No. 19 (Princeton, NJ: Robert Wood Johnson Foundation, Dec. 2009).

75 Kilo and Wasson, "Practice Redesign," 775.
76 See Richard A. Cooper, "States with More Physicians Have Better-Quality Health Care," *Health Affairs* 28 (2009): w91–w102; Blumenthal, "New Steam from an Old Cauldron," 1780–1787; Goodman, "Physician Workforce Crisis?," 1658–1661; Linda V. Green, Sergei Savin, and Yina Lu, "Primary Care Physician Shortages Could Be Eliminated through Use of Teams," *Health Affairs* 32 (2013): 11–19. But see Katherine Baicker and Amitabh Chandra, "Cooper's Analysis Is Incorrect," *Health Affairs* 28 (2009): w116–w118.
77 Green et al., "Primary Care Physician Shortages Could Be Eliminated," 11.
78 Using simulation modeling, Green and colleagues showed that two approaches used by large health systems such as the Geisinger Health System and Kaiser Permanente – "physician pooling and demand diversion" – allowed primary care practices to increase the "number of patients associated with a physician in a typical practice." Physician pooling, they explained, was a "shared practice arrangement" in which patients saw another doctor if their own doctor was unavailable. Demand diversion, on the other hand, referred to the use of "nonphysician professionals" and electronic forms of communication. "[B]y implementing partial pooling of patients by two or three physicians and diverting as little as 20 percent of patient demand to nonphysician professionals or using electronic health record–enabled electronic communication, or both, most if not all of the projected primary care physician shortage could be eliminated," they concluded. Ibid., 16–17.
79 Scott et al., *Institutional Change and Healthcare Organizations*, 265–311.
80 Stephen M. Shortell, Robin R. Gillies, David A. Anderson, Karen Morgan Erickson, and John B. Mitchell, *Remaking Health Care in America: Building Organized Delivery Systems* (San Francisco, CA: Jossey-Bass, 1996); Scott et al., *Institutional Change*; Gloria J. Bazzoli, "The Corporatization of American Hospitals," *Journal of Health Politics, Policy and Law* 29 (2004); Shay, "More Than Just Hospitals."
81 Martin Gaynor and Deborah Haas-Wilson, "Change, Consolidation, and Competition in Health Care Markets," *Journal of Economic Perspectives* 13 (1999): 143.
82 Lawrence Casalino and James C. Robinson, "Alternative Models of Hospital–Physician Affiliation as the United States Moves away from Tight Managed Care," *The Milbank Quarterly* 81 (2003): 334; Lawton R. Burns, Jeff C. Goldsmith, and Ralph W. Muller, "History of Physician–Hospital Collaboration: Obstacles and Opportunities," in *Partners in Health: How Physicians and Hospitals Can Be Accountable Together*, ed. Francis J. Crosson and Laura A. Tollen (New York: Jossey-Bass, 2010), 29.
83 Carol K. Kane and David W. Emmons, *New Data on Physician Practice Arrangements: Private Practice Remains Strong Despite Shifts toward Hospital Employment* (Chicago, IL: American Medical Association, 2013), 5–8; Lawton Robert Burns, Jeff C. Goldsmith, and Aditi Sen, "Horizontal and Vertical Integration of Physicians: A Tale of Two Tails," *Advances in Health Systems Management* 15 (2013): 41, 46, 52.

84 Lawton Robert Burns and Ralph W. Muller, "Hospital–Physician Collaboration: Landscape of Economic Integration and Impact on Clinical Integration," *The Millbank Quarterly* 86 (2008): 388–389.

85 Marc D. Halley, Peg Holtman, and Anthony D. Shaffer, "Physician Integration Economics: How Market Share Is Captured and Retained," *Becker's Hospital Review*, June 21, 2011. Available at www.beckershospitalreview.com/hospital-physician-relationships/physician-integration-economicshow-market-share-is-captured-and-retained.html.

86 Halley, "Physician Integration Economics."

87 Burns and Muller, "Hospital–Physician Collaboration," 388–389.

88 Scott J. Cullen, Mathew J. Lambert, and James J. Pizzo, *A Guide to Physician Integration Models for Sustainable Success* (American Hospital Association and Kaufman, Hall & Associates, 2012), 26.

89 Marc D. Halley, "Breaking Even with Hospital-Owned Practices," *Healthcare Financial Management*, Oct. 2014, 38–39. Available at www.hfma.org/Content.aspx?id=25370.

90 Ann S. O'Malley, Amelia M Bond, and Robert A Berenson, "Rising Hospital Employment of Physicians: Better Quality, Higher Costs?," Center for Studying Health System Change, Issue Brief No. 136, 2011, 1.

91 Jackson Healthcare, *Trend Watch: Physician Practice Acquisition*, 2015. Available at www.jacksonhealthcare.com/media/182032/practiceacquisition report_ebook0213.pdf. According to the American College of Cardiology, hospital employment of cardiologists increased from 11% to 35% between 2007 and 2012. Kane, *New Data*, 2.

92 O'Malley, "Rising Hospital Employment," 4; Halley, "Physician Integration Economics."

93 O'Malley, "Rising Hospital Employment," 3.

94 Ibid., 2.

95 Halley, "Physician Integration Economics."

96 Robert Kocher and Nikhil Sahni, the former a health policy expert and adviser to President Barak Obama, explained the financial trade-offs: "Hospitals lose $150,000 to $250,000 per year over the first 3 years of employing a physician – owing in part to a slow ramp-up period as physicians establish themselves or transition their practices and adapt to management changes. The losses decrease by approximately 50% after 3 years but do persist thereafter. New primary care physicians (PCPs) contribute nearly $150,000 less to hospitals than their more-established counterparts; among specialists, the difference is $200,000. For hospitals to break even, newly hired PCPs must generate at least 30% more visits, and new specialists 25% more referrals, than they do at the outset. After 3 years, hospitals expect to begin making money on employed physicians when they account for the value of all care, tests, and referrals. Skeptics note that often they already capture this value from physicians without employing them, through stable referral networks and hospital practice choices. Outpatient office practices of employed physicians seldom turn a profit for hospitals." Robert Kocher and Nikhil R. Sahni, "Hospitals' Race to Employ Physicians – The Logic behind a Money-Losing Proposition," *NEJM* 364 (2011): 1790.

97 Lisa Sprague, "The Hospitalist: Better Value in Inpatient Care?," National Health Policy Forum (Washington, DC: George Washington University, 2011), 3; "The Expanding Role of Hospital Medicine and the Co-Management of Patients," *Infocus* 21 (2013): 1. Available at http://hicgroup.com/sites/default/files/InFocus_Spring13_0.pdf.

98 Robert M. Wachter and Lee Goldman, "The Emerging Role of 'Hospitalists' in the American Health Care System," *NEJM* 335 (1996): 514–517; Jordan Messler and Winthrop F. Whitcomb, "A History of the Hospitalist Movement," *Obstetrics and Gynecology Clinics of North America* 42 (2015): 421.

99 Sprague, "The Hospitalist," 2; Messler, "A History of the Hospitalist Movement," 421.

100 Scott D. Smith and Khalil Sivjee, "Defining Training Needs, Core Competencies and Future Certification for Canadian Hospitalists," *Canadian Medical Association Journal* 184 (2012): 1557–1558; Donald A. Redelmeier, "A Canadian Perspective on the American Hospitalist Movement," *Archives of Internal Medicine* 159 (1999): 1665–1668; Kheng Hock Lee, "The Hospitalist Movement – A Complex Adaptive Response to Fragmentation of Care in Hospitals," *Annals Internal Medicine* 37 (2008): 145–150; M. Kingston, "Determining the Professional Attributes of a Hospitalist: Experience in One Australian Metropolitan Hospital," *Internal Medicine Journal* 35 (2005): 305–308.

101 Lee, "The Hospitalist Movement," 148; Arch G. Mainous, Richard Baker, and Stuart G. Parker, "Hospitalists for the NHS?," *Journal of the Royal Society of Medicine* 93 (2000): 504; Thomas E. Baudendistel and Robert M. Wachter, "The Evolution of the Hospitalist Movement in the USA," *Clinical Medicine* 2 (2002): 329; Carol Black and Ian Lister Cheese, "Hospitalists and Consultant Physicians in Acute Medicine," *Clinical Medicine* 2 (2002): 290; William Lancashire, Craig Hore, and Jennifer A. Law, "The Hospitalist: A US Model Ripe for Importing?," *Medical Journal of Australia* 179 (2003): 62.

102 Redelmeier, "A Canadian Perspective," 1665.

103 Adam Haley Rosenbloom and Alan Jotkowitz, "The Ethics of the Hospitalist Model," *Journal of Hospital Medicine* 5 (2010): 183.

104 Mark A. Marinella, "Hospitalists – Where They Came from, Who They Are, and What They Do," *Hospital Physician*, May 2002, 32. See also Robert M. Wachter and Lee Goldman, "The Hospitalist Movement 5 Years Later," *JAMA* 287 (2002): 487 (confirming Marinella's statements and observations).

105 Institute of Medicine, *To Err Is Human: Building a Safer Health System* (National Academy of Sciences, 2000), 1. Available at www.nationalacademies.org/hmd/~/media/Files/Report%20Files/1999/To-Err-is-Human/To%20Err%20is%20Human%201999%20%20report%20brief.pdf.

106 Flora Kisuule and Eric W. Howell, "Hospitalists and Their Impact on Quality, Patient Safety, and Satisfaction," *Obstetrics and Gynecology Clinics of North America* 42 (2015): 434; Sprague, "The Hospitalist," 4; Robert M. Wachter, "The End of the Beginning: Patient Safety Five Years after 'To Err Is Human,'" *Health Affairs*, published online Nov. 30, 2004,

W4-538–W4-540. Available at http://content.healthaffairs.org/content/early/2004/11/30/hlthaff.w4.534.short.

107 Kisuule and Howell, "Hospitalists and Their Impact," 434.

108 Steven A. Schroeder and Renie Schapiro, "The Hospitalist: New Boon for Internal Medicine or Retreat from Primary Care?," *Annals of Internal Medicine* 130 (1999): 382.

109 Wachter, "Renaissance," 1.

110 Messler, "History of the Hospitalist Movement," 423.

111 Sprague, "The Hospitalist," 6; Kisuule and Howell, "Hospitalists and Their Impact," 433.

112 Wachter and Goldman, "The Hospitalist Movement 5 Years Later," 492.

113 Lee, "The Hospitalist Movement," 147.

114 William E. Chavey, Sofia Medvedev, Sam Hohmann, and Bernard Ewigman, "The Status of Adult Inpatient Care by Family Physicians at U.S. Academic Medical Centers and Affiliated Teaching Hospitals, 2003–2012: The Impact of the Hospitalist Movement," *Family Medicine* 46 (2014): 94.

115 Wachter and Goldman, "The Hospitalist Movement 5 Years Later," 491.

116 Chavey et al., "The Status of Adult Inpatient Care," 94.

117 Sprague, "The Hospitalist," 3.

118 James P. Nolan, "Internal Medicine in the Current Health Care Environment: A Need for Reaffirmation," *Annals of Internal Medicine* 128 (1998): 857.

119 Sprague, "The Hospitalist," 3. See also Marinella, "Hospitalists – Where They Come from," 33 (stating that the "mean age of a hospitalist is approximately 40 years"); Robert M. Wachter and Abraham Verghese, "The Attending Physician on the Wards: Finding a New Homeostasis," *JAMA* 308 (2012): 977–978.

120 Baudendistel and Wachter, "The Evolution of the Hospitalist Movement," 327–329; Black and Cheese, "Hospitalists and Consultant Physicians," 290; Schroeder and Schapiro, "The Hospitalist: New Boon," 382; Richard Gunderman, "Hospitalists and Decline of Comprehensive Care," *NEJM* 375 (2016): 1011; Nolan, "Internal Medicine," 857.

121 Sheri Porter, "Family Medicine Match Rate Increases Slightly: Number Still Insufficient to Meet U.S. Demand for Primary Care," *AAFP News*. Available at www.aafp.org/news/education-professional-development/20120316matchresults.html.

122 Sheri Porter, "U.S. Medical Schools Still Underproducing Family Physicians," *AAFP News*, Oct. 21, 2016. Available at www.aafp.org/news/education-professional-development/20161021matchanalysis.html.

123 Wendy S. Biggs, Phillip W. Crosley, and Stanley M. Kozakowski, "Entry of US Medical School Graduates into Family Medicine Residencies: 2012–2013," *Family Medicine* 45 (2013): 645.

124 Margo L. Rosenbach and Debra A. Dayhoff, "Access to Care in Rural America: Impact of Hospital Closures," *Health Care Financing Review* 17 (1995): 32–33; Tyrone F. Borders, James E. Rohrer, Peter E. Hilsenrath, and Marcia M. Ward, "Why Rural Residents Migrate for Family Physician Care," *Journal of Rural Health* 16 (1995): 337–338, 342–347; Sarah L. Krein,

"The Adoption of Provider-Based Rural Health Clinics by Rural Hospitals: A Study of Market and Institutional Forces," *Health Services Research* 34 (1999): 33–34.

125 Rosenbach and Dayhoff, "Access to Care in Rural America," 32.

126 David C. Goodman, "Twenty-Year Trends in Regional Variations in the U.S. Physician Workforce," *Health Affairs*, DOI: 10.1377/hlthaff.var.90 (2004). Available at http://content.healthaffairs.org/content/early/2004/10/07/hlthaff.var.90.full.pdf+html.

127 Rosenbach and Dayhoff, "Access to Care in Rural America," 16 (Rosenbach and Dayhoff are reporting on the work of other researchers).

128 Scott R. Sanders, Lance D. Erickson, Vaughan R. A. Call, Matthew L. McKnight, and Dawson W. Hedges, "Rural Health Care Bypass Behavior: How Community and Spatial Characteristics Affect Primary Health Care Selection," *Journal of Rural Health* 31 (2015): 154; Rosenbach and Dayhoff, "Access to Care in Rural America," 16.

129 George M. Holmes, George H. Pink, and Sarah A. Freidman, "The Financial Performance of Rural Hospitals and Implications for the Elimination of the Critical Access Hospital Program," *Journal of Rural Health* 29 (2013): 140–141.

130 Rural Health Information Hub, "Critical Access Hospitals (CAHs)," available at www.ruralhealthinfo.org/topics/critical-access-hospitals; Michael E. Samuels, Sudha Xirasagar, Keith T. Elder, and Janice C. Probst, "Enhancing the Care Continuum in Rural Areas: Survey of Community Health Center – Rural Hospital Collaborations," *Journal of Rural Health* 24 (2008): 25.

131 Samuels et al., "Enhancing the Care Continuum in Rural Areas," 26; Flex Monitoring Team, "Location of Critical Access Hospitals," 2016, available at www.flexmonitoring.org/wp-content/uploads/2013/06/CAH_101216.pdf; Holmes et al., "The Financial Performance of Rural Hospitals," 141; American Hospital Association, "Fast Facts on US Hospitals 2016," available at http://www.aha.org/research/rc/stat-studies/fast-facts.shtml.

132 Holmes et al., "The Financial Performance of Rural Hospitals," 148. Critical Access Hospitals often shared the following characteristics: their average daily census was significantly lower than non-CAH hospitals; they relied heavily on government funds, particularly Medicare, to support their operations; their plants and equipment were often old and out-of-date; and they had difficulty attracting and retaining physicians, nurses, and other medical personnel. Larry R. Hearld and Nathaniel W. Carroll, "Interorganizational Relationship Trends of Critical Access Hospitals," *Journal of Rural Health* 32 (2016): 44.

133 Emily R. Carrier, Marisa Dowling, and Robert A. Berenson, "Hospitals' Geographic Expansion in Quest of Well-Insured Patients: Will the Outcome Be Better Care, More Cost, or Both?," *Health Affairs* 31 (2012): 827.

134 Samuels et al., "Enhancing the Care Continuum in Rural Areas," 29.

135 Hearld and Carroll, "Interorganizational Relationship Trends of Critical Access Hospitals," 51.

136 Ira Moscovice, Jon Christianson, Judy Johnson, John Kralewski, and Willard Manning, "Rural Hospital Networks: Implications for Rural Health Reform," *Health Care Financing Review* 17 (1995): 53–67.

137 Ibid., 60.
138 Ibid., 62; Michelle M. Casey, Anthony Wellever, and Ira Moscovice, "Rural Health Network Development: Public Policy Issues and State Initiatives," *Journal of Health Politics, Policy and Law* 22 (1997): 26, 28. The authors noted that federal antitrust laws potentially hampered network activity, but that several states had passed legislation to overcome this. In addition, the authors noted that the Department of Justice and the Federal Trade Commission had issued relevant guidelines.
139 Moscovice et al., "Rural Hospital Networks," 64–66.
140 Goodman, "Twenty-Year Trends in Regional Variations," VAR91–VAR95; Jayasree Basu and Lee R. Mobley, "Impact of Local Resources on Hospitalization Patterns of Medicare Beneficiaries and Propensity to Travel Outside Local Markets," *Journal of Rural Health* 26 (2010): 21; Jiexin Liu, Gail Bellamy, Beth Barnet, and Shuhe Weng, "Bypass of Local Primary Care in Rural Counties: Effect of Patient and Community Characteristics," *Annals of Family Medicine* 6 (2008): 128; Borders et al., "Why Rural Residents Migrate," 347; Samuels et al., "Enhancing the Care Continuum in Rural Areas," 29; Chul-Young Roh and M. Jae Moon, "Nearby, but Not Wanted? The Bypassing of Rural Hospitals and Policy Implications for Rural Health Care Systems," *Policy Studies Journal* 33 (2005): 379.
141 Goodman, "Twenty-Year Trends in Regional Variations," VAR95.
142 See, for example, CMS, "Primary Care Incentive Payment Program." Available at www.cms.gov/Medicare/Medicare-Fee-for-Service-Payment/PhysicianFeeSched/Downloads/PCIP-2012-Payments.pdf.
143 Biggs et al., "Entry of US Medical School Graduates into Family Medicine Residencies," 645. Doctors who established practices in rural areas also faced the prospect that significant numbers of rural residents, almost 50% in certain areas of the country, would bypass them for physicians and hospitals in larger towns and cities. A prominent factor in so-called rural bypass behavior concerned the shopping habits of consumers. Studies showed that consumers went to doctors who practiced in or near locations where they shopped. Big-box retailers, such as Wal-Mart, took advantage of these tendencies. Sanders et al., "Rural Health Care Bypass Behavior," 146–150; Liu et al., "Bypass of Local Primary Care," 124; Borders et al., "Why Rural Residents Migrate," 337, 338.
144 Samuels et al., "Enhancing the Care Continuum in Rural Areas," 27. See also Sarah L. Krein, "The Adoption of Provider-Based Rural Health Clinics by Rural Hospitals: A Study of Market and Institutional Forces," *Health Services Research* 34 (1999): 35.
145 Andrew B. Bindman, Arpita Chattopadhyay, Dennis H. Osmond, William Huen, and Peter Bacchetti, "The Impact of Medicaid Managed Care on Hospitalizations for Ambulatory Care Sensitive Conditions," *Health Services Research* 40 (2005): 21; Andrew B. Bindman, Kevin Grumbach, Dennis Osmond, Miriam Komaromy, Karen Vranizan, Nicole Lurie, John Billings, and Anita Stewart, "Preventable Hospitalizations and Access to Health Care," *JAMA* 274 (1995): 309.

146 Jon Christianson and Ira Moscovice, "Health Care Reform and Rural Health Networks," *Health Affairs* 12 (1993): 59.

147 See Francis J. Crosson, "The Accountable Care Organization: Whatever Its Growing Pains, the Concept Is Too Vitally Important to Fail," *Health Affairs* 30 (2011): 1254.

148 Tianna Tu, David Muhlestein, S. Lawrence Kocot, and Ross White, "Origins and Future of Accountable Care Organizations," Issue Brief: The Impact of Accountable Care, Part 1, Leavitt Partners/Brookings Institution, 2015, 2–3, available at http://leavittpartners.com/impact-of-accountable-care/; Lawrence P. Casalino, Natalie Erb, Maulik S. Joshi, and Stephen M. Shortell, "Accountable Care Organizations and Population Health Organizations," *Journal of Health Politics, Policy and Law* 40 (2015): 820–823; Robert A. Berenson, "Shared Savings Program for Accountable Care Organizations: A Bridge to Nowhere?," *American Journal of Managed Care* 16 (2010): 722.

149 Donald M. Berwick, Thomas W. Nolan, and John Whittingham, "The Triple Aim: Care, Health, and Cost," *Health Affairs* 27 (2008): 759–769.

150 Ibid., 765; Enthoven, "History and Principles of Managed Competition," 27, 37–39, 45.

151 Berwick incorporated the work of Elliott Fisher, John Wennberg, and others on clinical variation and shared accountability. In addition, his plan closely tracked the results of a demonstration project on physician group practices that the Centers for Medicare and Medicaid Services (CMS) began piloting in 2005 and completed in 2010. Tu, "Origins and Future of Accountable Care Organizations," 2.

152 Berenson, "A Bridge to Nowhere?," 724.

153 While traditional Medicare never abandoned fee-or-service, Medicare Advantage Plans included a variety of payment options.

154 Berwick et al., "Triple Aim," 763.

155 Ibid., 763.

156 Donald M. Berwick, "Launching Accountable Care Organizations – The Proposed Rule for the Medicare Shared Savings Program," *NEJM* 364 (2011): e32. Available at www.nejm.org/doi/full/10.1056/NEJMp1103602#t=article.

157 To become program eligible, ACOs among other things would have to "include primary care ... professionals ... sufficient for the number of Medicare fee-for-service beneficiaries assigned to the ACO" (5000 beneficiaries was the threshold). Social Security Act, secs. 1899(b)(2)(B),(C),(D) and (b)(3)(A), "Shared Savings Program."

158 In addition to those mentioned, see Christopher M. Pope, "How the Affordable Care Act Fuels Health Care Market Consolidation," *Backgrounder* (The Heritage Foundation, 2014) (criticizing the Act's endorsement of certain "anti-competitive arrangements"); Valerie A. Lewis, Carrie H. Colla, Kathleen L. Carluzzo, Sarah E. Kler, and Elliott S. Fisher, "Accountable Care Organizations in the United States: Market and Demographic Factors Associated with Formation," *Health Services Research* 48 (2013): 1840–1858 (arguing that the new law's requirements for ACO formation favor affluent areas and organizations that have the infrastructure to perform well on

certain quality measures); J. Michael McWilliams, "Accountable Care Organizations: A Challenging Opportunity for Primary Care to Demonstrate Its Value," *Journal of General Internal Medicine* 29 (2013): 830–831 (noting that cost savings from primary care relating to preventive care coordination and disease management "may be minimal").

159 Berenson, "A Bridge to Nowhere?," 722–723.
160 "Until the value-based payment models – bundled payments, episode-based payment, capitation, risk-adjusted global budgets and expenditure targets – reach a threshold of a hospital's business, hospitals are unlikely to significantly change their strategy from maximizing the inpatient margin to maximizing the total margin," Stephen Shortell and colleagues predicted. Stephen M. Shortell, Sean R. McClellan, Patricia P. Ramsey, Lawrence Casalino, Andrew M. Ryan, and Kennon R. Copeland, "Physician Practice Participation in Accountable Care Organizations: The Emergence of the Unicorn," *Health Services Research* 49 (2014): 1530.
161 Casalino et al., "Accountable Care Organizations and Population Health Organizations," 820.
162 Zirui Song and Thomas H. Lee, "The Era of Delivery System Reform Begins," *JAMA* 309 (2013): 35. ACOs were not the only form that the Affordable Care Act prescribed for controlling costs and improving quality. The new law contemplated several other options. See Thomas C. Tsai, Karen E. Joynt, Robert C. Wild, E. John Orav, and Ashish K. Jha, "Medicare's Bundled Payment Initiative: Most Hospitals Are Focused on a Few High-Volume Conditions," *Health Affairs* 34 (2015): 371–380.
163 Deborah A. Savage, "Professional Sovereignty Revisited: The Network Transformation of American Medicine?," *Journal of Health Politics, Policy and Law* 29 (2004): 675; Burns and Muller, "Hospital–Physician Collaboration," 393; American Hospital Association, "Clinical Integration – The Key to Real Reform," *TrendWatch*, Feb. 2010, 1–3.
164 Burns and Muller, "Hospital–Physician Collaboration," 380.
165 Sayaka Nakamura, "Hospital Mergers and Referrals in the United States: Patient Steering or Integrated Delivery of Care?," *Inquiry* 47 (2010): 228; Burns et al., "A Tale of Two Tails," 42.
166 Burns and Muller, "Hospital–Physician Collaboration," 393.
167 See Bonnie Lefkowitz, *Community Health Centers: A Movement and the People Who Made It Happen* (New Brunswick, NJ: Rutgers University Press, 2007); Starfield et al., "Contribution of Primary Care," 464.
168 The principal providers of primary care in medically underserved areas (MUAs) across the United States are federally qualified health centers (FQHCs). FQHCs encompass community health centers, migrant health centers, health care for the homeless health centers, and public housing primary care centers. Federal grants to FQHCs cover approximately one-third of operating costs. The rest of the money comes from philanthropic sources, Medicare/Medicaid reimbursements, and private insurers. In communities or neighborhoods that do not have an FQHC, but nonetheless have significant numbers of poor and uninsured individuals, free clinics may exist

to fill the gap. Free clinics do not receive their funds from insurers or federal grants. Most of their money comes from individual donors, philanthropic entities, or community foundations. I and my colleagues have conducted grant-funded field research over the past fifteen years in communities where FQHCs or free clinics are the principal sources of primary care: certain areas of Oshkosh, WI (2003), Richmond, VA (2012), and Omaha, NE (2015). In every instance, resources were spread thin, funding was uncertain, wait times to see physicians often were long, and coordination of care was difficult to achieve. See Saltanet Liebert and Carl F. Ameringer, "The Health Care Safety Net and the Affordable Care Act: Implications for Hispanic Immigrants," *Public Administration Review* 73 (2013): 810–820.

Index

accountable care organizations (ACOs), 15, 100, 119–20, 122, 170n157, 170n158, 171n162

Advisory Board for Medical Specialties, 27, 134n77

Aetna, 97

Affordable Care Act (ACA), 16, 100, 104, 119–20

Allied-Signal Corporation, 95

ambulatory surgery centers (ASCs), 108–9, 113

American Academy of General Practice (AAGP), 79

American Association for Labor Legislation (AALL), 40

American Board of Ophthalmology, 27

American College of Physicians (ACP), 27, 77, 110

American College of Surgeons (ACS), 27, 33, 48, 74–77, 149n75

American Hospital Association (AHA), 67, 72–73, 75–77, 114

American Medical Association (AMA), 18, 39, 48, 114, 129n69, 157n60
  and antitrust, 40, 57–62, 93, 143n119, 144n133
  and comprehensive health care reform, 40–43, 52, 62, 90
  and contract practice, 45, 53, 143n103
  and educational reform, 23–24
  and Code of Medical Ethics, 29–37, 53, 84, 135n101
  and Joint Commission, 76–77, 150n79
  and managed care, 105
  membership in, 46–47, 51, 64, 103
  and nurse practitioners, 110–11, 163n64
  reorganization of, 46–47, 140n61
  and specialty certification, 27–28, 75, 79
  and state licensing, 19
  See also American College of Surgeons (ASC); Committee on the Costs of Medical Care (CCMC); corporate practice of medicine; group practice; Joint Commission; managed care; medical staff organizations (MSOs); nurse practitioners (NPs)

American Public Health Association, 65, 67

Arizona v. Maricopa County Medical Society, 93

Arnold, Thurman, 57–63, 93, 103, 143n119, 144n133

Australia, 2, 7–8, 11, 44, 123n2

Barker, Lewellys, 52

Bates v. Arizona State Bar Association, 31

Baylor University Hospital, 72

Berenson, Robert, 95, 120

Berwick, Donald, 119–20, 170n151

Biggs, Hermann, 66

Billings, Frank, 40, 46

Bismarck, Otto von, 43

Blue Cross, 16, 67, 69, 71–74, 80–81, 90, 97

Blue Shield, 16, 73, 80, 82, 84, 90

Bodenheimer, Thomas, 101, 105, 107

Boerma, Wienke, 11

increasing inflexibility, hoped to reverse or at least moderate the association's position. After some discussion at the AMA's annual convention in 1926, fifteen "frustrated delegates" established a Committee of Five to examine the problem of rising health costs and report at the next annual meeting.[93] Rather than deal with the issue of social insurance, which the AMA now firmly opposed, the Committee of Five focused on ways to reduce costs through health system reorganization. Many of the committee members came from the academic ranks. They included Winford Smith, director of Johns Hopkins Hospital; Lewellys Barker, a Johns Hopkins Medical School professor; Walton Hamilton, an economist at the Brookings Institute; C. E. A. Winslow, a public health professor at Yale University; and Michael Davis, the director of the Boston Dispensary whose writings had inspired many of Lambert's recommendations.[94]

At the AMA's national convention in 1927, the Committee of Five secured the support of Ray Lyman Wilbur, Stanford University's president. Wilbur reportedly met with several persons at the 1927 convention who were interested in pursuing the cost issue.[95] Though the AMA endorsed the effort, the CCMC was an independent undertaking. Funds for its activities came from eight philanthropic foundations, among them the Rockefeller Foundation, the Carnegie Foundation, and the Milbank Memorial Fund. Comprising physicians, economists, social scientists, public health officials, and other notable members of the health care community, the CCMC was large (forty-six individuals signed portions of the final report). The backgrounds and perspectives of its members were disparate. Wilbur chaired the committee.[96]

In the five years of its existence, from 1927 to 1932, the CCMC published twenty-seven reports providing much useful information on health expenditures, cost allocations, and case studies of hospital plans and private group clinics.[97] But when committee members met to assemble a final report, they could not reach consensus. Thirty-five members of the committee recommended some form of group practice and group payment. "[M]edical service," they said, should "be furnished largely by organized groups of physicians, dentists, nurses, pharmacists, and other associated personnel, [and] the costs of medical care be placed on a group payment basis."[98] Nine persons, eight of them private practitioners, opposed the majority's recommendation. In a separate, "minority" report, these nine persons stated: "Our understanding of the majority report is that ... [t]he medical profession is to be formed into large or small groups, preferably large, and these groups are to furnish medical care under some type of contract with groups of laymen ... Over against

Yet no effective steps were taken to address the situation. As indicated, doctors and hospitals could not be expected to pursue an approach that failed to advance their economic interests. Doctors "saw community hospitals as supports for and extensions of a private practice that gave priority ... to acute manifestations of chronic disease," health scholar Evan Melhado noted. Hospitals, for their part, Melhado wrote, "failed to sustain an 'outward glance' toward the community but consistently preferred an 'inward vision' that emphasized in-house provision of technologically advanced, acute-care services and that depreciated or ignored chronic care."[138]

Unless government weighed in, there would be little progress. But 1960s reformers did not focus on the specific concerns of Brown and Dorsey, that is, the lack of community-based primary care. Instead, a new breed of urban planners emphasized the plight of teaching hospitals. Because voluntary hospitals had gained advanced medical technology, the money to pay for it, and the specialists who knew how to use it, they could offer many of the same services that teaching hospitals provided.[139] Facing competition from voluntary hospitals for middle- and upper-income patients with insurance coverage, teaching hospitals sought financial support from politicians and policymakers.[140] Successful lobbying by teaching hospitals and their supporters in Congress led to a shift in federal funding from rural to metropolitan areas under the 1964 Hill-Harris amendments to the Hill-Burton Act.[141] The new orientation advanced the "modernization" of teaching hospitals in large urban centers.[142]

The shift from "rural hierarchies" to "metropolitan areawide planning," as urban planners called it, emphasized the benefits of medical research, scientific inquiry, and advanced technology. Viewed from the perspective of planners, academic physicians, and leading specialists, health care should be organized to enhance the flow of scientific knowledge downward and outward so that all could enjoy it.[143] Unfortunately, the approach overlooked the need for basic services. While the building of small- and medium-sized hospitals in small towns and small cities emphasized the middle of the health care pyramid, the shift in Hill-Burton funding in order to save teaching hospitals stressed the top of it.[144] There was little accounting for the lack of primary care services at the bottom.

To be sure, many medical schools and teaching hospitals in the 1960s sponsored neighborhood health centers. But health centers were not part of a broader scheme or overarching design to deliver primary care to all doctors and other participants. Accountable care organizations – not the doctors, hospitals, or others involved – would incur any financial loss.[156]

Unlike Enthoven, Berwick would see his idea come to fruition when Congress established the Medicare Shared Savings Program for ACOs in the 2010 Affordable Care Act. During his brief stint as administrator of the Medicare and Medicaid programs, Berwick would shepherd the ACO model through the agency rulemaking process.[157]

The ACO model had its critics, of course.[158] Robert Berenson noted that "there are no downside penalties for missing [certain] spending targets."[159] Stephen Shortell observed that hospitals "may be reluctant participants given that the new value-based payment models are likely to adversely affect hospital admissions and financial viability."[160] Lawrence Casalino and colleagues questioned CMS's "narrow" construct of the phrase "population health" contained in the Affordable Care Act. CMS's interpretation failed to consider "socioeconomic factors such as poverty, poor education, and inadequate housing," Casalino and colleagues claimed.[161]

Though the ACO model was far from the ideal that ardent reformers had envisioned – a regional delivery system that coordinated care over a wide spectrum – it was a beginning, a tentative first step toward government-designed health care delivery.[162] While the Affordable Care Act made joining ACOs an entirely "voluntary" undertaking, it nonetheless opened the door to the development of agency specifications for private organizations seeking Medicare funding. There were precedents – the HMO Act of 1973 and CON legislation – but neither conditioned federal payment for services on the formation of a specific legal entity that performed certain functions. As such, ACOs straddled the fence between government inducements and government involvement in health system design.

CONCLUSION

Each of the events related in this chapter is the logical extension of what happened before. However viewed, these events were decades in the making, the accumulation of years of struggle and conflict among doctors, reformers, and, more recently, entrepreneurs. The backlash against managed care in the 1990s and the current predominance of preferred provider organizations has roots in American medicine's egalitarian tradition, coupled with the belief that patients should have free choice of physician. Though Medicare and Medicaid now offer managed care plans, a majority of enrollees still choose the traditional option.

146 Ibid., 367–374.
147 Fox, *Health Policies, Health Politics*, 208.

Chapter 5

1 Campion, *AMA and U.S. Health Policy*, 278.
2 Ibid., 278. The US Department of Health, Education, and Welfare (HEW) was created in 1953. HEW changed its name to the Department of Health and Human Services (DHHS) in 1979 when the education part of HEW split off to form the Department of Education (DE). Today's DHHS encompasses the Medicare and Medicaid programs under the auspices of the Centers for Medicare and Medicaid Services (CMS).
3 Ibid., 279.
4 W. Richard Scott, Martin Ruef, Peter J. Mendel, and Carol A. Caronna, *Institutional Change and Healthcare Organizations: From Professional Dominance to Managed Care* (Chicago, IL: University of Chicago Press, 2000), 206.
5 Stevens, "History and Health Policy," 471; Timothy Stoltzfus Jost, "Medicare and the Joint Commission on Accreditation of Healthcare Organizations," *Law and Contemporary Problems* 57 (1995): 22; Scott et al., *Institutional Change*, 206; Starr, *Social Transformation*, 377.
6 42 U.S.C. sec. 1395 (1988).
7 This was known as "deeming" authority. Hospitals would be "deemed" to be in compliance with federal standards if the Joint Commission accredited them. Lisa Sprague, "Hospital Oversight in Medicare: Accreditation and Deeming Authority," National Health Policy Forum, Issue Brief No. 802 (2005): 2; Bugbee, "The Physician in the Hospital Organization," 901; Jost, "Medicare and the Joint Commission," 31–32.
8 Campion, *AMA and U.S. Health Policy*, 276.
9 Rick Mayes and Robert A. Berenson, *Medicare Prospective Payment and the Shaping of U.S. Health Care* (Baltimore: Johns Hopkins University Press), 18.
10 Melhado, "Health Planning," 394.
11 Ameringer, *Health Care Revolution*, 56–57; Mayes and Berenson, *Medicare Prospective Payment*, 16–29; Jennie Jacobs Kronenfeld, *The Changing Federal Role in U.S. Health Care Policy* (Westport, CT: Praeger, 1997), 80–85; Lawrence D. Brown, ed., "Introduction to a Decade of Transition," in *Health Policy in Transition: A Decade of Health Politics, Policy and Law* (Durham, NC: Duke University Press, 1987), 1–3.
12 Milton Friedman, *Capitalism and Freedom* (Chicago, IL: University of Chicago Press, 1982), 15; Melvin W. Reder, "Chicago Economics: Permanence and Change," *Journal of Economic Literature* 20 (1982): 31–32.
13 Mancur Olson, ed., *A New Approach to the Economics of Health Care* (Washington, DC: American Enterprise Institute, 1982), 4, 5.
14 Ibid.
15 US Congress, Senate, Committee on the Judiciary, Subcommittee on Antitrust and Monopoly, 93rd Cong., 2nd sess., 1974, 1041, 1083 [Statement of Clark Havighurst].